Contents

Acknowledgments, *vi*

Introduction, *1*

1. The Myth of Indonesian Economic and Political Development in East Timor, *9*
> *Political and Military Control, 10*
> *Information Control, 12*
> *The Politics of Aid to East Timor, 15*
> *Economic Incorporation, 21*
> *Population Control and Demographic Engineering, 25*
> *The "Opening Up" Policy, 30*
> *Conclusion, 35*
> *Notes, 37*

2. Perez de Cuellar on East Timor, *41*

3. An East Timorese Reconciliation? *45*

4. Appeal to US Asianists on "Death Squads" in East Timor, *51*

5. Australia, the Timor Gap, and the World Court, *57*
> *Implications of the Ruling, 62*
> *Australian Appeasement of Indonesia, 63*
> *Appeasement of Domestic Lobby, 67*

6. In Memory of Denis Freney, East Timor Activist *Par Excellence*, *69*

7. East Timor and the Japanese Media, *73*

8. Chinese Maps? *77*

9. The "Blue Book" and East Timor, *83*
> *Namibia: lessons from a former trusteeship, 88*
> *The Cambodia Analogy, 90*
> *Western Sahara: the lessons of voter registration, 93*
> *El Salvador: lessons from the Cold War, 97*
> *Eritrea: lessons from history, 99*
> *Mozambique: lessons from Frelimo, 101*
> *Recommendations, 102*
> *Notes, 104*

WANDSWORTH LIBRARY SERVICE

Documents

Document 1 *UNGA RESOLUTION 3485 (XXX)–12 DECEMBER 1975*, 107

Document 2 *UNSC RESOLUTION 384 (1975)–22 DECEMBER 1975*, 109

Document 3 *UNSC RESOLUTION 389 (1976)–22 APRIL 1976*, 111

Document 4 *UNGA RESOLUTION 37/30–23 NOVEMBER 1982*, 112

Document 5 *Joint Statement by the Permanent Representatives of the People's Republic of Angola, the Republic of Cape Verde, the Republic of Guinea Bissau, the Republic of Mozambique and the Democratic Republic of São Tome and Principe to the United Nations on 18 November 1991*, 114

Document 6 *Declaration on the Situation in East Timor issued at Brussels on 3 December 1991 by the European Community*, 116

Document 7 *Situation in East Timor: Report of Secretary-General, 10 February 1993*, 117

Document 8 *Report by Special Rapporteur, Mr. Bacre Waly Ndiaye, on his mission to Indonesia and East Timor from 3 to 13 July 1994*, 139

Document 9 *UNCHR Resolution on East Timor, 49th Session, March 1993*, 172

Document 10 *UNCHR Resolution 1997/63, 53rd Session, Situation of Human Rights in East Timor, 10 April 1997*, 175

Document 11 *UNCHR Situation in East Timor. Report of the Secretary-General, 21 February 1997*, 177

Document 12 *UNHCR Statement by José Ramos-Horta, 1996 Nobel Peace Prize Laureate, 7 April 1997*, 181

Document 13 *Statement from Xanana Gusmão, head of the National Council of Maubere Resistance, to the U.N. Decolonization Committee in New York, July 27 1992*, 188

Document 14 *UNGA, 22 June 1995, Special Committee on the Situation with regard to the Implementation of the Declaration on the Granting of Independence to Colonial Countries and Peoples*, 195

Document 15 *Letter dated 28 February from the Permanent Representative of Portugal to the United Nations addressed to the Secrtary-General/Letter handed on 22 February 1991 to the Minister of Foreign Affairs of Australia by the Ambassador of Portugal at Canberra,* 211

Document 16 *ICJ Press Release: World Court Decides it cannot Adjudicate Dispute on Exploitation of East Timorese Continental Shelf, 3 July 1995,* 216

Document 17 *Statement by Secetary-General's Spokesman on East Timor, 17 September 1993,* 218

Document 18 *UNGA Document: Question of East Timor: Progress Report of the Secretary General* (16 September 1994), 219

Document 19 *UN Press Statement of 9 January 1995,* 221

Document 20 *UNGA Document: Question of East Timor: Progress Report of the Secretary-General (September 1995),* 223

Document 21 *Communique of UN Talks Issued at the Conclusion of the Seventh Round of Talks on the Question of East Timor (16 January 1996),* 226

Document 22 *Communique Issued at the Conclusion of the Eighth Round of Talks on the Question of East Timor, 27 June 1996,* 227

Document 23 *Declaração de Burg Schlaining, Austria, 1995,* 228

Document 24 *Burg Schlaining Declaration, Austria, 1996,* 230

Document 25 *European Parliament Resolution on Indonesia, 19 June 1996,* 232

Document 26 *European Union's Common Position on East Timor, 25 June 1996,* 234

Document 27 *Letter to Javier Perez de Cuellar, U.N. Secretary-General from Bishop Carlos Filipe Belo, Apostolic Administrator of Dili, 6 February 1989,* 236

Document 28 *Announcement of the Norwegian Nobel Committee, 11 October 1996,* 237

Document 29 *Statement by the Spokesman of the UN Secretary-General on Award of the 1996 Nobel Peace Prize,* 238

Index, *239*

Acknowledgments

The author wishes to acknowledge the assistance of the following individuals in the preparation of this volume: in Australia, Jefferson Lee; in Macau, António Luiz Mota; in Bangkok, Sonny Inbaraj; in Japan, Jean Inglis, Akihisa Matsuno, and various individuals in Nagasaki. Naturally, all responsibility for errors and interpretations rests with the author. The author also wishes to acknowledge permission granted by Peter Limqueco to republish in modified form chapter one originally published in Gunn with Lee, *A Critical View of Western Journalism and Scholarship on East Timor*, Journal of Contemporary Asia Press, Manila, 1994.

For publication support, the author also wishes to express thanks to the Southeast Asia Research Center of the Faculty of Economics, Nagasaki University.

Introduction

Arriving in Dili, the capital of East Timor, some eight months after the Santa Cruz massacre of 12 November 1991 (to distinguish this massacre from other massacres committed in Dili) and almost two decades after my last visit to what was then a Portuguese colony naturally provoked strong emotions. Nothing was quite like what I imagined, although enough of the familiar remained. Half expecting to find buildings riddled with bullet holes or destroyed in the Indonesian naval shelling of Dili, it was some comfort to find most structures still standing and recognizable, if sadly derelict. Still, the proliferation of new structures all over town left me wondering as to their real function and relevance. I also could not avoid noticing that where in the past the reef was littered with the remains of presumably Japanese landing barges, legacy of World War II battles between invading Australian and Japanese forces, today it is the debris of the Indonesian invasion that stamps its character upon Dili's harbor.

First impressions count, however. Arriving on the midday Merpati Airlines flight from Kupang in west (or Indonesian Timor), what immediately struck me was the lack of commercial activity in the town center. While Dili always slept during the long siesta, what was disconcerting was that the late afternoon brought no discernible increase in street activity. That evening, retracing my steps down Dili's once vibrant and elegant promenade, I found it both run-down and deserted. Most people, it seemed, found it prudent to keep off the streets after dark. In any case, I noted, motorized army patrols were beginning to move around, sometimes at a dangerously high speed.

The shadows, however, provided my first opportunity to make meaningful conversation. This was with João, a teenage orphan who, with no prompting whatsoever, filled me in on the infamous massacre—the casualties, the missing, the horror. The military are such cowards, he told me, afraid even to venture to the hills, that they turn their guns on civilians. Born under the Indonesian occupation, he spoke freely in Bahasa Indonesia. "Australia has recognized *integrasi* (integration with Indonesia), hasn't it?", he asked me dolefully. "But what about the UN?", he continued in an equally rueful voice. He also told of the invasion of immigrants, tension between Timorese and immigrants, the general sense of hopelessness at finding employment, and the iniquity of a medical system that benefited only those with the money to pay for the services. João described his own condition and that of his people as "traumatized." We both walked uneasily off into the dark in different directions. This was to be the first of many whispered conversations.

Later, discovering that the currency of Bahasa Indonesia now extends to just about all strata of Dili society I sought to extend the range of my contacts and conversations. From a peasant's eye view, fishermen on the rocks near Farol lighthouse offered their own version of the Dili massacre. What most concerned this group of two was the extreme youth of the victims. They pointed at my son, exclaiming "Just like him." To my question of how many victims, they replied, *seratus enam puluh*" tracing by way of emphasis the numerals 160 in the sand. Noone, I asked (and the matter came up in many conversations) offered a figure of less than this, and many offered a larger number including the missing.

On the second day of my first return visit to East Timor under Indonesian occupation, I ventured to Maubara, site of an old Dutch fort and legacy of a near 400 year old struggle between the Dutch and the Portuguese for control over this part of the island of Timor. I witnessed a Timorese wedding, I heard men strumming home made guitars singing a *fado* of sorts. Several kilometers back along the lonely road to Dili, I accosted an old farmer. We exchanged salutations. I shot at him in Bahasa Indonesia, the question. "How do you feel about Indonesia in Maubara?" Nonplused at the sight of a foreigner looming out of nowhere, much his impertinence, he rejoindered, "*Merah-putih masih ditimbangkan di desa ini*" (lit. "The Indonesian presence is still being weighed up in this village") which I took to mean that the Indonesians were still on trial in this part of the woods, a diplomatic answer to be sure on the part of a survivor.

Appearances in the new Dili can sometimes be deceptive though. Such was my experience when hailing a "Timorese" taxi driver on arrival at Comoro airport. This erstwhile local—who curiously enough met me at the airport on my third visit—turned out to be from Flores. But if conversation falls flat around crowds and around Indonesians in general—and if this is good reason to be slightly paranoid about the system of spies and informers which also extends to visitors—there are still enough bona fide East Timorese taxi drivers to engage any number of "sociologists" who will listen to them.

En route to Comoro market in an ancient taxi, my Timorese driver Manuel generously expanded with great excitement on the theme of Fretilin victories, naming with great pride José (Xanana) Gusmão, António (Mau Hunu) Gomes da Costa (both then still leading the armed resistance from the maquis), along with some others whose names I could not catch. The faster he drove, it seemed, the more he was given to elaborations—and exaggerations—his conversation checked only as we slowed to pass road blocks and the ubiquitous uniformed presence. *"Saya tidak bohong"* ("I am not telling lies"), he called out, as we parted company. If Manuel was given to over-optimism as to the guerrilla struggle, not so the next bearded Timorese taxi driver I accosted. While appearing to share his countryman's pride in the knowledge of the armed resistance, he nevertheless had arrived at a sober estimation of Australian political attitudes towards Indonesia's annexation of East Timor. "But, Canberra has already sold us out to Jakarta," he retorted, "You tell me how the Indonesians can be removed from this place." But paranoia probably works both ways as well. José, my driver on an excursion by taxi over the mountain to Hera, would only answer in monosyllables.

While in the past my journeys to Timor had been made during the rainy season, often recalling Conrad's famous description of Timor as "that pestilential place," my recent return journeys, in August 1992, and in July and September 1993, were in the middle of the long dry season. The distinction is important, especially as the agricultural cycle is different as indeed is the lay of the land. Whereas the rainy season can make life a general misery, especially for travel, the converse is the case during the dry. In any case, as others before me have noted, the occupiers have seen to a major improvement in the road system. What used to be a day's journey now takes only several hours by public bus—as much as the ubiquitous military convoy. Timor today is much smaller for it, more homogenous, less intimate.

It also soon became apparent to me that East Timor society today is bifurcated between locals and foreigners. Nowhere is the gap between occupier and occupied more apparent than in the system of controls imposed by the former upon the latter. More than once I became a victim of this particularly iniquitous system—down to body searches behind walls by automatic weapon bearing blue berets—so it is not hard to empathize with those who endure it day in, day out.

Once on a bus at a checkpoint outside Manatutu, the largest town on the north coast route between Dili and Baucau, a young Balinese soldier of the Udayana Kodam demanded identity cards, mine included. These were taken to a desk, checked, and then returned by the process of calling names. Just how ludicrous and outrageous the Indonesian occupation of East Timor was soon became apparent when the soldier revealed to all out loud that he could not pronounce Latin names. "V-i-n-c-e-n-t d-a H-o-r-n-a-y, J-o-v-i-t-a d-a C-o-s-t-a, he stuttered, and to which the passengers responded with sniggers of derision. (It also struck me as remarkable that there were scions of the ancient rival families still around and on board the same bus, but that is another story).

To the extent that Australians of my generation travelled to Asia, Baucau, named Villa Salazar on prewar maps, was for many their first "Asian" port of call. Yet it was utterly unlike any other Southeast Asian town. It was both a profoundly Melanesian yet African setting with respect to its cultural roots and its colonial structures. Driving down the escarpment of the plateau from the airport and emerging out of the mists into the marketplace of Baucau was to step back in time as much as place. This time around, lodging in the old Pousada da Baucau/Hotel Flamboyant, I surveyed the wreckage of this picturesque town, human and otherwise. Having been occupied by the military and used as a detention center and for other nefarious purposes, the hotel was in sad disrepair. As the "opening" of this hotel was announced several days before the arrival of myself and family, it is possible that we were the first paying "tourists" since 1975. In this once bustling market center the *mercado* or market had precious little to offer in the way of fruits or vegetables. Both misery and poverty showed on the faces and skeletal frames of, especially, the women and children. It was my son who pointed out children with distended bellies, the surefire sign of malnutrition. It was my wife who noticed the chronic eye condition of many, especially the children, even the children of the military privileged to reside in the precincts of the hotel.

Faced with a somewhat rebellious family, not tempted to eat anything, and not finding much worth eating, I decided that one night in old Baucau was about as much nostalgia as I could stand. With my son complaining of fever and with Conrad's description of Timor in mind, I decided to backtrack to Dili the following morning.

Still, I wished to survey the land. Woken by the cries of Baucau's famous cocks I set off on foot alone to Baucau beach. This seven-kilometer route takes one down the forested limestone escarpment to a bucolic world of peasant households, a veritable vista of thatched huts set among domestic gardens, coconut groves, and paddy fields watered by ancient irrigation systems. It is not far removed from a self-sufficient economy. Again it recalls another age. A horseman lurches out of the mists. "Bom Dia," he salutes. For the first time in my sojourn in East Timor, I have the sense of not being under surveillance. Even so, the signs of the Indonesian presence are everywhere. First one passes a monumental colonial-era school, now well and truly harnessed to Indonesia's project. "Hello Mister," the children shout in unison. One hundred meters further down the road, the Sang Merah Putih, the Indonesian national flag, flies over what is clearly a cemetery for Indonesian soldiers fallen in battle with their Timorese adversaries. It must have been a terrible attrition all around. There are nearly a hundred tombstones, about half Muslim, half Christian, all piled in together. Another two hundred meters further down this road appears a very large cemetery. There are some grave diggers at work. This is for Timorese and Chinese. Going by the inscriptions on tombstones, I note, many were buried here in 1975/ 76, the year of the Indonesian invasion. Further down the mountainside and looking back at Baucau, one sees the walls of what looks like a prison. "Penjara?", I ask a man tending buffaloes. He nods in the affirmative. Another symbol of the Indonesian occupation, a communications antenna, also looms on the mountain above.

At the beach, to my relief, there is a cantina. I join a group— *mestiçao* by appearance— under an ancient banyan tree, hailing them in Portuguese. There are some sailing boats from the Indonesian island of Wetar at anchor in the lagoon. A large, colonial-era structure lies abandoned on the foreshore while further along is a modern warehouse belonging to Bulog, the Indonesian rice procurement and distribution agency. A Timorese lady brings coffee. "Obrigado", I reply and the conversation continues in Portuguese. "Are you Australino?", one bearded fellow asks me in very confident Portuguese. "Si!", I reply. "We have heard about (former Australian Prime Minister) Bob Hawke" says another, also in Portuguese. "What are you doing here, anyway"? interrogates another. "We know all about Canberra," accuses a third. "The Santa Cruz massacre, the crosses vigil in Canberra, the Australian Labor Party, it's a disgrace, it's unbelievable. We are alone in our struggle. Who are you anyway?", this latter accuses. Pleading inadequacy in Portuguese, I revert to Bahasa Indonesia. Oblivious, my interrogators continue in Portuguese, "Senhor. Do you know how much a coffee farmer in Ermera receives for a kilo of coffee beans today. I will tell you. 800 rupiah.

Rice. Who gets to eat rice?" He waves in the direction of the Bulog warehouse. "The suffering, the suffering". The conversation shifts tack. We talk of travel and its dangers. "The *resistência*, Senhor! With Fretilin out there (he gestures to the east), even the Indonesians are afraid to travel at nighttime." This is met with great guffaws of laughter. I have a lot to learn, I tell them. I take my leave. "Adios." "Adios Australiano".

Back at the hotel, my son now awake and feverish is asking where I have been so early in the morning? "Oh," I reply, "just for a short walk, nothing much really." One year later I returned to the cantina at Baucau beach. To my regret, my bearded interlocutor and his Timorese *companheiros* were no longer to be found.

Returning again in September 1993, I found that the Indonesian authorities were doing their best to promote a sense of normalcy, of people (at least in Dili) going about their lives as ordinary "Indonesians." Centerpiece of this strategy, it appeared to me, was a "hearts and minds campaign" to socially engage Indonesians, including military families, and East Timorese, not just through such institutions as the school system or the armed forces but as fellow "Indonesians." While ordinary Timorese would not be in the least deceived by this carrot-and-stick strategy, I sensed that it was one that was designed to impress future visiting delegations with no historical perspective on East Timor who "see what they see". In any case, the bankruptcy of this policy was exposed with finality in late 1994 as resentment on the part of East Timorese against Indonesian immigrants and military abuses exploded into anger in the form of riots and a virtual Palestinean-style *intifada*.

Nothing shows up the contrast between the old and the new today in East Timor as much the rituals of state imposed upon the East Timorese people by Indonesia. The obligation of almost all Timorese to partake in the celebration of Indonesian anniversaries is very much part of this process. Although I was spared the spectacle of Indonesian Army Day as it was celebrated in East Timor in September 1993, I did witness certain of the preliminaries of this bizarre and irrelevant event, notably jogathons and bicycle races, beach calisthenics, and martial arts displays complete with a whistle-blowing march-past by schoolchildren.

On the Sunday morning of my last departure from Dili, attracted by a sign which read in English "Mountain fun bike 93," I followed on foot a parade of overweight nylon-outfitted cyclists from their starting position in front of the "Kantor Governor." My walk took me around the leafy Farol quarter, down streets with names like

Jalan Mozambique. Each and every one of these distinctly Latino but sadly decayed tiled and stuccoed villas today serve as the squatts and residences of the Indonesian officer cadre. It may have been the case that East Timorese only entered this suburb as house boys, but that still appears to be so. In front of one of these houses—the grandest "Wisma" of all—I found the finishing line of the bicycle event. This was in front of the "Rumah Panglima" or the Indonesian military commander's residence. Here, under the shade of banyan trees and to the tunes of a rock band, were assembled military, their wives and offspring and their unsmiling and hapless red and white tee-shirted Timorese *anak buah* or camp followers. I backed off for a bit of sanity to the Motael church still overflowing for the late morning mass. After all, it is the church in East Timor which provides the sole buffer and sanctuary for the people against the foreign occupier.

The Book

While, as mentioned above, I had previously visited Timor during colonial times, I was not especially engaged in the Timor "problem" in this period—in any case, an honor that owes to people like Denis Freney, as profiled in chapter 6. But, as with many travellers who criss-crossed Timor on the back of a pony in the late 1960s and early 1970s, I came to appreciate the hospitality of the Timorese people, while learning something of their culture and traditions. All the more so, when, for a period of several weeks in 1971, I found myself literally abandoned on Timor's remote south coast, having worked my way out of Darwin as deckhand on a ship conducting a hydrographic survey. While it happens that, later in the same year, I was privileged with a meeting in the Tanzanian capital of Dar Es Salaam by local represeratives of Frelimo, then waging a classic guerrilla war against the Portuguese in Mozambique, I was soon drawn back to Southeast Asia. For my generation and nationality, the Vietnam War was an obsession and, so it happened, when Indonesia invaded Dili, I was resident in Vientiane, Laos, where I witnessed the revolutionary takeover the same month. While these events became the major focus of subsequent research, it was not until offered a teaching position in the University of New South Wales in 1986 that I was in a position to place the international question of East Timor on my teaching agenda.

This book presents my advocacy on East Timor via a number of media, namely, print, conference, and electronic conference. The central theme concerns the need for UN intervention in East Timor. It is not that the UN is not engaged in the problem. It is, and has been ever since Portugal engaged the attentions of the UN on the question of granting independence to non-self-governing territories in 1960. But the failure of Indonesia, obviously, to observe the relevant UN resolutions condemning its 1975 invasion of East Timor and calling on it to withdraw its army of occupation, as much as the failure of the UN to act on its own resolutions, are perplexing questions. This is especially the case given the almost sacred character of the UN charter forbidding the aggression of one state against another. It is all the more surprising given the particular and disquieting character of the Indonesian occupation of East Timor and the mounting documented evidence of gross and cruel violations of human rights committed by the Indonesian armed forces in the territory, monitored not only by interested non-governmental organizations, but by the highest organs of the UN itself. While to be sure, at this writing, the UN Secretary-General, upon whose office the East Timor question devolves, has stepped up the diplomatic tempo on the East Timor question, notably in the form of Ministerial meetings between Indonesia and Portugal and, since 1995, an intra-Timorese dialogue, it is regrettable that the world body continues to hold back from the logical procedural consequences of this process, namely the establishment in East Timor of a permanent UN presence, inter alia, monitoring human rights violations, pending preparation for a referendum on East Timor's future.

As a foil to the arguments and recitation of facts presented in this book, I have also appended a selection of relevant UN documents and/or official press releases relating to East Timor. While these documents are eloquent of the problem, it should be recalled that even the Indonesian (and Australian) Foreign Ministries have not stood back from the production of documentary compilations puporting to justify Jakarta's annexation of the territory, unabashed in even the recycling of relevant—and damning—Security Council documents on the question. Necessarily, documentary studies demand contextualization. Where appropriate, I have sought to link the text with the relevant UN documentation. Also, by presenting the documents in thematic rather than in a strictly chronological order I have sought to facilitate consultation. Either way, then, this book can be read as analytical study or as documentary reference.

Geoffrey C. Gunn
Nagasaki

1

The Myth of Indonesian Economic and Political Development in East Timor

One of the arguments that Indonesia presents to the world to justify its armed annexation and occupation of East Timor is that it has achieved more development than Portugal accomplished in several hundred years. While this argument is a novel reading of the UN Charter, to say the least, an examination of the facts reveals that Indonesian-style military development in East Timor has actually come at the expense of the livelihoods and lives of large numbers of East Timorese. Indonesian occupation also negated East Timor's own autonomous development plans as developed embryonically by Fretilin in the last months of 1975. As East Timorese independence leader Xanana Gusmão stated after his capture and incarcerartion by the Indonesian armed forces: "I have always said to all those that wanted to listen to me that the Maubere people don't like the word 'pembangunan' (development). The problem is that it is not free. Freedom is what my people value, the aim of their struggle." [1] Versions of this chapter were presented in public seminars at the Centre of Southeast Asian Studies, Monash University (October 1992) and in Macau (December 1992). A printed version appeared in the author's work (with Jefferson Lee), **A Critical View of Western Journalism and Scholarship on East Timor** *(Journal of Contemporary Asia Publishers, Manila, 1994)*

This chapter seeks to dispose of two myths—the myth of economic development in East Timor and the myth of political development in the territory—by the Indonesian state. My observations are derived both from numerous fields trips *in situ* in the pre-1975 period as well as return visits in August 1992 and June and September 1993. I also draw upon the existing published literature on East Timor since 1975, to the extent that this engages development issues. Confronting the question of Indonesia's development claims is important as the arguments that East Timor is economically unviable, that the former colonial power, Portugal, achieved nothing in Timor in 450 years and that Indonesia's development project in East Timor vindicates its aggression are powerful propaganda indeed. Such arguments have been variously accepted not only in Indonesian circles, but also in official Australian circles (overtly) and in the case of Indonesia's largest trading partners, Japan and the United States, have not met with demurral.

Whereas in Cambodia, for example, the aid agencies that commenced to gain access to the country in 1979 were able to wield influence in a political arena where four major factions contended for political power and, eventually, in a development and security environment shaped by the UN, inside East Timor it was—and still is— the Indonesian government that determines the dispensation of rewards, sets the development agenda, and even determines which agency may or may not maintain a presence in the territory. The failure of the UN to act on its resolutions in favor of East Timorese self-determination has meant an appalling blackmail over the Timorese people, prolonging their agony in terms of development needs in the areas of poverty elimination, basic health services, and nutrition support. [2]

Political and Military Control

Following the full-scale Indonesian invasion of East Timor in December 1975, Jakarta moved quickly, not only to secure military dominance, at least in the capital, but to seek out an appropriate cadre of collaborators as the basis of a new administrative set-up. In the meantime an appropriate political formula had to be arrived at— even over the objections of the international community—to politically incorporate the territory. On 16 July 1976, Indonesia proclaimed East Timor as the 27th province of the Republic and placed it under the rule of a Governor. As mentioned in the introduction, Dili today is an Indonesian town, albeit a garrison town, peopled not by the inheritors of a Latinized culture but by the army of the invader, their *anak buah* or civilian adjuncts and, in turn, their camp followers, a reference to immigrants from outside East Timor who continue to infiltrate the former Portuguese colony.

It follows that as East Timor became administratively incorporated into greater Indonesia, all other ancilliary Indonesian government agencies made their appearance. These include such agencies and departments of government as health, public works, education, information, agriculture, not to mention—the highest profile of all —police and military. No less obviously, Indonesian currency replaced the Portuguese unit while Indonesian banks, private as well as public, replaced Portuguese. By 1987 there were 10,527 civil servants or *pegawai negeri* on the Indonesian government payroll in East Timor, not including military personnel. By 1991 the number of these privileged *Korpri* or state officials had risen to 11,036. While certain of this number were locals, by definition, those holding key positions within the Indonesian occupation bureaucracy were outsiders.

It goes without saying that in implanting a new administration in the occupied territory, the Indonesian authorities dismantled the old. Commensurate with its status in Jakarta's design as an Indonesian "province," East Timor has been obliged to accept the full panoply of the Indonesian political and administrative apparatus along with codes of behavior, bureaucratic rituals, and underpinning national ideology. While noone inside East Timor has any illusion that power rests with any other body than the military, Jakarta has also assiduously promoted civilian institutions to match their Indonesian counterparts. The most visible symbol of this political *léger de main* in East Timor is the office of the Provincial Governor, in theory elected by members of District Representative Councils (DRRD) and confirmed by the Provincial Representative Council (DPRK) which convenes in Dili. The fiction of Timorese political participation in national Indonesian affairs is also evidenced by the existence in East Timor of such institutions as Golongan Karya (Golkar), the quasi-governmental party in Indonesia which all military personnel and civil servants are obliged to join, as well as the pro-Muslim Partai Persatuan Pembangunan and the more secularly oriented Partai Demokrasi Indonesia (PDI). While these organizations nominally serve as political parties in their Javanese setting (witness the brutal crushing of the PDI under the leadership of Megawati Sukarnoputri by the military in Jakarta in late July 1996) obviously in East Timor they act as further agents of political recruitment for the Indonesian cause. It may be the case, as Lapian and Chaniago declare, that participation in the Indonesian general election of 4 May 1982 by East Timorese was their first opportunity in history to vote; it is more dubious that they have yet tasted the freedom to make even basic choices concerning their national destiny, as Timorese or as Indonesians.[3] A similar observation might be made apropos the 1992 general elections which, compared with the results of the 1987 exercise, saw electoral gains by the two erstwhile pro-government parties at the expense of Golkar.

In any case, the civilian administrative structure in East Timor is overarched by the military, police, and security apparatus. In East Timor, the Indonesian armed forces (known by its Bahasa Indonesia acronym ABRI) has never comprised less than a dozen combat-ready battalions. In turn, the ABRI presence is considerably swollen by the addition of units of Timorese adjuncts, the armed equivalent of civilian collaborators. But just as the army commander in East Timor answers directly to the Indonesian commander-in-chief, the President, so it is the rule of the gun that sets the limits to civilian actions in East Timor. Above all it is the highly visible, all-intrusive and intimidating presence of this army of occupation that gives the lie to Indonesian propaganda of the mental or mystical integration of East Timor with the motherland.

Information Control

At the heart of the endeavor to "integrate" East Timor into an Indonesian administrative structure has been the use of information. Taking a leaf from modernization theory that would see primordial loyalties broken down the more the bounds of the state intrudes upon the domain of little traditions outside the mainstream, so has Jakarta sought to engineer change in the realm of language, education, and ideology. Where Portugal was laggard in extending its presence below the level of *suco*, Indonesia has moved in with the full panoply of mass media; film shows, exhibitions, print media, radio, and television, not to mention the superimposition upon the Timorese people of a new language and concept of state.

It almost goes without saying that strenuous efforts have been made by the Indonesians to eliminate Portuguese language media in East Timor. It would appear, on surface at least, that the possession of a book in Portuguese constitutes a crime in East Timor today. Indeed, the only Portuguese language publications on sale in Dili today are those found in the Catholic Bookshop, a pitiful collection of ancient prayer books and religious tracts. Otherwise, the Dili Diocese Press is the single exception to the Indonesian stranglehold on the media in

East Timor. The single offering on sale observed during the author's visit was the pastoral of the Bishop of Dili, Carlos Filipe Ximenes Belo, of 17 September 1991, "The position of the Catholic Church as to the visit of the Portuguese delegation." [4] The only books publically available in Dili today are of foreign (meaning Indonesian) origin and mostly keyed to meeting the curriculum needs of local children obliged to attend local Indonesian schools. Except for a thin Tetum-Bahasa Indonesia wordbook and grammar, none of the Indonesian-language books on sale in Dili observed by this writer spoke directly to the East Timorese.

The foregoing also relates to the recovery of Timorese history. While the Historical Archive of Goa and the Macau archives remain extant, accessible, and celebrated, under respectively Indian and essentially Chinese protection, the same cannot be said of the historical patrimony of the East Timorese under Indonesian occupation. Indeed, there is a real fear that the record has been irretrievably lost, just as the New Order regime of General Suharto sought to physically eliminate some half-million members of the Indonesian Communist Party along with Sukarnoist camp followers in the 1965-66 period, as much the historical memory surrounding that epoch, so in East Timor the occupier has sought to wipe clean the nationalist slate of the erstwhile enemy. Timorese tell that Portuguese books in East Timor were simply destroyed in the frenzy of the invasion. Their near total absence makes this version of events highly plausible. [5] Commencing from a new year zero, the history of integration effectively replaces national Timorese history. Thus the nineteenth century Javanese anti-Dutch Muslim rebel Diponogoro replaces Boaventura, the anti-Portuguese Timorese rebel leader, just as Suharto, the "Father of Development," replaces Xanana Gusmão, leader of the umbrella resistance grouping CNRM (a Portuguese acronym standing for the National Council of the Maubere Resistance) and now (in incarceration) common criminal. Even the 1959 Viqueque rebellion, fomented by Indonesian separatists, is now portrayed as a historical prelude to integration.

Central to the Indonesian project of *integrasi* or integration has been education. Indeed, the construction of educational infrastructure has been one of the more impressive developments brought by Indonesia to East Timor. According to an Indonesian source there were (in 1991) some 130,000 children enrolled in the school system. These were distributed through 580 primary schools, 94 middle schools, 44 higher middle schools. Additionally, scores of Timorese students secured places in Indonesian universities. [6] This means that within a decade or so Indonesia has fundamentally altered not only the mental horizons of a subject people but also the spatial hierarchy of the education system. For a generation of East Timorese, Jakarta—not Lisbon—is at the apex of the education hierarchy. Graduates of Indonesian universities return as administrative collaborators if they play the game. In a situation of widespread graduate unemployment in East Timor, not to play the game spells social and economic death.

Besides propagating an essentially Jakarta-centric world view it is important to note the function of Bahasa Indonesia as the carrier of an Indonesian cultural crusade. In replacing Portuguese, Bahasa Indonesia thus becomes the print language of the Timorese as, in the main, the indigenous languages of Timor are untranscribed languages. Whereas some 67 percent of the population of Timor (1980 census) used only a local language (Tetum is predominant) and whereas 77 percent remain illiterate, the Indonesian project to expand primary education thus becomes the cutting edge in the battle for the hearts and minds of Timorese. Already a generation of school-age Timorese has emerged not only ignorant of Portugal and its mission, but linguistically competent in Bahasa Indonesia. It follows that the Lusophone culture that linked Timor with its modern history has been expunged or is at least in the advanced process of eradication. Tetun and other languages in Timor also become threatened as little cultures give way to the assimilationist thrust of the new cultural and political center, as of course does a nationalist curriculum that would speak to the Maubere people.

One concession to the past was the Externato de São José school, referred to by East Timorese as the "Portuguese school," established in 1964 under the auspices of the St.Joseph Foundation. Although closed after East Timor's annexation by Indonesia, the school was reopened in 1983 under the patronage of Bishop Belo for the benefit of young Portuguese who were left behind at least pending their eventual return to Portugal. But when most of the youths in this category returned to Portugal in 1987, the school continued to function, offering courses in Portuguese outside the national curriculum and in Bahasa Indonesia, but only as a second language. Located about 100 meters from the Santa Cruz cemetery, the site of the massacre in November 1991, the school was ordered to be shut down by the military authority in East Timor the following April. Students from the school were alleged to have been involved in the anti-Indonesian demonstration during the visit to East Timor by Pope John Paul in 1989 and also in the Santa Cruz cemetery demonstration. [7]

Besides the network of primary and lower and upper secondary schools established by the Indonesians in East Timor, local higher education opportunities are afforded by the church-run Fatumaca Senior Technical school in the Baucau district, the "private" Universiti Timor Timur with 800 students and 60 lecturers, and the Dili Polytechnic at Hera, a showcase institution, at least by appearances. But illustrative of the use of schools for the political projects of integration are the statistics for those who had graduated through P4 or Pancasila courses in the year 1989 alone, namely 39,730 junior and senior high school students. This is a reference to an obligatory exposure to or indoctrination in the mores of the Indonesian national ideology.

One constraint in the full development and extension of the Indonesian education project in East Timor, however, has been a chronic teacher shortage, in part complicated by the unwillingness of Indonesian teachers and Indonesian-trained East Timorese teachers alike to serve in East Timor. According to one Indonesian press report, the "province" was not only in need of an additional 2,500 teachers for its schools but also housing for teachers, as well as books and other educational aids. A no less telling comment on the education crisis in East Timor is the dearth of East Timorese in the teaching profession. For whatever reason, there is only one high school teacher of East Timorese origin in the local education system. [8] No doubt, self-esteem as much as the system of offering employment priority to outsiders explains this abject situation.

The Politics of Aid to East Timor

Despite representations to the Indonesian government by a "queue" of international aid organizations, only two were permitted to operate in East Timor up until the early 1980s. These were the International Committee of the Red Cross (ICRC) and the US-based Catholic Relief Services (CRS). The picture is not much different today. While certain groups such as the Australia-based Community Aid Abroad sought to take advantage of the "opening" and actually mounted a survey of needs in East Timor just prior to the Dili massacre, the ensuing repression put an end to even this limited opportunity. While the World Bank has been indirectly involved in the funding of transmigration projects, the Australian government working through AIDAB has sought to channel aid directly to East Timor in such areas as agricultural projects and the provision of water to Dili. Similarly the US is represented inside East Timor by USAID working out of Jakarta. Indonesian charities, including the Palang Merah Indonesia (PMI) [Indonesian Red Cross], have also set up shop in East Timor.

As discussed in a study by the Australian Council for Overseas Aid (ACFOA), those groups permitted to operate inside East Timor have been severely compromised and have been obliged to play a subservient role to the Indonesian government and, in the case of one organization, additionally to the US government. While this study looks at the role of exclusively the ICRC and the CRS some of its conclusions apply equally to the role being played out by the World Bank in East Timor and, particularly, the Australian government. Indeed, the price of Australian governmental assistance to East Timor, as shown, has been acknowledgement of Indonesia's *de facto* and *de jure* incorporation of the territory with the additional bonus for Jakarta of negating the claims of the Australia-based NGOs to operate inside East Timor. [9]

It became apparent in 1979, as reports of famine inside East Timor reached the international press, that the only permissible conduit for overseas aid, the PMI, was not coping. Over the objection by Indonesian authorities that the situation was "normal," the Australian government and World Vision together managed to send two barge-loads of relief materials from Darwin to Dili in late 1978 and early 1979. The price for this operation was recognition of Indonesian sovereignty over East Timor. Only in late 1979, however, did the Indonesian government readmit the ICRC, whose officials confronted a situation "as bad as Biafra and potentially as bad as Kampuchea." The ICRC swung into action with a A$7-million programme spanning a six-month period and funded mainly by Western governments, including A$3 million from the Australian government and Red Cross societies. Yet a month after this program was launched, it was described as a mere holding operation keeping large numbers of people "just above starvation." [10]

According to the ACFOA critique, the ICRC program was severely compromised. General operations were under the control of the PMI, allowing minimal involvement by trained ICRC personnel. Such traditional ICRC concerns as prison visits, monitoring of the Geneva Convention, the location of missing persons, etc., were disallowed, although permitted under the Fretilin administration four years previously. Indeed, it would appear that negotiations on this question of mandate with the Indonesian authorities bogged down with the overall result of setting back the commencement date of ICRC operations in East Timor. [11]

In September 1978, then US Ambassador to Indonesia Edward Masters visited East Timor and learned at first hand of the horrendous situation. Reporter David Jenkins, who accompanied Masters to Remexio, described the inhabitants of this hill-town south of Dili in the *Far Eastern Economic Review*, as "emaciated....undernourished and desperately in need of medical attention." [12] Such sentiments were echoed in the Melbourne *Herald,* which also reported that the diplomats and newsmen who visited Remexio were convinced that "a major international relief effort is necessary." [13]

Yet, as Budiarjo and Liem have clarified, it was another 13 months before the military authorities allowed a relief program to begin. This was after the "encirclement and annihilation campaign" of 1977 and 1978 had thoroughly accomplished its objectives. [14] The blandishments of Ambassador Masters before a US Congressional committee of enquiry on East Timor and the failure of the US State Department to even acknowledge the need for assistance until June 1979 were exposed by Cornell Indonesia expert Ben Anderson, addressing another session of the committee in February 1980 with these words:

> Ambassador Masters *deliberately* refrained, even within the walls of the State Department, from proposing humanitarian aid to East Timor. Until the generals in Jakarta gave him the green light, Mr. Masters did nothing to help the East Timorese....Adding further distortions to the record, Mr. Masters made no mention whatever of Indonesian counter-insurgency operations or their effects when he testified before this Committee last December 4. In fact he had the effrontery to suggest that the appalling plight of the East Timorese was primarily their own fault. It was a consequence, he said, of the "extreme backwardness of the East Timorese economy." [15] (emphasis original.)

When relief operations eventually commenced in October 1979 it ostensibly came under the cover of an independent humanitarian organization, CRS. According to the ACFOA critique, CRS worked in East Timor, as it had done earlier in South Vietnam, as subcontractor of the US government. As such, CRS served in East Timor as "an extension of American foreign policy the purpose of which is to secure and complete the Indonesian takeover of an unwilling East Timor." Of the US$7.2 million spent by CRS in Timor up to December 1979 US$6,969,662 was from direct US funds. While the ACFOA report praised the CRS operation as "vigorously and effectively conducted" and for saving many lives, like the ICRC, its *modus operandi* in East Timor was seriously compromised, being obliged to work entirely with the Indonesian government and not through the local church or any other agencies. But most damaging, the CRS program of focussing upon "resettlement areas" (*daerah pemukiman*) created by the Indonesian armed forces as part of their population control exercise, reveals the full ambiguity of the US-CRS exercise. As ACFOA argues, and as shown below, the "resettlement sites" cannot serve as centers of self-sufficiency and development, but rather deepen the structure of dependence of the people upon food imports and the occupier." Masters, accompanied by CRS officials, had earlier surveyed the "resettlement sites" where CRS was to concentrate its relief efforts. [16]

One Australian journalist who saw through the Indonesian smokescreen on famine conditions inside East Timor was Peter Rodgers. He claims that the price he paid for exposing the reality on the humanitarian situation inside East Timor in the *Sydney Morning Herald* on 31 October and 1 November 1979 was the failure of the Indonesian government to extend his residence visa. Worse in the eyes of the Indonesian authorities, he claims, were accompanying photographs of starving East Timorese children also published on 1 November, even though these had been taken in the company of military escorts. As the then Jakarta correspondent for the *Sydney Morning Herald*, *The Australian Financial Review*, *The National Times* and the *Far Eastern Economic Review*, the expulsion cannot have been made lightly. The issue, claims Rodgers, was not so much the representation of the reality in East Timor but the question of reporting which engenders official Indonesian hostility. [17]

To a certain extent the Indonesian attempt to impose an information *cordon sanitaire* over East Timor failed at this juncture, not necessarily in the Australian but in the international press. In November 1979, the *Financial Times* of London carried the headline "Tragedy in Wake of Indonesian Invasion" while the Manchester *Guardian* led with "Starvation drive against Timor." The famine and information distortions were also given exposure in the *Washington Post*. Breaking with the ASEAN consensus on East Timor, the Bangkok *Nation Review* carried a long interpretive article by the Thai Muslim writer and politician Surin Pitsuwan, headlined "East Timor: the other famine" (17 February 1980). As this author wrote of the US State Department version of events in East Timor provided to the 4 December 1979 House Subcommittee on Asian and Pacific Affairs, "they offered arguments that would have driven George Orwell to drastically revise his famous essay on politics and the English language." Yet, one senses, without concerted government action the humanitarian outrage generated by these articles was soon dissipated and the East Timor humanitarian cause lost among a welter of competing claims.

While a marginally greater plurality of interests is represented by the Indonesian press than its government-controlled counterparts in Malaysia/Singapore, it is hard to find even a single Indonesian press article on East Timor that challenges the assumptions of integration. Indeed, the way that East Timor is reported in the Indonesian media conforms precisely to the prescribed official role for the press in Indonesia as a "Pancasila press." To wit, *Antara* (18 October 1979) released a statement from the Indonesian Ministry of Foreign Affairs shamefully denying Australian press reports of hunger in East Timor. While this newsagency revealed that the PMI worked in the field with the Badan Urusa Logistik or Bulog, the official rice procurement and distribution agency (about which more later), *Berita Buana* (8 December 1979) was even more candid in revealing that CRS worked hand-in-hand in the field with both civil and military agencies Pemda and Korem (sub-regional military commands). While there is nothing particularly novel in using the armed forces of a nation in civil relief operations, as explained below, it was the counterinsurgency operations of the Indonesian Armed Forces in East Timor which created the conditions for the disaster evocatively described by José Ramos-Horta, external delegate for the resistance, as like scenes from Dante's *Inferno*. [18]

The famine issue was revived in mid-1982, not at all by the visit to East Timor by former Prime Minister Gough Whitlam, but by American journalist Rod Nordland, whose reports were published in the *Philadelphia Inquirer* and republished in *The Age* (10 June 1982). [19] Nordland reported that, try as they might, the Indonesian authorities could not even hide a hunger situation in the capital much less strife-torn districts of Baucau and Viqueque. Nordland also reported on the difficulties under which the ICRC then operated in East Timor. *The Age* (18,20 October 1983) also reported that the ICRC was unable to visit any prisons or assess requirements for humanitarian aid in East Timor, except for Atauro Island. But basically it was only in such publications as ACFOA's *East Timor Report* that the full dimensions of the hunger problem were exposed.

Taylor[20] writes that as the news of the food shortages leaked out in 1982 the military was obliged to take some action to avoid further adverse international reaction. Once the "fence of legs" counterinsurgency operation was completed in September of that year, the ICRC was again permitted to gain access to military-controlled areas to survey needs. Again the results were devastating and again the attempt to apply aid on a more systematic basis to meet massive harvest shortfalls was frustrated by military corruption and abuses.

Although UNICEF, along with the World Food Program and UNHCR, had been mandated by the UN General Assembly (resolutions 34/40 and 35/27) to render all possible assistance to the Timorese people, it is a pointed commentary upon the attitude of the world body as much the world community that in over two decades of the illegal Indonesian occupation of East Timor, of all the UN agencies, only UNICEF has had some minimal degree of engagement inside East Timor and even then this body fell into line with the Indonesian diktat that it work through the PMI. Ramos-Horta writes that its programs amounted to little more than offering Bahasa Indonesia lessons to relief workers, contributing little more than assisting Jakarta's Indonesianization of East Timor. [21]

While the rhetoric of development became the major Indonesian propaganda justification for its integration for both an international and domestic Indonesian audience, certain sections of the Australian press were willing to play along. Notable was the journalism of John Hamilton in the Melbourne *Herald*. Following a six-day guided tour in early 1983, Hamilton reported supportively on the reconstruction of Dili, the new airport, the paved roads and the new schools. As the authors of an article in the American publication, *Southeast Asian Chronicle*, wrote of this kind of journalism, it failed to note that these kinds of improvements benefit the Indonesian occupiers rather than the local population. [22] By the mid-1980s Australian government officials, notably officials of the right-wing Northern Territory government, including the Chief Minister, had also fallen hostage to Indonesian propaganda on the developmentalist virtues of integration.

In the wake of the Santa Cruz massacre and just before the visit to Jakarta by then Australian Prime Minister Keating in April 1992, the Australian government unveiled a plan to supply A$30 million in aid to East Timor over a period of five years. This included A$11.5 million for the financing of a water supply project for Dili. This announcement brought forth immediate protests from such Timorese groups in Australia as the East Timorese Independence Committee (ETIC) and ACFOA. The spokesperson for ETIC welcomed Australian aid to East Timor but asserted that unless it was administered by an "accountable" non-Government body the aid would otherwise serve to entrench Jakarta's control over the occupied territory. [23] The ACFOA spokesperson, in turn, contended that by declining to link aid to respect for human rights in East Timor, Keating was merely giving comfort to the military government while subverting true and equitable development. [24]

Economic Incorporation

One gloss on the official Indonesian view on economic incorporation has been put forth by M. Hadi Soesastro, an official scholar attached to the Jakarta-based CSIS. While he dismisses the Portuguese legacy as one of "utter neglect" he also concedes that, as in the case of Indonesia since 1976, the Portuguese government was obliged to bank-roll much of the "modern sector." At the center of his discussion is the question of "economic viability, absorption and the distribution of gains for development," meaning the integration of East Timor into the "national economy" in a way that would reduce its "aid dependence" on Jakarta. This is not a view that would entertain for a minute the prospect of an independent East Timor but, commensurate with official Indonesian ideology and contrary to UN resolutions, accepts the territory as politically incorporated. Neither does this view spell out the political parameters surrounding Indonesia's occupation and annexation, much less the human and economic cost arising from these bloody actions. In this account, the CNRM-led resistance against political incorporation is dismissed as the work of "disaffected groups" although, in the same breath, Indonesia's failures in East Timor are attributed to "security considerations." Overall, then, this writer is silent on attributing population loss—a differential of some 112,000 between the 1973 and 1980 censuses—to the actions of the Indonesian military inside East Timor. Similarly, massive damage incurred to East Timor's fragile agricultural economy, especially in output of maize, rice, sweet potatos, cassava, and cattle, is attributed to "civil war" and not at all to the sustained and ongoing counterinsurgency operations of the Indonesian armed forces. [25] This is making light of an aggravated situation which some aid-workers compared to the famine situation confronted in wartime Biafra.

The central theme in Indonesian propaganda over its version of *pembangunan* or development in East Timor, then, is that the "province" of East Timor has received since 1976 by far the largest central government allocations on a per capita basis of any region in the country. This is undoubtedly the case if one includes the budget for the army of occupation. The scale of the Indonesian political investment in East Timor is also pointed up by comparisons with development spending in neighboring islands of the Lesser Sunda chain, by far the most backward in development of any region of the country, a legacy of both colonial and post-colonial neglect.

Such triumphalism is also sounded by Soesastro, who points out that during 1983-86 the East Timor economy is estimated to have grown at almost 6 percent per annum or 50 percent higher than the national rate. Trade is another area where growth has been significant (although most licenses have been issued in Dili, not up country). As this author points out, to understand this rate of increase we have to look to the role of government spending in the East Timor economy. In a situation where the local economy contributes only some 7 percent of current expenditure (1986/87 figures), clearly it is the government—especially the military share of government expenditure—which dominates. This includes salaries paid to regional (East Timor) government personnel that accounts for less than one half of total government salaries and salaries paid to central government civil servants and armed forces personnel stationed in East Timor. Even though a considerable part of the salaries paid to military personnel end up in time deposits in banks in Dili and are repatriated at the end of their tours, it is undeniable that the government is responsible for a large part of the monetized economy. Accordingly, construction, utilities, services, road-building, and a host of other activities depend crucially on government spending. [26] Soesastro neglects to mention, however, that capital works like the construction of airports and roads—especially the new and upgraded roads linking west Timor with East Timor—serve more than just the circulation of goods and economic extraction: they are central to the military pacification of the annexed territory. As is obvious to any traveller in East Timor, military transport exclusively dominates strategic roads, at certain times.

In a situation where agriculture contributes 50 percent of economic activity, argues Soesastro, East Timor must look to comparative advantage even if that means remaining a net food importer. Rather, he counsels, East Timor should boost its export sector, especially the export of cash crops like coffee. Accordingly, the government has committed "substantial financial resources" to rehabilitating East Timor's coffee plantations and to increasing yields. This would require the free movement of seasonal plantation labor. Manufacturing is not accorded high priority in the Indonesian schema, contributing less than 1 percent of GNP and restricted to handicrafts, coffee processing, furniture-making, etc. Mining is even less significant and restricted to quarrying. Oil exploitation awaited the signing of the Timor Gap Agreement between Indonesia and Australia. Road building and sea communications serve the purpose of further integrating the economy with the "national" economy [27] and, although not mentioned, the counterinsurgency effort of the government.

All in all, he argues, there is no alternative to increased national economic integration. "It was a belief that an independent East Timor was not economically viable that provided one of the justifications for its incorporation into Indonesia," he reveals. [28] The hidden assumption in this line of argument, also echoed by the Australian Indonesian Lobby, is that if an economically viable East Timor had been allowed to develop under national East Timorese auspices it might have held up an attractive anti-model to the kind of military-sponsored development and political repression that has become a staple in Indonesia itself. But that was far from the Indonesian invader's intent. Political incorporation encouraged by the US, Japan, and Australia followed a crude Cold War logic and never had people's livelihood or niceties of history and culture in mind.

No doubt it also suited the comparative advantage of Indonesian businesspeople *cum* carpetbaggers that the handicraft sector of East Timor be destroyed. One would not have to be a specialist on Timorese folk art to observe that the *tais* (woven blankets) being touted in Dili today are fakes and possibly not even woven in East Timor. It says something also about the destruction of Timorese society by the invader that the bonds uniting the Timorese family and community, as symbolized by the production of *tais*, has been broken, perhaps irremediably. Indeed, as someone who has worked in the no less war-ravaged societies of upland and lowland Laos, I would hazard that handicrafts, including local versions of *ikat*, have better survived in those societies than even in Timor.

As Budiardjo and Liem emphasize, "From the moment Indonesian troops landed in East Timor interests closely linked with the military began to engage in business"—notably P.T. Demok Hernandes International. Although unlisted, this was an army-controlled company managed by a Chinese businessman and backed by General Benny Murdani, with close links to trading and finance houses in neighboring countries, notably Singapore. Within six months of the capture of Dili this company had shipped 500 tons of coffee to Singapore followed by a second shipment of 800 tons earning Demok US$3.1 million for the first year of "*integrasi*." In achieving this "market niche," Demok assumed the confiscated plantation lands and estates owned by SAPT, the Portuguese state enterprise. [29]

The only exception to the Demok monopoly was coffee land returned to the former Indonesian-appointed governor's brother and coffee smallholders allowed to work on land also assumed by the Indonesian state. Demok's monopoly, invigilated by the military, also extended to other cash crops including sandalwood, a commodity it "rapaciously" collected, as well as a monopoly over the importation of a variety of food products and consumer goods. Contributing to Demok's success were the rocketing world coffee prices during 1976-77 and demand for Timor's esteemed coffee. [30]

The link between military owned companies in Indonesia and joint ventures between the military and private capital in post-occupation Timor has also been made by one student of Indonesia's political economy under the generals, Richard Robison. While the origins of this arrangement go back to the "guided economy" period, commencing with the Indonesian New Order of General Suharto, the military further ventured into the area of forced purchases of smallholder crops below market prices. By buying cheap and selling dear in Singapore, this company made an estimated profit of US$20-25 million on its business dealings in East Timor between 1976 and 1980. [31]

In a second phase, according to Budiardjo and Liem, and moving beyond that of plunder and the collection of war booty, Indonesia set about establishing the basis of a plantation economy "like the Portuguese did before them, but....more systematically." To this end, an additional 10,000 hectares of land have been turned over to coffee (from 45,321 hectares in 1976 to 51,960 hectares in 1992) and a million clove seedlings planted. Also in line with the rapid conversion to cash-crop cultivation, coconut plantations have all been expanded. In this phase, Indonesia's policy has been to concentrate on introducing new techniques and new forms of agricultural organization such as the largely USAID-funded "integrated rural development" program. While, they concede, the application of science and technology to agriculture was sadly neglected by Portuguese colonialism, the Indonesian development program in East Timor bears some strong qualifications. First, Timorese themselves—at least those not confined to concentration camps—are denied access to fertile lands and, second, they are required to subordinate their food-growing activities to the security criteria of the occupation forces. While Budiarjo and Liem do not deny the possibilities inherent in this form of accumulation, they write:

It will mean nothing to them if East Timor sooner or later becomes a surplus producer of rice while at the same time the Timorese people themselves are prevented from returning to their former land and from engaging in their former agricultural pursuits. [32]

Observation reveals that East Timor has not even achieved food self-sufficiency under Indonesian rule. While mass famine is no longer the condition of the East Timorese, such as occurred with devastating consequences through the 1980s, death from starvation was still being reported in 1992 in such places as on the island of Atauro [33] and malnutrition remains the lot of most Timorese. Fishermen in Dili told me they could not afford to eat the fruits of their catch but shared with their compatriots a meagre diet of maize and cassava. While these foodstuffs figure as the staple of the Timorese peasantry, the urban classes in Portuguese times came to depend upon a diet of rice. But rice today is a luxury and control over the procurement and distribution of rice falls to the military-controlled Bulog agency. Timorese drivers for Bulog—and there are many—informed me that Bulog maintains a network of strategic rice depots across East Timor, especially in such rice-deficient regions as Baucau in the east. But the presence of a Bulog-controlled rice store in Baucau could bring little cheer to native Timorese when malnutrition and physical debilitation, especially among women and children, is written on their faces. In fact, Bulog-military control over rice can also be viewed as a strategic weapon used in population control and in the war against the people. Rice, a luxury commodity, is a reward for compliance and collaboration, its denial a punishment. So much for the perverse doctrine of "comparative economic advantage."

Population Control and Demographic Engineering

The key element in population control, however, concerns the creation of a system of resettlement villages that reminds this observer of the "strategic hamlets" created by the United States armed forces in Vietnam and the force-paced urbanization also foisted upon certain montagnard groups by the US in Vietnam and Laos alike. While such social engineering measures take manifold forms in East Timor today, obviously the counterinsurgency ends of the occupier invariably take priority over people's social or economic needs. This strategy of removing the fish from the guerrilla ocean seeks to break the people's spirit and deny sustenance to the rebels. This strategy never worked in Vietnam beyond the montagnard zones, but in tiny Timor, out of the gaze of the Western press and conveniently bottled up for seventeen years, the Indonesians got away with and are getting away with the murder of a people and its culture. Some scores of these hamlets, always under the gun, litter the countryside of East Timor. Even where the gun has been lowered, the chains of dependence built up as a result of forced resettlement are not easily broken. The prospect of returning to broken villages is too daunting. Indeed, in many parts of East Timor, a "traditional" village life is now more the exception than the rule.

From observation it is apparent that the very demographic profile of East Timor has been restructured. Absent of course is the Portuguese segment of the population, absent as well is the embryonic Timorese middle and professional classes, including the Latin *mestição* classes, absent as well are the Timorese-Macanese-Chinese and even the African segment of East Timorese society. In a word, the cream of Timorese society, the inheritors of national power in Timor, are either dead or in the diaspora. Even more sinister, at least for those familiar with pre-1975 urban life in Timor, is the virtual absence from the streets and parks of Timorese. Although Sunday church services bring out the Timorese *en masse*, the levels of intimidation inhibit all but the car-owning classes from venturing out in the evening. Forget about the famous evening promenade.

Just how many East Timorese died as a result of the Indonesian invasion and annexation? This question has been subject to much guesswork and even more propaganda. We think that the statistics issued by the Church in East Timor are eloquent of the tragedy and, indeed, speak of mass murder if not genocide. According to these figures, East Timor suffered a population loss of 134,581 between 1974 and 1980 or the difference between a total population of 688,769 in 1974 and 554,188 for 1980. The corresponding figures for 1984 are 609,603; 1985 (624,328); 1986 (649,674); 1987 (666,412); 1988 (683,585); and 1989 (701,196). [34] As a foil to the Church figures, it is of interest to note that the base figure for 1974 is not out of line with the official Portuguese census figure for 1970 giving a population of 609,477. Using this figure as a starting point and assuming a 1.7 percent annual growth rate (the average population growth rate for the period 1960-1970) it is not unreasonable to impute a figure of 700,000 in 1975, especially bearing in mind the tendency in Portuguese times to disguise the number of family members as a way of evading the head tax. The veracity of the 1980 figure is not disputed by Indonesian sources, only the interpretation as to the population decrease. Be that as it may, it should also be clear that the 1980 figure is inflated by immigrants entering East Timor in numbers far greater than those of East Timorese leaving the territory as refugees or those killed in the civil war. Whether working from Church figures or extrapolations from the official Portuguese census figures, it is apparent that between one-fifth and one-third of East Timor's population was eliminated between 1976 and 1980. Refugee exodus, deaths in the brief civil war of 1975, and disrupted food production will not explain these harrowing but revealing statistics. [35]

As noted, Dili has been transformed into an Indonesian garrison town, *par excellence*. All prime real estate such as that formerly occupied by Portuguese state officials has been sequestered by the army of occupation and, indeed, resemble veritable blockhouses. As evoked in the Timothy Mo novel, *A Redundancy of Courage*, [36] the new tenants of villas have imported both their lifestyles and their fetishes from Jakarta. The former middle-class suburb of Comoro has been voided of its Latin *mestiçâo* inhabitants and replaced by the auxiliaries of the army of occupation. From Liquisa in the west to Baucau in the east, the commercial centers of towns are voided of their former Chinese tenants. Chinese schools, it goes without saying, are derelict across East Timor. To a certain extent, though, new Chinese from Surabaya and elsewhere in Indonesia have profited from the opportunity afforded by Indonesia's extension of boundaries to set up shop in East Timor, mainly in the capital.

While ethnic Timorese have been pushed back to outer suburbs like Santa Cruz, they too are obliged to live cheek-and-jowl with the occupier. No quarter of Dili is far from a military unit or police post. No urban Timorese is out of sight of the watchful eye of one or another government agency or its agents. This is all too apparent to the visitor as spontaneous conversation is practically lacking. While the military is omnipresent in any Indonesian town, the analogy for East Timor is closer to that of the West Bank of Jordan under the Israeli gun. Indeed, for a Timorese the right to live and travel is a right conferred by the occupier. Only the possession of an Indonesian-issued identity card ensures this right, while the presentation of this card to whatever uniformed—and more often than not, un-uniformed authority—has become an obligatory trial and ritual for ordinary Timorese going about their daily business.

The other major demographic distortion in East Timor, also related to the Indonesian project of political and cultural control, is immigration. This a reference to a deliberate policy on the part of Jakarta to effect demographic change in East Timor along "Indonesian" lines, a policy pioneered with some mixed success in the ethninically Melanesian province of West Irian. Under this state (and World Bank) sponsored scheme, "transmigrants" are brought into Timor from Java and Bali and resettled in designated zones. According to an Indonesian account, such zones are projected to support a population density of fifty persons per square kilometer, half of them locals and half transmigrants. [37] While accurate statistics on the number of arrivals of officially sponsored transmigrants are lacking, it appears that the fertile alluvial plains of such southwestern parts of East Timor as Covalima have been major destinations.

From direct observation, far more numerous are the job-seekers from Sulawesi, East Java, Bali and other provinces of Indonesia including West Timor and Flores. Numbering in the tens of thousands, such "spontaneous" immigrants have now indelibly imprinted their social character upon the Timorese landscape. In residential terms they have entered the hearts of towns across East Timor. Lacking title to land, they have been permitted by their military protectors to squat wherever they can erect their temporary dwelling of plywood and tin. Thus, in Dili, street after city street are lined with the shanty towns of the immigrants. Sanitation and infrastructure are lacking. In 1989–90 this influx was particularly rapid, although tapering off in the following year. By September 1990, there were an estimated 100,000 non-indigenous people in East Timor whose population was given by the Djaelani Commission as 755,950. [38] As reported by one journalist, the national passenger shipping line disembarks 500 of these foreigners a week while only fifty make the return journey. [39] As one Timorese taxi-driver put it to me, "Dili is no longer a Timorese town."

While certain of the immigrants share Roman Catholicism with their Timorese co-religionists, most in fact are Muslims. Whereas in pre-1975 society this faith was shared exclusively by a small group of Arab families living in the Comoro suburb, including that of the Fretilin representative in Mozambique, Mari Alkatari, today corrugated iron mosques have become as much a part of the urban landscape as churches, if less imposing. No less intrusive has been the appearance in the East Timorese landscape of Pentecostalist missions, which like Islamic institutions, are under the patronage of the military and serve the religious needs of the military, their auxiliaries, and the immigrants. [40]

While such apparent multiculturalism sits well with the Indonesian state doctrine of Panca Sila which theoretically underpins religious tolerance within a secular state system, it also denies East Timorese the fundaments of their own national culture and identity.

While the West rewards the Indonesian New Order for its invigilation of fundamentalist Islam, the cost for East Timor is its survival. As seen above, there is no place in the Indonesian schema for even a Chinese-Timorese identity much less a separate Timorese identity. Moreover, with its Sanskritized signs and codes, Panca Sila severely stigmatizes the animist beliefs of the East Timorese as beyond the morality of the state ideology and acceptable cultural forms.

While the Catholic Church has emerged under Indonesian rule as the major crutch for a traumatized people and indeed remains the major buffer between the military and the people—especially under the leadership of Bishop Belo—religious affairs in the territory come under the ambit of the Departemen Agama Propinsi or the Provincial Department of Religion set up in Dili in 1978 and assisted by 93 regional branches throughout East Timor. While the Church in East Timor still answers to the Vatican and not Jakarta, ecumenical questions and, *ipso facto*, erstwhile communal questions engaging other faiths and sects are handled and managed by the state bureaucracy.

But it is in the marketplace that the new immigrants are currently dominant. More aggressive and entrepreneurial than the Timorese, historically sidelined by the Chinese, the immigrants have quickly asserted themselves in petty business and market activities. A visit to any marketplace makes this obvious. Whereas imported goods used to find their way into the marketplace through the ubiquitous Chinese commercial outlets, now it is the new immigrants who have totally cornered this niche. Moreover, the place of origin and even the nature of the commodities has changed. Whereas in the pre-1975 period, items of daily consumption originated from Macau, Hong Kong, or Singapore, today they are overwhelmingly of Indonesian origin. Everything from bottled water to soap to tweezers is imported. As mentioned below, the doctrine of comparative advantage sees to it that East Timor's role in the New Order economy is as supplier of raw materials and prebends. Import substitution has no place in this schema. As Timorese lament, in this situation it is the skilled and even unskilled migrants arriving from Indonesia who reap the major economic benefits. Unemployment and disguised employment falls the lot of the East Timorese. As one of my informants told me, "We are foreigners in our own land. Even our professional people cannot find employment." Undoubtedly such frustrations fueled the anger behind the Santa Cruz demonstrations.

Having withstood the onslaught of deliberate genocidal policies wrought by ABRI, it is the unfortunate lot of the East Timorese women to be subject to birth control measures under the banner of family planning and prenatal health care. While this ideology may have some meaning in the densely populated areas of Indonesia, in the traumatised war zone of East Timor such population engineering can only be interpreted as war on the East Timorese women's uterus. In the East Timor context, "family planning" is a highly organized management exercise carried out in tandem with such agencies as transmigration, information, and education and the armed forces. According to a 1993 press report, 30 percent of *Pasangan Usia Subur* (PUS) or women of child bearing age were recorded as "*akseptor aktip*" or recipients of birth control measures that include obligatory use of the highly controversial contraceptive drug Depo Provera and forced sterilization. The "PUS" target for 1993–94 was set at a staggering 40 percent. As one propagandist of this project boasted, without the slightest consideration of the very special human and demographic conditions of East Timor as opposed to say Bali, "This means that the success of Family Planning in the province will be the same as in other provinces of Eastern Indonesia." East Timorese women now targeted for birth control are those of Los Palos and Baucau precisely from areas that have been most impervious to Indonesian rule. [41] The World Bank also had its hand in this insidious venture. [42]

The "Opening Up" Policy

The decision to "open up" East Timor, which formally took effect on 1 January 1989, was undoubtedly taken by General Suharto, following his visit to Dili in October 1988. But whatever the logic of the decision, writes Feith, whether for political reasons, getting back at opponents in the military elite, economic reasons, "breaking rackets," pragmatic reasons, or for engineering demographic change by facilitating the in-migration of outsiders, the result was the same, that is, stimulating the latent anti-Indonesian nationalism of the East Timorese. Not only was the decision a watershed in the history of East Timor, Feith continues, but "It may also go down as one of the major political mistakes of Soeharto's long period as President." [43] Soesastro earlier argued that the closed door policy not only worked against facilitating private investment but created "aid dependence." The author also criticized defenders of the closed door policy who asserted that more entrepreneurial immigrants would dislodge indigenous people from their market niche. While he acknowledged "abuses" committed by certain outside interests, he saw labor mobility, such as bringing in more plantation workers and entrepreneurs, as the price to be paid for full opening and full integration. [44] As discussed above, this logic has a cold calculus. All in all, Soesastro has unwittingly exposed the dimensions of Jakarta's recolonization of East Timor. Having escaped from hundreds of years of subjugation under Portuguese colonialism, East Timorese have now been subjected to the crudest form of military occupation, plunder, and developmentalism. Indeed, military dominance of the economy in East Timor is reminiscent of the case of US aid policies *vis-à-vis* Vietnam and Laos in the 1960s, which worked to preempt national development outside the hands of a comprador class, entirely urban, living off windfall profits generated by the aid largesse.

In a country known for a system of corruption that massively benefits the holders of power, it would not be surprising if corruption did not extend beyond mere military-initiated plunder. The bare facts on corruption inside East Timor were revealed by the outgoing Indonesian-appointed Governor of occupied East Timor, Mario Carrascalão. In August 1992 he revealed that Rp.90 billion (US$45 million) out of Rp.900 billion provided by the central government for various development projects had been misappropriated by unscrupulous officials since 1975. His allegations were also echoed by the newly elected chairman of the DPRK, António Freitas Parada. Specifically, Parada blamed three institutions for corruption in East Timor, namely governors and former governors, governor's assistants for development affairs, chiefs and former chiefs of the provincial development planning agency Bapenda. In answer to such sweeping allegations of mismanagement of development funds, the state audit agency, BPKP, reportedly sent a team to East Timor to investigate the matter. [45] In a separate report Carrascalão complained that while he encountered no problem in investigating local Timorese officials involved in corruption cases, high flyers in the ministries appointed by Jakarta were removed from the province or posted abroad to prevent them being brought to justice inside East Timor. [46]

One visitor to East Timor in 1991, Borsuk, writes that the "opening" policy has eased the military's dominant role in the economy. A case in point is that the former army-controlled port is now in the hands of civilian port authorities. He contends, moreover, that the Demok affiliate, PT Batara Indra, now accounts for only slightly less than 60 percent of trade and construction work in East Timor. "There is competition where there wasn't before." But still that is no great news for coffee farmers who are victims of low coffee prices worldwide. [47] But who *have* been beneficiaries of this development spending by Jakarta?

A visit to Ermera, the heart of the coffee plantation country, reveals that army-Demok control over the purchasing, transport, warehousing and export of coffee appears total even though other military-private joint ventures such as PT Salazar Perkebunan, PT Sai Diak Utama, PT Ina Racik, and CV Algarve dan Timor have also muscled into the business in recent years. In 1992, the second year of the "opening up," these companies together raked in a total of US$7,861,150 for a total of 6,255 tons of coffee exported. [48]

From observation in Ermera I can confirm that at the point of purchase, where smallholders sell their produce to buyers—who also check for quality—there is no other outlet but Demok although sellers may believe that they are dealing with a KUD or village cooperative. While peasant farmers could probably live with a price of Rp. 2,500 a kilo, the purchase price for coffee beans in the range Rp.600–1,400 a kilogram over the last five years has given cause to major grievances by growers throwing them back upon the brink of subsistence. This is all the more intolerable as no evident hardship besets the middlemen and outsider interests who dictate prices, who set quality control, and who repatriate the profits to metropolitan Java. While the Association of Indonesian Coffee Exporters (AEKI) have made their grievances known through the press and other counsels that "fierce and unfair competition" by such multinationals as Nescafe have forced their 1,400 members onto the brink of bankruptcy, the shoe is on the other foot inside East Timor, where the Army-Demok monopoly is the direct cause of peasant smallholder grievance, not multinational capital. In other words the plight of the Timorese coffee smallholder is of a qualitatively different order from that of rest of the 1.4 million families reportedly earning their living from coffee elsewhere in Indonesia. [49]

But poverty in East Timor is not only the lot of the coffee smallholder. Various classes and strata of people in East Timor live below the poverty line, however defined. While there has always been poverty in East Timor in a near subsistence economy, the Indonesian invasion and occupation has thrown up new categories of poor outside traditional community support systems. There are urban poor and rural poor, there is poverty and malnutrition that appears to afflict particularly women and children, there is poverty and malnutrition that is specific to certain regions of East Timor and which is in part seasonal, there is a whole category of widows and orphans, there are the unemployed and underemployed urban poor—the scavengers and day laborers and the walking wounded. One would expect that after two decades of military occupation, the massive injection of "development" funds into East Timor would lead to the discernible improvement in the life and lot of the East Timorese. In fact, official statistics give the lie to this argument. In 1991 the average annual per capita income in East Timor was given as Rp.410,534 (US$196) or between Rp.190,000 (US$90) and Rp.700,000 (US$335). [50] While these bare figures suggest a significant improvement over pre-1976 figures—reflecting a more monetized economy—they also point to failure, especially if we consider the way that income is distributed in East Timor. In 1993 another unintended consequence of the "opening up"—inflation—registered upon the economy.

Seldom in any colonial situation has the occupier appeared so fat and sleek and the occupied so physically emaciated and so obviously mired in a situation of gross deprivation. Economic failure in East Timor under Indonesian colonial auspices is now so patently obvious that it can't be dismissed. Yet it is now dismissed with such explanations as the negative legacy of "geographical and human factors" or, as the Indonesian-appointed puppet Governor Abilio Soares would have us believe, East Timor is such a special case that it can't be compared in development terms with provinces in Indonesia owing to the negative legacy of Portuguese colonialism. [51] While, to be sure, the East Timor economy has special features bequeathed by history, so has the Indonesian version of counterinsurgency-related developmentalism indelibly stamped its destructive mark upon the human ecology of the territory.

Another consequence of the "opening up" has been tourism— or at least the entry of observers from the outside otherwise excluded for seventeen years. Evidently the scrutiny of outsiders was the cost/ risk that Suharto was prepared to make/take, perhaps on the basis that the physical and mental integration had somehow been achieved. But not many have grasped the opportunity, not many have cared to expose themselves to the kind of routine physical and psychological harassment meted out to locals and visitors alike in East Timor by *"intell"* and their auxiliaries. In 1989, the first year of the opening, 1,190 "wisata" or "tourists" visited the territory, in 1990, another 1,317; and in 1991, some 1,935 visitors entered East Timor (of these, 757 were listed as Australian). The second largest group were Japanese followed by other ASEAN nationals. No holders of Portuguese passports, East Timorese included, have been able to avail themselves of the so-called "open-door" policy, nor have many East Timorese holders of other passports flocked back to East Timor under Indonesian occupation.

By 1992 the picture had changed. The erstwhile tourist paradise had attracted the justified image of a charnel house. The number of visitors in that year dropped away to 936. Besides numbering my wife and nine year old child, this statistic mainly includes visiting diplomats and officials from missions in Jakarta along with the odd carpet-bagger from mainly Australia and Japan.

In important ways the 12 November 1991massacre in Dili can be viewed as both cause and effect of, respectively, the opening and the administrative shakedown in the province in its aftermath. Although Governor Carrascalão, who had served two terms as Governor of the province, was obliged under Indonesian law to step down at the end of his term on 18 September 1992, the choice of his successor in a runoff "election" of four candidates was in a number of ways unforeseen. Whereas Jakarta had been prepared to live with the former governor, largely seen by Timorese as a champion of their cause, his appointed successor, Abilio José Osorio Soares, the former Bupati of Manatutu and a former Apodeti man, is seen as a sop to the hardline rule enforced by the military in East Timor in the wake of the massacre. Soares has subsequently been credited with the statement that "even more should have died in Dili", [52] although subsequently retracted under pressure. The irony of the situation is that the major concession made by the President in his enquiry into the massacre was to replace the "soft-line" General Rudolf Warouw and as overall commander of ABRI in East Timor with Brigadier General Theo Syafei, an individual who answers directly to Prabowo Subiato, son-in-law of the President, rising star in the military-intelligence complex, and a former battalion commander in East Timor.

Still, ABRI did not always have it their own way, at least until the widescale arrests and draconian repression occurred, especially in Dili in the wake of the capture of Xanana Gusmão on 20 December 1992. The logic of the situation is perhaps captured in the revelation by Syafei that "seven out of the eight defendants in the trial for the 12 November incident in Dili were members of *Korpri* and worked for Government institutions." According to this admission, the worst possible scenario for Jakarta, even Fretilin (more accurately, members of the resistance) hold valid Indonesian identity cards and even Fretilin members or supporters have infiltrated *Korpri*. Thus, if ABRI could infiltrate Timorese society, so remarkably could Fretilin, after nearly two decades of repression, turn the tables on Jakarta. [53]

As revealed by one press article on the military management of the first anniversary of the massacre, the policy of tolerating small-scale protests, as in the past, has been replaced by a strategy of overall suppression of sentiments of nationalism by Timorese. This has translated into a hard line against the Roman Catholic church. Notable was the transfer out of East Timor of two priests regarded as close to the most vocal opponents of Jakarta's rule. The Bishop of East Timor and outspoken defender of Timorese rights, Ximenes Belo, has been under considerable duress since the massacre. In March 1993, as on so many other occasions, Indonesia announced that it was preparing to end its "special" military command in East Timor and to scale back the number of battalions in East Timor, hitherto never less than twelve. But for the Timorese people the rotation of military personnel and the change of commands is but a cosmetic change as the full apparatus of coercion and control is not disturbed in the least by such exercises. While Indonesia continues to assiduously promote the ideology of "normalcy" in East Timor, courting international tourism as much as foreign investments, the events down to 1996 discussed and documented below give the lie to that cannard.

But for the visitor to East Timor today, one is struck by the almost comatose condition of East Timorese, both urban and rural. While it is a fact that young Timorese reaching the outside world as refugees almost invariably require psychological counselling to adapt to a non coercive and "normal" environment, for those who remain, one is reminded of chapter five of Franz Fanon's *The Wretched of the Earth*, namely "Colonial War and Mental Disorders." While Fanon was speaking of French repression of the Algerian independence movement, the analogy of individual East Timorese at the hands of their Indonesian tormentors would seem an entirely accurate match for Fanon's catalogue of psychological symptoms under colonialism, namely, cases of natives and colonizers alike suffering symptoms of mental disorders of the "reactionary type," illness stemming from the atmosphere of total war, "affective-intellectual modifications and mental disorders after torture" and "psychosomatic disorders." The listless, almost zombie-like condition of too many East Timorese today attests to the profoundly disorientating and destructive impact of Indonesia's forced occupation and integration upon individual Timorese. The language of *pembangunan* can never make up for this tragic loss of identity, self-esteem, and peace of mind.

Conclusion

It is apparent from the above analysis that there is practically no manufacturing industry in East Timor today. It follows that there is no program of import substitution and therefore no value added to East Timor's exports. This is a serious indictment of Indonesia's development project in East Timor. It may serve Indonesian economies of scale to relegate the East Timor economy to that of a supplier of raw materials and prebends to Indonesian intermediaries, but such a direction merely reinforces East Timor's colonial dependency.

As Roger S. Clark has observed, in international law there is no suggestion that a lack of economic viability is grounds for delaying independence to a non-self-governing territory. On the contrary, he asserts, there is every reason to believe that East Timor possesses the natural resources with which to build a viable economy. [54] As we have seen, this most certainly is the case provided that Timor's resources are not siphoned off to Jakarta, are not diverted to sustain an occupation army, and are otherwise directed towards building both a national and an ecologically sustainable economy.

How has the process of accumulation in East Timor proceeded under Indonesian auspices? As seen, the Indonesian state backed by international lending agencies and its own oil-generated windfall profits wields a vastly larger "development" budget than that deployed by Portugal in the past. In privileging East Timor in its overall budget disbursement, however, it is patently obvious that Indonesia seeks, first, to accelerate the military pacification of East Timor and, second, to simultaneously achieve the economic, political, and social integration of the half-island into a larger regional economic ensemble. As seen, this has been achieved at the expense of the domestic economy. Wracked by war and devastation, the possibilities of domestic accumulation are more limited than even in the past. Both the subsistence economy and the handicraft sector have been massively distorted by the iniquitous system of population controls as well as unequal competition in the marketplace stemming from the uncontrolled entry of immigrants. Also, as seen, the embryonic professional and middle class that emerged in the last decades of Portuguese colonialism has been extirpated. Even an indigenous proletariat has not been permitted to form, much less labor consciousness. Indonesia has compensated by importing its own labor, a project which, as we have seen, has both political and economic consequences.

More so for Indonesia than even Portugal, the imperative to politically incorporate and maintain Timor under the metropolitan flag negates the strictly uneconomic imperialism arguments that the center is pouring more funds into the periphery than it is taking out. The promise of dividends stemming from exploitation of Timor oil following "re-pacification" of East Timor alone makes the project worthwhile, much less as seen, the handsome dividends paid individuals within the armed forces stemming from control over the coffee plantation economy. While the Indonesian state looks to long term advantage from its costly adventure in East Timor, there is no denying that individuals and capitalist blocs within the heights of ABRI-Cukong (Chinese crony) networks have already emerged as major economic beneficiaries of the rape of Timor.

As seen, the finely differentiated social structure of the East Timorese as much their language, their mores, their domiciles, their communities, and their livelihoods have been massively and deliberately disturbed and shaken by the experience of the Indonesian occupation. As Taylor has observed, while the military occupation initially sought to bring about an ideological and political convergence of the East Timorese through reeducation, resettlement and restructuring of the agricultural mode of production, post-1983 and faced with the stubborn resistance of the survivors, the Indonesian state went over to a policy of total change and eradication of all traces of indigenous society and culture. [55]

Today, there are disturbing signs that the sheer weight of the armed Indonesian presence has prevailed, especially given the demographic reconstitution of East Timor and the complex web of collaborative relationships built up over the years. Only the sacrifice of the martyrs of Santa Cruz stands as testimony to the collective memory of an age before the Indonesian war which makes the pre-1976 era seem like a golden age by comparison.

Notes

1.   Defence Plea by Xanana Gusmão, Member of CNRM, Commander of Falantil, Dili, 27 March 1993, translation by Tapol.

2.   The contradiction between the response of aid organizations to the Cambodian tragedy and the world's response to East Timor has been detailed by José Ramos-Horta in "The Quality of Mercy," an aptly entitled chapter in his work, *Funu: The Unfinished Saga of East Timor* (Trenton, N.J.:Red Sea Press, 1987), pp.191-204.

3.   A.B. Lapian and J.R. Chaniago, *Timor Timur Dalam Gerak Pembangunan*, Proyek Inventarisasi dan Dokumentasi Sejarah Nasional, Direktorat Sejarah dan Nilai-Nilai Tradisional, Direktorat Jenderal Kebudayaan, Departmen Pendidikan dan Kebudayaan, 1988, pp.21-22.

4.   *Posicao da Igreja Catolica Perante a Visita da Delegacão Parlamentar Portuguesa*, Imprensa da Diocese de Dili, September 1991.

5. As told in Julius Pour, *Benny Murdani: Profile of a Soldier States-man* (Jakarta: Yayasan Sudirman, 1993), p.336. General Murdani's mission on arrival in Dili on 10 December 1975 was precisely to capture and remove to Jakarta all Fretilin and Portuguese documents.

6. *Tempo*, 23 November 1991; and see analysis on education in John J. Taylor, *Indonesia's Forgotten War: The Hidden History of East Timor* (London: Zed, 1991), pp.125-7.

It should not be forgotten that the Indonesian system of state schools in East Timor overlaps with the Catholic school system as operated by Yayasan Pendidikan Santo Paulus or Saint Paul Education Foundation. According to church sources, the Foundation operates 93 primary schools across East Timor, in addition to 30 lower secondary schools, 11 upper level secondary schools and 4 technical schools. While certain of these schools (eg., the Missi Baucau, which traces its origins to 1916) were established prior to the Indonesian occupation, most emerged in the late 1970s and 1980s. As such, all the Catholic schools in East Timor are obliged to conform to an Indonesian curriculum.

7. Paul Jacob, *Straits Times*, 31 March 1992.

8. "East Timor Needs More Teachers and Better Teaching Facilities," *The Jakarta Post*, 5 September 1992.

9. ACFOA Dossier, pp.16-18.

10. Ibid.

11. *The Age*, 8 May 1978 cited in ACFOA Dossier, pp.16-18.

12. David Jenkins, *Far Eastern Economic Review*, 29 September 1978.

13. *Herald*, 12 September 1978.

14. Carmel Budiarjo and Liem Soei Liong, *The War Against East Timor* (London: Zed Press, 1984), p.77.

15. Anderson cited in Budiarjo and Liem, p.79 and see Noam Chomsky, *Myth and Ideology in US Foreign Policy* (New York: East Timor Human Rights Committee 1981), p.23.

16. ACFOA Dossier, pp.20-21 and see John G. Taylor, *Indonesia's Forgotten War: The Hidden History of East Timor* (London: Zed Books, 1991), p.122.

17. Peter Rodgers, *The Domestic and Foreign Press in Indonesia: Relations*, Research Paper No.18, May 1982, School of Modern Asian Studies, Griffith University, May 1982, p.27.

18. Ramos-Horta, op.cit., pp.195.

19. Rod Nordland, "Famine signs clear in East Timor," *The Age*, 10 June 1982.

20. Taylor, op.cit., p.121.

21. Ramos-Horta, op.cit., p.197 and see "Kerjasama PMI dan UNICEF untuk TT," *Kompas*, 26 May 1982. Indeed, a computer print-out from the ESCAP library in Bangkok on UN reports/publications on East Timor brought to light only a couple of speeches by the Portuguese President and–in line with Ramos-Horta's argument–nothing on UN agency activities inside East Timor..

22. John Hamilton, "Timor–then and now," *Herald*, 29&30 April 1983, 4 May 1983 critiqued by M.A. Browning and Susan Vitka, "East Timor and Diplomatic Pragmatism," *Southeast Asia Chronicle*, Issue No. 94, 1984, pp.18-23.

23. Mark Metherell, "Keating criticised over Timor aid," *The Age*, 18 April 1992, p.4.

24. Amanda Meade, "PM attacked on aid to Jakarta," *Sydney Morning Herald*, 20 April 1992, p.3.

25. M. Hadi Soesastro, "East Timor: Questions of Economic Viability" in Hal Hill (ed.), *Unity and Diversity: Regional Economic Development in Indonesia since 1979* (Kuala Lumpur: Oxford University Press, 1989), p.210.

26. Ibid.

27. Ibid., pp.210-19.

28. Ibid.

29. Carmel Budiardjo and Liem Soei Liong, *The War Against East Timor* (London: Zed Books 1984), pp.103-6.

30. Budiardjo and Liem, 1984, op.cit.

31. Richard Robison, *Indonesia: The Rise of Capital* (Sydney: ASAA/ Allen and Unwin, 1986), p.269n. By the 1980s Suharto family business interests were also turning to East Timor with interests in, besides coffee, the mining of marble and construction (interests held by Suharto's wife) and, most recently, transport/tourism.

32. Budiardjo and Liem, op.cit., p.107.

33. According to a Reuters report (*New Straits Times*, 4 March 1992), famine killed several people on the East Timorese island of Atauro in early 1992. In the words of a peasant farmer quoted in this report: "We have no corn or rice. We have had to eat the fruit of palm trees to survive." Atauro was the site of major concentration camps and, like the rest of the country, proclaimed out of bounds for international relief agencies.

34. See P. Drs. Gregor Neonbasu, *Keadilan dan Perdamaian di Diosis Dili, Timor Timur* (Dili: Komisi Komunikasi Sosial Diosis Dili Timor Timur, 1992), p.76.

35. see "East Timor: How many people are missing?," *Timor Information Service*, No.28, February 1980 for the official Portuguese census figure.

36. Timothy Mo, *A Redundancy of Courage* (London: Chatto and Windus, 1991).

37. Lapaian and Chaniago, op.cit., pp.107-8.

38. Herb Feith, an unfinished paper for the Asian Peace Research Association conference, Christchurch, New Zealand, 30 January-4 February 1992.

The other side of the coin of the labor influx has been the crude attempts by Indonesia to lure East Timorese workers to factories in Java with promises of better pay. Exposed by Asia Watch in a paper entitled "Deception and Harassment of East Timorese Workers," it transpires that not only were these workers (several hundreds) exploited but were subject as well to political harassment.

39. Richard Borsuk, "Killings Breed Antipathy in East Timor," *Asian Wall Street Journal*, 9 December 1991. By 1993 the balance between arrivals and departures on this shipping service appeared to me to be more even.

40. Such a view has also been expressed in one Indonesian study undertaken in East Timor by Indonesian academics from Gadjah Mada University, albeit without denying the assumptions of integration. See Prof. Dr. Mubyarto, Dr. Loekman Soestrisno etc, al., *East Timor: The Impact of Integration: An Indonesian Anthropological Study* (trs) (Melbourne: IRIP, 1981), p.54, who write, "The flood of newcomers will create competition with the indigenous inhabitants which could sow the seeds of communal conflict. Within indigenous East Timorese circles a feeling of hatred has arisen towards the Makassarese and Bugis. They are seen as a new group of extortioners who stand in the way of their economic advancement." They also noted communal incidents directed against Javanese prostitutes in Dili.

41. See "BKKBN propinsi Timtim menyatu dengan rakyat," *Suara Timor Timur*, 13 Mei, 1993, p.3.

42. See Taylor, op.cit., pp.158-9.

43. Feith, op.cit.

44. Soesastro, op.cit.

45. "Administration asked to be on alert for corruption in E. Timor," *The Jakarta Post*, 1 September 1992.

46. "Carrascalão says punishment of corrupt officials goes on," *The Jakarta Post*, 5 September 1992.

47. Borsuk, op.cit.

48. "Masyarakat Jepang doyan kopi, kita kebagian peluang," *Suara Timor Timur*, 15 Mei 1993, p.5.

It comes as no surprise, then, that in July 1995, international press reports revealed that coffee farmers in Gleno, 65 km west of Dili, burned down a local market in protest over low coffee prices. The farmers complained that local businessmen (ie., agents of Indonesian procurers) were only willing to pay between 700 and 1,500 rupiah per kg.. The farmers called upon the government to raise prices to at least 1,500 per kg. (Reuter, Dili, 10 July 1995).

49. *Jakarta Post*, 1 September 1992.

50. "Rendah, pendapatan per kapita Tim Tim," *Suara Timor Timur*, 19 Mei 1993.

51. "Jangan bandingkan Tim Tim dengan propinsi lain," *Suara Timor Timur*, 24 Mei 1993.

52. Tom Hyland, "'Even more' should have died in Dili: Governor," *The Sydney Morning Herald*, 4 November 1992.

53. *Indonesian Times*, 30 May 1992.

54. Roger S. Clark, "The Decolonization of East Timor at the United Nations: Norms of Self-Determination and Aggression," *The Yale Journal of World Public Order*, Vol. 7:1 (1980).

55. Taylor, op.cit., p.157.

2

Perez de Cuellar on East Timor

While the UN General Assembly vote of 1982 repeated its call for self-determination for East Timor, with 50 in favor, 46 against, and 50 abstentions, the motion also instructed the UN Secretary-General, then Javier Perez de Cuellar, to initiate consultations with all concerned parties in order to "achieve a comprehensive settlement of the East Timor issue." In the 1984, 1985, and 1986 sessions of the General Assembly it was agreed to defer discussion of the East Timor question pending submission of reports by the Secretary-General on talks between the Portuguese and Indonesian governments as specified in the 1983 General Assembly resolution. Matters drifted, until 14 September 1989, when Perez de Cuellar released a report on the current state of progress, concluding that a proposed visit by a Portuguese Parliamentary Mission to East Timor would help create an atmosphere conducive to an internationally acceptable solution. Instead, expectations raised by the proposed visit—eventually cancelled—led to a surge of East Timor independence sentiment, leading to the Santa Cruz cemetery massacre of 12 November 1991 by Indonesian armed forces. This infamous event prompted the Secretary-General to decry the events as "an unjustified act of aggression" and a "crime that has to be punished." On 1 December 1991, the Secretary-General tasked his personal envoy to investigate the killings.

The following is a dialogue between myslf and Perez de Cuellar, on East Timor, conducted in the course of a public lecture on the theme of UN involvement in conflicts around the world at Universiti Brunei Darussalam, Bandar Seri Begawan, Brunei Darussalam, on 9 September 1993. This was originally released on 22 September 1993 on the electronic mail server "Apakabar" moderated by John

MacDougall and with an estimated audience of 80,000 (1995). The
original exchange was otherwise closely monitored by officials of
the Brunei Darussalam Foreign Ministry.

In this lecture, the former UN Secretary-General underscored the lofty
UN principle that "all UN resolutions have to be implemented impartially." To this end he instanced the role of the UN body in solv-
ing such conflicts as the Namibian problem, the Iran-Iraq war, the
Gulf War, the Afghanistan question, and the Cambodia question.
Noting the end of the Cold War had usefully facilitated the settlement of such conflicts, the destruction of the former Yugoslavia also
revealed that old rivalries had been resurrected.

In responding to Perez de Cuellar's speech from the floor, I offered strong endorsement of his remarks on the UN body's key role
in bringing to fruition an apparent resolution of the Cambodia problem. I also reminded the former Secretary-General that his stated
mistrust of the Khmer Rouge in the lead up to constitutional talks
around the question of the future form of government in Cambodia
and the constitutional role of Prince Sihanouk had to be seen alongside his own previous role in offering the UN seat to that party. While
I concurred with the UN Secretary-General as to his broad remarks
on Cambodia [and the pivotal role of Prince Sihanouk], I pointed out
that it was an oversight to neglect the case of East Timor, the "back
door," so to speak, of the Southeast Asian country in which he was
delivering his speech.

I observed that Indonesia was bound by two Security Council
resolutions [384 (22 December 1975), 389 (1976)] and one General
Assembly resolution [3485 (12 December 1975)] to facilitate East
Timor's self-determination, to withdraw its occupation forces, and
to facilitate the role of the UN Secretary-General to bring together
all parties concerned to achieve the decolonization of the territory. I
noted that the Secretary-General had protested the horrific massacre
which occurred in Dili on 12 November 1991 and had called for an
impartial enquiry, but that the Secretary-General's special emissary
sent to East Timor, Amos Wako, had yet to table his report [at least
not made public] and, in any case, as reported in the local (Brunei)
press on 8 September ["Jakarta Interfered in UN Probe: US", *Borneo
Bulletin,* 8 September 1993, p.7], was subject to the manipulation of
evidence. I further noted that it was the former Secretary-General
himself who, in 1982 [General Assembly resolution 37/30], had initiated proceedings towards this dialogue—a process still in train—

and with a meeting between the Portuguese Foreign Minister and his Indonesian counterpart pending in New York (on 16 September 1994). I further noted that provision was made in this resolution for the participation in this dialogue of representatives of the East Timor people.

However, I pointed out, the distinguished and acknowledged representative of the East Timor people, Xanana Gusmão, was at this moment incarcerated in an Indonesian prison, having been tried in an Indonesian court house in Dili and sentenced to life imprisonment (commuted to twenty years). Why, I asked, was this man not present at the UN-initiated dialogue in New York in line with the principles established by the office of the UN Secretary-General, namely dialogue "with all concerned parties"? More the irony, I said, that this man was not permitted to deliver his defense plea in Portuguese. All the more appropriate, I added, that I read from a section of that defense plea, otherwise leaked to the international press:

> May I recall that Saddam Hussein reminded the international community that there was already a precedent for disregarding the principles of international law, expressly mentioning East Timor. What value does Indonesia give to the resolutions of the Security Council and the General Assembly? (Xanana Gusmão, Dili, 27 March 1993).

I then asked the former Secretary-General to reply. In return, Perez de Cuellar responded by acknowledging that he had failed to mention the East Timor case in his speech. He then added that he felt that the respondent knew something that he did not in respect to the Wako report. Acknowledging that he had been out of office for 18 months, he felt that in fact the report had been tabled. [This was true, but in fact the report had not yet been publically released].

The Secretary-General indicated that he saw his past role on the East Timor question as that of a go-between. He acknowledged that the Indonesian occupation of East Timor has not been recognized by the UN and that Portugal was considered by the UN as the administering power in that territory.

He also specified that he expects Indonesia to be especially careful on human rights and not to indulge in "excesses of force."

The former Secretary-General expressed the view that a solution to the the East Timor problem could only be brought about through negotiation. Moreover, this solution had to be in line with pending UN Resolutions.

In defending his role in establishing the mechanism for achieving a comprehensive settlement, he reiterated that no solution could be achieved without "dialogue."

In concluding his remarks, the former Secretary-General noted that the question of territorial waters and resource allocation [a reference to the Timor Gap Accord signed between Indonesia and Australia and Portugal's challenge to that Accord in the World Court] significantly clouded the East Timor question.

While the Secretary-General held back from asserting the right of the East Timorese people to self-determination, his scrupulous emphasis upon the "totally impartial implementation" of UN resolutions appeared not to rule this option out.

Envoi

As a footnote to the preceding, the Portuguese Newsagency Lusa reported on 26 October 1995 that Perez de Cuellar condemned Indonesia for "continuing to resist" the UN resolutions regarding East Timor. "I very much regret that Indonesia not make a final political decision of complying with the [UN] decisions," he stated. He further described Indonesia's defiance of the decisions of the UN Security Council, together with the disregard by other governments of the UN's decisions, as leading to "the loss of credibility" of the organization. For the UN to be credible, he pointed out, "It is very important that the member countries have the necessary political will for that the [UN] decisions be complied with."

3

An East Timorese Reconciliation?

As a result of agreements reached between the Portuguese and Indo-
nesian Foreign Ministers during the fourth and fifth round of UN-
hosted negotiations in May 1994 and January 1995, respectively,
the first UN-sanctioned inter-Timorese talks were held between 3–5
June 1995 in Stadtschlaining, a medieval castle, 140 km south of
Vienna in Austria. This meeting, the first "All-Inclusive Intra-
Timorese Dialogue" (AII-TD) was significant in the way that it per-
mitted a Timorese voice in negotiations otherwise restricted to Por-
tugal and Indonesia. But, while financed by the UN and with a UN
official in attendance, the talks were not permitted to address the
political status of East Timor or to replace the Ministerial negotia-
tions. In the run-up to this meeting, the UN Secretary-General initi-
ated contacts or so-called "cross-meetings" with Timorese of vari-
ous political persuasions. But in drawing up a list of 30 partici-
pants it galled the resistance that the line-up favored Jakarta's pro-
integrationist appointees. While the Apostolic Administrator of Dili
and Nobel Peace Prize-nominee Bishop Ximenes Carlos Belo was
invited, the jailed resistance leader, Xanana Gusmão was shunned.
Even so, the meeting had to be postponed to meet further Indone-
sian objections. Notwithstanding the grave misgivings held by José
Ramos-Horta, Special Representative of the National Council of
Maubere Resistance, as to the dominant pro-Indonesian composi-
tion of the meeting, the results turned out an unexpected victory for
the resistance. All members present signed the document known as
the Burg Schlaining Declaration [see Documents]. Inter alia, the
Declaration affirmed GA resolution 37/30 [see Documents], the need
to protect human rights, and the desirability of further inter-Timorese

talks under UN auspices. Otherwise, the atmosphere of reconciliation achieved at Burg Schlaining affirmed a strong sense of Timorese nationalism vis-à-vis Indonesia. This was too good to be true, however, as scarcely was the ink dry on the document than Indonesian intelligence working out of the Indonesian Embassy in Vienna pressured the East Timorese travelling on Indonesian passports to repudiate the document, thus throwing a cloud over the entire process. Alone, Bishop Belo refused to sign a separate document swearing allegiance to Indonesia.

Earlier, a representative of the UN had graced a meeting of pro-integrationist Timorese, along with a group of fence-sitters, who, in September 1994, met under Indonesian auspices in Chepstow in the UK, the second edition of a farce which I exposed in print as follows. Both meetings were financed by Siti Hardiyanti Rukmana (Mbak Tutut), Suharto's eldest daughter, working through the so-called "Portugal-Indonesia Friendship Society".

*This article was originally published as "Voices of hope—or of oppression," **The Nation** (Bangkok), 11 January 1994.*

In late December wire agencies (*South China Morning Post*, 27 December 1993, p.8) reported that East Timorese exile Rogerio Lobato, a former senior member of Fretilin along with former Portuguese General Galvao de Melo and member of the revolutionary council which ended the dictatorship in Portugal in May 1974 would visit Indonesia from 4 January "in the latest move in Jakarta's efforts to mute international attacks on its role in East Timor." How did this extraordinary turn of events eventuate? What is the meaning of this diplomacy outside the ambit of the United Nations? What risks does this private and erstwhile secret diplomacy entail?

Between 14 and 15 December, a meeting occurred in a house outside London between two groups of Timorese. One consisted of pro-Indonesian East Timorese along with Indonesian officials, while the other comprised self-appointed representatives of the East Timorese people in exile. Styled the "Reunião fraternal entre lideres Timorenses da Indonesia e da diaspora" (fraternal reunion between Timorese leaders from Indonesia and the diaspora), this meeting can be seen as a diplomatic triumph for the Indonesian side. Not only had a section of the Timorese-in-exile been lured into dialogue with their pro-integrationist compatriots but the Indonesian side had managed to sow discord amongst the overseas Timorese while at the same time conferring legitimacy on "acceptable" as opposed to "unacceptable" leaders of that community.

The matter can be further illustrated by examining the dramatis personae of those involved in the London meeting. Chief front man for the Indonesian side at London was, not surprisingly, former Timorese Democratic Union (UDT) supremo turned Indonesian collaborator, currently presidential appointee cum roving ambassador for Indonesia on East Timorese affairs, Francisco Lopes da Cruz. Having started his political career in colonial Timor as a representative of the Caetanoist Acção Nacional Popular party, Lopes da Cruz did not arrive alone at the London meeting, however. Besides top Indonesian diplomats from the London Embassy as well as from Indonesian missions in Spain and France, representatives of Indonesian military intelligence including figures close to presidential confidant and *eminence gris*, Minister for Research and Technology, B.J. Habibie, were also in attendance.

While Lopes da Cruz spoke long at this meeting of the tragedy of the "grand Timorese family" separated by time and space, of the need for "unity of all for the good of all," it was after all the language of *"integrasi,"* not a formula that envisaged an independent Timor outside of Indonesia. Besides the exercise in London designed to win over the cream of Timorese society in the diaspora, Lopes da Cruz has also been active on Indonesia's behalf over the past twelve months in an albeit unsuccessful attempt to win over the Vatican to Jakarta's views. Taken together, this diplomatic push by Indonesia seeks to remove two major obstacles to the legitimation of its rule in East Timor, major opposition from the Church and, no less, from the most troublesome and least manageable quarter of all, the leadership of the overseas Timorese who have hitherto showed one face and stood for one supreme goal, the liberation of their homeland.

Heading the "reconciliation" group of overseas Timorese was erstwhile senior or rather expelled Fretilin leader, Abilio Araujo. Styling himself "Head of Delegation of Leaders of the Diaspora," Araujo in an opening speech declared the meeting "an exciting historical moment for our beloved Timor."

While the presence at London of Rogerio Lobato, founder of the Fretilin armed forces or Falantil and brother of the late Fretilin commander Nicolau, might be taken as a diplomatic coup on the part of Jakarta, it should be recalled that Jakarta's new "ally" also served long time in a Luanda prison on the charge of trafficking in diamonds and abusing Angolan diplomatic privileges. [Rogerio Lobato was subsequently expelled from Fretilin for such activities.]

Besides these Portugal-based leaders, the "reunion" also attracted a strong push from Macau led by lawyer Dr. Manuel Tilman, a former Timorese member of the Portuguese parliament (1980-81) [Independent Social Democratic Party] and self-styled UDT President in Macau. Other members of the so-called "grupo do seis" or group of six from Macau included the highly respected Timorese community leader Father Francisco Fernandez.

No communiques issued forth from this meeting except the decision taken that this would be the first of a series of talks. [While there was speculation that a subsequent meeting would be held in an ASEAN country, in fact the second meeting was held in London.] Given the secret and private nature of the diplomacy, one can only speculate as to the *quid pro quo* offered by the Indonesian side in return for the extraordinary gesture of granting visas to Rogerio Lobato, Tilman and others to visit Indonesia (and East Timor?).

It appears now that notwithstanding obvious divisions between UDT and Fretilin among the overseas Timorese, Jakarta has successfully opened up a rift between those who support the so-called "reconciliation" process and those who resist. This is not surprising as neither Fretilin leadership (José Ramos-Horta nor Mari Alkitari) nor for that matter UDT leadership (João Carrascalão) are in agreement with this diplomacy. Neither has Portugal nor, for that matter, the UN lent its endorsement to the Indonesian initiative.

While individual members of the East Timorese leaders' delegation assert that they still claim self-determination is the objective, that they still regard Xanana Gusmão as the rightful leader of a future independent East Timorese state, that the reconciliation talks are not out of line with the ongoing UN sponsored dialogue on East Timor, the affair raises more questions than it answers.

While impatience on the part of the East Timorese with the snail's pace of the UN-initiated talks is understandable, the rush to embrace the Indonesian government in private diplomacy obviously carries enormous risks. First, it plays directly into the hands of Indonesian propaganda aimed at splitting the fragile unity of the East Timorese nationalist movement, namely between "acceptable" leaders (Abilio Araujo) and unacceptable leaders (José Ramos-Horta and Mari Alkatiri). Second, it is a delusion to expect Indonesia to offer the slightest concessions on self-determination on East Timor to any single group of East Timorese when Jakarta has shunned the international community and ignored the numerous UN resolutions on the issue for almost two decades. Neither, for that matter, would recent outbursts by the Indonesian president against pro-democracy activists in the Indonesian capital offer any hope for the East Timorese self-determination cause in any quarter. Third, it might be said, by focussing minds on leadership questions—which have always bedevilled the East Timorese freedom cause—Indonesia detracts from the unity of resolve required by the Timorese if ever and whenever the UN pushes Indonesia to honor an internationally acceptable referendum on self-determination. Finally, by entering into a secret diplomacy with Indonesia, the "reconciliation" group threatens to prejudice the ongoing UN-sponsored dialogue on East Timor. Pushed to extremes—unless this too is the Indonesian strategy—the splittist tactics pursued by Jakarta in dealing with the Timorese threatens to recreate the devastating conditions of civil war such as transpired in East Timor in 1975.

Clearly, what concerns Jakarta is the creation in Lisbon last August of the all-party Coordinating Committee for the Diplomatic Front, under which the three major elements of the Timorese resistance seek to take a common stand especially on UN-initiated discussions on East Timor such as at the third round of talks on East Timor held in New York on 17 September 1993 [see Documents].

Those East Timorese leaders behind the push for reconciliation with Jakarta would be well advised to direct their energies towards obliging Indonesia to adhere to the letter and spirit of the 17 September 1993 meeting, notably the stipulation set down by the UN Secretary General that Indonesia facilitate unconditional access to the territory by UN agencies, including human rights monitors and other interested parties including journalists (respectively, the fourth and sixth points of the statement by the UN Secretary-General's spokesperson on East Timor). Bargaining for visa rights with Indonesia to enter East Timor pending the implementation of these determinants and, indeed, pending the fourth round of UN-sponsored talks on East Timor to be held in Geneva on 6 May 1994 is tantamount to trading with the devil and should be condemned as such.

Envoi

A second "All-Inclusive Intra-Timorese Dialogue" (AII-TD) was conducted under UN auspices on 19–22 March 1996. This meeting, also held in Austria, brought together a total of fourteen exiled representatives of the East Timorese resistance along with fifteen living under Indonesian rule. As with the format of the previous meeting, there was to be no debate on the issue of self-determination and no discussion on the political status of East Timor. The former Indonesian-installed governor of East Timor, Guilherme Goncalves, and signatory of the so-called "Balibo Declaration" on integration was prevented from attending by the Indonesian authorities. Gonclaves had earlier outraged Indonesia by repudiating the "Balibo Declaration," otherwise not recognized by the UN. Bishop Ximenes Belo, who played a key mediating role at the June 1995 meeting, also did not attend. In his case, however, this owed to Indonesian pressure upon by the Papal Nucio in Jakarta. Nevertheless, the Bishop—duly awarded the 1996 Nobel Prize for Peace along with José Ramos-Horta—was ably represented by Dili Diocesan Vicar-General Father José António da Costa. Bishop Belo sent a message to the participants urging them to work towards finding consensus, taking into account the cultural identity, religion, and history of East Timor and the need to safeguard the future of Timorese youth. While the document which ensued from the meeting [see Documents] was no repeat of the declaration of June 1995, and otherwise short on specifics, members of the resistance nevertheless lent their signatures in the interest of keeping up the momentum of the Dialogue and, to a large extent, not wishing to be seen as the obstructive party. Still, from the account of one of the participants, that did not prevent Francisco Lopes da Cruz, Suharto's so-called "Special Ambassador on East Timor," from seeking—unsuccessfully— to have paragraphs 6 and 8 refering to UN resolution 37/30 removed from the June 1995 Burg Schlaining Declaration.

4

Appeal to US Asianists on "Death Squads" in East Timor

It is of more than passing interest that in December 1995 ABRI announced its intention to "wage a war of words" on the Internet because of anxieties over "anti-Indonesian" articles circulating on various electronic networks. In the words of the ABRI chief-of-staff behind the move, the activities of these networkers is "agitational and propaganda" aimed at destroying Indonesian national unity. Meantime, Indonesia has answered back with ABRI.mil.net for the armed forces and Hankam.gov.net for the Department of Defense.

On 22 February 1995, the East Timor Action Network (ETAN), a coordinating center for East Timor support groups in the US and major lobby for political action on East Timor, disseminated an "Action Alert" on the disturbing actions of "death squads" inside East Timor. Then a subscriber to H-Asia, a US-based moderated E-mail conference of professional historians of Asia, I was requested to pass comment. The following was my response.

The ETAN/US Action Alert on "death squads" in East Timor [22 February 1995] certainly gives one some pause. While it comes as no news to close followers of the East Timor scene, it undoubtedly merits a larger audience among Asianists.

As mentioned in the Alert, the levels of military-initiated violence have increased dramatically inside East Timor since the APEC summit in Bogor, Indonesia, in November 1994. As well noted in international news media, the East Timorese saw in this gathering an ideal opportunity to publicize their claims for independence. While the media focussed upon the activities of East Timorese in Jakarta, namely the dramatic entry into the US Embassy compound of a group of pro-independence East Timorese, parallel events in Dili, the capital of East Timor, were less reported but, nevertheless, are of far greater importance as to the overall status of the occupied territory and the aspirations of the East Timorese people.

This is a reference to the unprecedented outbreak of communal violence in Dili, in part provoked by tensions besetting ethnic Timorese, overwhelmingly Catholic, and Muslim immigrants, especially from the southern Sulawesi province of Indonesia. Never before in the history of Indonesian occupation of East Timor has there been such obvious acts of civil resistance on the part of large numbers of ordinary Timorese. Unlike, say, the Dili massacre of November 1991, today's *"intifada"* (to use a Palestinean analogy) has also spread to other towns in East Timor, notably Baucau in the east, as well as to a number of towns in the interior. Certain triggers to the violence which first errupted in the capital can be traced to acts of religious provocation committed by immigrants or non-Timorese against the Catholic Church. But one should not impose entirely communalist interpretations upon what has clearly been an outpouring of pro-independence sentiment, especially on the part of East Timorese youth, including students of the University of East Timor. Neither should one ignore the pro-active role of Indonesian or pro-Indonesian *agents provocateurs* in stirring this violence or in presenting it as purely communalist. In this confusing situation, Indonesia also mounted demonstrations of pro-Indonesian support.

While some of this was reported in the international press, Indonesia wasted no time in bundling visiting members of the international press out of the country and, now, has re-imposed strict controls upon outsiders wishing to visit East Timor. But, no sooner had the APEC conferencees dispersed, and the press spotlight shifted, than the repression of pro-independence activists commenced inside East Timor. This was a predictable pattern of events. Certain of this violence is documented in the Alert. Certain of the ongoing violence perpetrated by the military against East Timorese has also been carried in the fairly regular bulletins circulated by Amnesty International. What the ETAN Alert doesn't mention is that the mounting civil unrest, and its repression in East Timor, concides with a damning report on Indonesia released in January by Mr. Bacre Waly Ndiaye, the UN Special Rapporteur on extrajudicial, summary, and arbitrary executions. *Inter alia*, this report criticizes Indonesia's account of the Dili massacre of November 1991 and its failure to account for the disappeared [see Documents].

As highlighted in the Alert, it was in these general circumstances that the so-called Ninjas or criminal gangs raised their ugly heads. Such was the deteriorating situation in Dili that, on 14 February, the Apostolic Administrator of East Timor, Bishop Belo, was obliged to call for a meeting with Indonesian civil and military authorities to plea for the re-entry into the city of police patrols to impose order upon an anarchic situation where citizens were subject to the random terror of military-linked gangs otherwise operating with impunity. The natural instincts of East Timorese to administer their own justice did not improve matters. At this point the Indonesian-installed "governor" of East Timor, Abilio Soares, was removed to Jakarta to attend a "mentalization" course, believed [incorrectly] to be a prelude to his dismissal. Where Abilio Soares had proven to be too autonomy-minded, no such lapse is anticipated on the part of the acting governor, Brigadier Johannes Haribowo.

To the extent that the West focused attention on East Timor in recent weeks, it has been over the killings of six Timorese by members of the Indonesian armed forces in a place called Liquisa. An outcry by the East Timorese, monitored by human rights organizations, was evidently strong enough to prompt the intercession with Indonesia on the part of the US, the Netherlands, Japan, and Canada. It is understood that the US Ambassador to Indonesia, Robert Barry, raised this matter with the Indonesian authorities. Jakarta responded to these interventions with unusual dispatch and, in a seldom-seen gesture on the part of the armed forces, sent an investigating team to East Timor. As far as East Timorese opinion is concerned, the killings were those of unarmed villagers. The military authority in Dili alleges that the victims were members of "Fretilin," invariably referred to in official parlance as "outlaws." As I write these lines, news has arrived that General Feisal Tanjung, Indonesian armed forces commander, has told a parliamentary hearing in Jakarta that four of the dead were informants for Fretilin, and that two were armed members. To all intents and purposes, the military enquiry, the result and the sequel, has all the trappings of the official coverup of the Dili massacre, so eloquently exposed by Waly Bacre Nyiade in his report.

To finish on a personal note, I visited Liquisa in August 1992 and June 1993. I particularly wanted to show my Japanese wife (and child) the site where the Portuguese administration of the colony were interned in appalling conditions during the Japanese occupation of the island. This we accomplished but not without some degree of physical harrassment by the local military authorities, not the kind of treatment your everyday Japanese and Western tourist in Bali comes to expect. I think that my family had never before seen automatic weapons at such close quarter.

Located about an hour's bus-ride to the west of Dili, Liquisa resembles a series of villages sprawled across a mountain-side that plunges into the sea, otherwise softened by the presence of a white coral sand beach. Shuttered shop-houses, old colonial-era structures and thatch-roofed village houses all seem to lie buried beneath flowering bougainvillea. The peace is deceptive, however. For some reason or other, the Chinese of Liquisa were killed by invading Indonesian forces in 1975–76. None remain, and neither have other Chinese sought to return. The notion that armed Fretilin guerrillas would hide out in Liquisa strikes me as both unlikely and absurd. Located astride the highway linking Dili with West Timor, Liquisa and its neighborhood have long been under Indonesian military control, neither does the barren mountainside of Liquisa offer much in the way of cover. Also, as I experienced at first hand, the Indonesian military presence is ubiquitous and so is its system of informers. While armed resistance activity continues at a low level in the extreme east of the island, why and how would Fretilin/Falantil regroup in Liquisa?

As the Alert requests, a permanent UN presence in East Timor is urgently needed, and the more agencies engaged, the better. This would be entirely in line with standing UN resolutions on East Timor and would, of course, fall in with current UN concerns as to the modus operandi of East Timor's decolonization.

Envoi

Unquestionably, the Liquisa shootings had important sequels, at least in producing a flurry of administrative memorials on the question of human rights. In March 1995, to salvage the situation, the National Commission on Human Rights set up by Suharto three years earlier in the way of salvaging international credibility in the wake of the Santa Cruz massacre, accused the military of human rights violations with respect to the Liquisa killings and later announced the creation of a Dili-based office of the Commission.

In December 1995, however, visiting UN Human Rights Commissioner, Jose Ayala Lasso, failed to override Suharto's objections that a UN Human Rights Office could not be opened in Dili, as requested, and as urgently required, but only in Jakarta. While the creation of a Jakarta office could in itself play an important role in protecting human rights in Indonesia and East Timor, at this writing, the realization of even this office has yet to transpire. While a Dili branch of the pro-Indonesian human rights office belatedly opened its doors in 1996, serious concerns have been raised about its ability to function effectively. Notably, it is located opposite the district military headquarters. Moreover, its director is not a speaker of Tetum, the major local language, while other employees are former local government staff. Alone, the Commission on Peace and Justice established by Bishop Belo in August 1994 has shown its worth.

In fact, as revealed in the appended documents, with the exception of 1993 and 1997, the UNCHR has issued only two resolutions on East Timor since the Dili massacre, along with a series of "consensus statements" (1992, 1994, 1995, and 1996). Such watered-down or minimalist statements have allowed Indonesia, a member of the Commission, to treat the UN body with contempt. Apart from allowing the Special Rapporteur on Extrajudicial Killings and the UNHRC Commissioner to visit East Timor, nothing contained in the earlier statements has actually been implemented. It remains to be seen whether Indonesia acts upon the letter and spirit written into the 1997 resolution, especially as the Indonesian Foreign Ministry answered back on 25 April 1997 that it "refuses and will never accept" the stationing of UN human rights officials in Jakarta to monitor East Timor.

5

Australia, the Timor Gap, and the World Court

As explained in a World Court press release of 3 July 1995 [see Documents], the Court was unable to pass a ruling on the dispute between Portugal (acting for East Timor) and Australia over the exploitation of Timor's oil, as Indonesia did not accept the jurisdiction of the Court. While Australia subsequently claimed a technical victory, at least in the way that its immoral exploitation of East Timor's resources remains unchallenged, the reiteration by the Court that East Timor remains a non-self governing territory and that its people have a right to self-determination vindicates the Portuguese challenge and comes as a major vitiation of Indonesia's claims of historical consolidation over East Timor during the past twenty years of military rule.

*This chapter was originally commissioned by Jean Inglis of the Japan-East Timor Coalition for publication in **Higashi Chimoru Tsushin** (No.35, April 1995, pp.3-12). The English language version, as reproduced below, was published as a two part series in **The Nation** newspaper (Bangkok) as (Part 1), "Australia, the Timor Gap and the World Court" (25 April 1995, op ed page) and (Part II) "Coddling Indonesia in the Name of Business" (26 April 1995, op ed page).*

One of the givens of international relations is that while politics change, geography remains fixed. For Australia and Australians there is no escaping the reality of neighborhood with the sprawling archipelago that Indonesia inherited as successor state to the Netherlands East Indies.

That was just as much the case under the left-leaning Sukarno as it is with his successor, the New Order military-backed regime of General Suharto. But whereas Sukarno's version of economic and political nationalism was perceived by the West as drawing Indonesia into the communist bloc of countries, Suharto was—and still is—rewarded by the West for his rescue of Indonesia from leftist threats and economic penury and, in the bargain, for delivering up the resources-strewn archipelago for economic plunder. But whereas Indonesia—and the West—could live with Portuguese Timor as a decadent outpost of the Salazar-Cataeno order, the political-developmental model espoused by Fretilin in the period of Portuguese-sponsored decolonization represented an ideological threat and anti-model to the very underpinnings of the Suharto regime.

While the act of cleaning up the map on East Timor implied by the Indonesian invasion of 1975/76 also heralded the naked plunder of East Timor's resources by military-linked companies, few observers at the time would have foreseen a brazen re-divisioning of East Timor's marine resources between Indonesia and another power. This is a reference to the Timor Gap Treaty signed between the Australian government and Indonesia in December 1989.

Not incidentally, the Timor Sea, lying between East Timor and northern Australia, is believed to contain the world's 23rd largest oil field, with estimated reserves of five billion barrels of oil and 50 trillion feet of liquid natural gas.

The Timor "Gap," then, is an area, approximately 25 kilometers long, which had been excluded from the seabed boundary line negotiated between Australia and Indonesia in October 1972. But where Indonesia conceded to Australia on the question of delimitation in line with the continental shelf principle, Portugal held out over the principle of demarcating Timor's sea boundary with Australia according to the median point.

Indonesia, meanwhile, wasted no time in seeking negotiations with Australia on the "Gap" subsequent to its annexation of East Timor. During a state visit to Jakarta in October 1976, then Australian Prime Minister Malcolm Fraser offered recognition of Indonesia's *de facto* incorporation of East Timor, although the East Timorese resistance led by Fretilin was then in control of large swathes of the territory and the ink was hardly dry on the UN Security Council resolutions condemning Indonesia's armed invasion and calling for withdrawal [see Documents].

As the Indonesian newspaper, *Kompas* (18 December 1978), later made known, Mochtar Kusuumatmadja, Indonesia's Foreign Minister at the time, instructed his Australian counterpart that negotiations on the continental shelf boundary could not begin without Australia first recognizing Indonesian sovereignty over the whole island, especially as the south coast of Timor formed one of the survey base lines. Sure enough, in January 1978, the ruling Australian conservative government recognized Indonesia's *de jure* sovereignty in East Timor, only holding reservations as to the method of takeover.

In a stroke, Australia acknowledged Indonesian sovereignty over East Timor, by implication and contrary to UN law, derecognized Portugal's legal responsibility for the decolonization of East Timor and, in the bargain, cleared the way for negotiations on the Timor "Gap." Commenced in February 1979, the negotiations over the Timor Gap Treaty were concluded some ten years later in December 1989 by the Australian Labor government which had assumed office in 1983. In early 1991 the Timor Gap Zone of Cooperation Treaty was signed, otherwise determining the allocation and administration of spoils.

In essence, the Treaty divides an area of some 62,000 square kilometers lying between the northern coast of Australia and East Timor into three exploitation zones. The northernmost is to be reserved for exploitation by Indonesia with some provision for profit-sharing by Australia while, in the southernmost zone, the position is reversed. The middle zone—touted as a creative diplomatic solution to resource sharing— involves the joint Indonesian-Australian management, exploration, and exploitation of the zone. Exploration contracts have been awarded and drilling has commenced.

It is this Treaty which Portugal protests at the International Court of Justice which initiated proceedings at The Hague on 22 February 1991. In placing Australia in the dock over this issue, Portugal is cognizant that there are two potential third parties to the claim, the people of East Timor and Indonesia. The people of East Timor, in legalese, have no standing before the Court, and can only be represented by a State having that status (eg., Portugal). While Indonesia stands as the obvious culprit in this affair, it has not accepted the jurisdiction of the Court and no case can be made against it. Australia, on the other hand, which prides itself as being a responsible member of the international community, will, doubtless, be morally obliged to adhere to a ruling by the Court.

Also known as the World Court, the International Court of Justice is the principal judicial organ of the UN. Established in 1945, the 15-judge body rules on cases submitted to it by governments and provides advisory opinions or rulings. Judges are chosen in elections held concurrently by the UN Security Council and General Assembly.

In general terms Portugal asserted in its application before the Court that Indonesia's claims to sovereignty over East Timor stemming from its illegal 1975 invasion are invalid, and that Australia's negotiations with Indonesia and its own domestic legislation apropos the Treaty are illegal acts *vis-à-vis* Portugal, the legal authority as far as East Timor is concerned. Moreover, Portugal argues, the Treaty violates the rights of the people of East Timor, notably by denying their right to self-determination and access to and sovereignty over natural resources in the relevant maritime zones.

At the time of lodging its application (28 February 1991), Portugal stated that Australia had caused "particularly serious legal and moral damage to the people of East Timor and to Portugal" which would, in turn, become "material damage" if the exploration of resources were allowed to go ahead.

Portugal, which recognized East Timor as a non-self-governing territory under Chapter XI of the UN Charter as of July 1974, otherwise supports its case by reference to relevant UN resolutions passed after the 1975 invasion, *inter alia*, reconfirming the right of East Timorese to an internationally acceptable act of self-determination. Portugal is also asking the Court to demand of Australia that it pay reparations for losses. Portugal also claims that it is not in pursuit of oil riches, but, rather, is concerned to uphold a matter of principle. In taking the case to the Court, it is clear that Portugal seeks from an influential international institution a firm declaration that, in the context of international law, the invasion of East Timor was illegal.

Before considering the case, the Court had to determine certain facts as to its admissibility, notably as to Portugal's "standing" as an interested party to the claim and that it had not lost its standing, say as implied by its "abandonment" of the colony in 1975.

Coming before the Court on 30 January this year (1995), Portugal initiated the substantive legal arguments by filing a memorial or detailed justification for its Court action. Australia followed up with a counter-memorial. Portugal then filed a reply, Australia a rejoinder. Then the oral arguments began.

It is worth replaying these arguments, as they tell us much about colonial history and about the processes of "settler colonialism," not to mention intra-colonial and imperial competition. In its counter-memorial, the Australian side launched into a tirade against Portugal's "neglect" of Timor in its 400-year-old rule. Portugal, it was alleged, did little once the (Indonesian-backed) coup of August 1975 broke out, indeed withdrew its administration to the island of Atauro, where it stayed until just after Indonesia's invasion of Dili. Gratuitously, Australia contends, "No action could have been more calculated to encourage outside intervention in the affairs of East Timor."

In a bitter indictment of Australia's East Timor policy reaching back to the Second World War, Portugal charged that Australian actions in occupying Timor over Portuguese protests in December 1941, while "allegedly intended to forestall a Japanese landing.... may very well have triggered it." Moreover, at war's end, and with hegemonistic designs over the south-west Pacific, East Timor included, Australia made every attempt to stop Portugal reestablishing sovereignty in the territory. Portugal had to appeal to other Allied countries to protest a second violation of East Timor by troops sent to receive the Japanese surrender.

Turning to the boundary-delimitation question, Portugal then alleged that, beginning in 1970, Australia sought to persuade Portugal to divide the continental shelf on terms advantageous to Australia so as to include a geological structure known as "Kelp" believed to contain huge petroleum reserves. Australia's interest in East Timor post-1974, Portugal contended, was guided by its interest in natural resources.

Moreover, when in 1974 Portugal sought to initiate the process of decolonization in East Timor, Australia offered no meaningful help. Former Australian Prime Minister Gough Whitlam told President Suharto in September 1974 that he did not think that East Timor would be a viable independent state and would welcome its joining Indonesia. In the period after Portugal moved its administration to the offshore island of Atauro (27 August 1975), Australia refused to allow talks to be held in Australia between Portugal and East Timorese factions, it refused to allow a Portuguese warship to take supplies in Darwin, and, in the weeks following Indonesia's invasion at the height of the Indonesian massacre of East Timorese, Australia took measures to help isolate the territory internationally, namely, banning radio and ship communication. "Contrary to what it claims in its defense, Australia has not been a mere innocent spectator of the tragic events which have led to so much bloodshed," Portugal asserted. Noting Australia's fervent desire not to displease either Indonesia or the United States, Portugal summarized that: "It was its designs on East

Timor's petroleum that carried more weight than all the rest....only this greed can explain the *de jure* recognition of an annexation by force at the cost of over 100,000 lives."

In its rejoinder, Australia said that it was "astonished" that Portugal had questioned its motivation and integrity. Australia contended that it was not its policy to support Indonesian use of force in East Timor. Australia had always expressed regret at the way Indonesia forcibly annexed East Timor. It did not care whether negotiations over the seabed boundary were with Indonesia or with Portugal.

In written submissions, released when the Court began hearing oral pleadings, Australia contended that Portugal's legal actions against Australia would more likely harm than help the East Timorese people. Australia argued that if Portugal wins the case and the Treaty is ruled invalid, the real winner will be Indonesia which will be able to claim the right to all the resources in the Timor Gap against the best interests of the East Timorese. "In effect, Indonesia would be at large to pursue its own interests, unencumbered by any agreement with the neighboring State." Accordingly, it would be the responsibility of the UN to ensure that the East Timorese received an equitable share of the profits Indonesia made from the agreement. More dubiously, the Australian side argued, if Portugal won the case, "the people of East Timor would lose any prospect of benefit from the treaty." In particular, Australia argued, the real target of Portugal's suit is not Australia but Indonesia.

Implications of the Ruling

Undoubtedly the ruling by the Court on the Timor Gap will also have commercial implications for the oil industry. Since the Treaty was signed, considerable exploration activity has started in the Timor Gap, notwithstanding the murky legal title to the claims. At least 16 wells have been sunk. While first results have not been promising, prospects look much better following the announcement by Australia-based Woodside Petroleum of a big oil flow at its Laminaria-1 well, 12 miles outside the zone. But wells inside the zone, namely those on a BHP-operated permit, have flowed as well. These include discoveries made by the Brisbane-based oil and gas company Petroz NL in the Elang field, said to hold up to fifty million barrels of oil.

Some legal experts contend that a ruling against Australia would leave the status of permits granted by the joint-authority as very questionable. A number of permits granted by Australia prior to the signing of the Timor Gap Treaty have been canceled. Security of title to a lease bestowed by Portugal on Denver-based Oceanic Exploration was also not guaranteed. One Australian company involved, Western Mining, has sued the Australian government for this revocation of title and won in the federal court.

In "On Trial over Timor," the *Sydney Morning Herald* (31 January 1995) opined that while a ruling by the Court might not make all that much difference to the way that oil companies exploit the oil resources of the "Gap," nevertheless: "Ultimately, the main effect of this excursion to the rarefied heights of international law will be political. From Portugal's point of view—whether it wins or loses at The Hague—it is bound to succeed politically in refocusing attention on East Timor's claims to self-determination." It concludes that many Australians are uneasy at the signing of the Treaty and "feel that this is one international event where it is not-all important that Australia comes out winner."

Australian Appeasement of Indonesia

It is clear, then, that in its ingenuous and egregious defense Australia has been obliged to appease both Indonesia and hostile domestic opinion. It is known that Australian Foreign Minister Gareth Evans went out of his way prior to the World Court hearing to brief his Indonesian counterpart on the defense that Australia would take. In making this defense public on Radio Australia prior to the hearings, Evans dodged between the standard official Australian appeasement-of-Indonesia line and the mounting crescendo of Australian public opinion (and even opinion within his own Australian Labor Party) that would see Indonesian policy (and *ipso facto* Australian policy) on East Timor as a failure. In this demarche, and for Indonesian consumption, Evans reiterated that Australia recognizes Indonesian jurisdiction over East Timor. However, in a line of argument that has puzzled observers, as it had never before been publicly stated, he also declared that recognition of Indonesian sovereignty over the island is not in contradiction to the recognition of East Timor's right to self-determination according to the principles of the UN. The rub is, however, that the self-determination question would have to be brokered according to new realities, namely, on the basis of which power, Portugal or Indonesia, held sovereignty.

While Evan's language is as diplomatic as his logic is tortured, intimations of the real Australian position have recently been laid down with startling clarity by former Australian diplomat Richard Woolcott [*International Herald Tribune*, 6 March 1995]. Australia, he asserts, has never denied an East Timor right to self-determination, but holds that this could only be carried out within the framework of Indonesian sovereignty. Woolcott, Australian Ambassador in Jakarta at the time that Indonesia launched its campaigns to destablize and invade East Timor, also claims—wishfully—that Portugal has long forfeited any credible claim to be seen as administering authority of East Timor and that the time for a UN-supervised act of self-determination has "probably" passed.

Woolcott also observed that there has never been a UN-supervised Act of Self Determination in Mozambique, Angola, or Guinea Bissau. This is true, but neither were these countries invaded by a neighbor, at least not before they proclaimed their own versions of Unilateral Declaration of Independence (UDI). In fact, it was Mozambique's UDI which encouraged Fretilin to do the same, but whereas Frelimo in Mozambique prevailed and has since gained international recognition, in East Timor, by contrast, Fretilin were overwhelmed by the Western-backed Indonesian invasion, making its UDI irrelevant or "illegal" and otherwise preempting an internationally acceptable Act of Self Determination.

But what is the meaning of Evan's admission/concession or revelation, as it comes to most Australians, that Canberra all along finds no contradiction in recognizing Indonesian sovereignty over East Timor and the right of East Timorese to self-determination? Does it represent a softening of Australia's position, or is it pure chicanery? Is it a position that can be exploited by supporters of East Timor's independence?

Undoubtedly, back in 1976, when Australia framed its policy on post-invasion East Timor, the caveat that Australia disapproved of the method of "incorporation" was entered into as a way of appeasing fairly hostile Australian public opinion. While the caveat remained obscured in the long intervening years, especially as an academic, political, and media consensus emerged on East Timor in Australia that portrayed it as a fringe Left-wing issue hardly meritorious of serious support, this duplicious bit of manipulation came to be challenged by the events surrounding the Dili massacre of 12 November 1991. Yet, notwithstanding the horrors surrounding the massacre and the iniquitous system of military abuses that it exposed, Evans was still prepared to accept Indonesian blandishments and call the event an "aberration." While Australian public and official opinion appeared to be deeply affronted by the human rights abuses committed by Indonesia at Dili, still no editorial leader in any mainstream newspaper in Australia spoke out for self-determination or independence for East Timor at that juncture.

But with the quiet reengagement of the UN in the East Timor question, now leading up to the first intra-Timorese dialogue under UN, later this year, Australia has now found itself out of step with a growing body of world opinion on East Timor that simply finds the situation there morally reprehensible. The release in November last year of the damning report on the Dili massacre by UN Special Rapporteur Waly Bacre Ndiaye is a case in point. The credibility gap of the Keating Labor government in Australia over East Timor has been further exposed by the events of the last few months, notably the escalation of military-initiated terror in the occupied territory.

But while external criticism of the Suharto regime appears to be reaching a new level, internal evidence suggests the regime is facing terminal crisis. This is, in part, a reference to the succession question. History has shown that there has never been a bloodless transition of regime in Indonesia and no-one is betting on a smooth changeover to a post-Suharto order. While the hallmark of the New Order regime has been its ability to win economic legitimacy, the demography/resources relationship suggests that poverty elimination has its limits within the present development parameters, notably an economy that privileges cronies surounding the palace, including the infamous *cukong* or Chinese billionaires, and a system which prioritizes high technology industry, the brainchild of Minister Habibie. While economic development in Indonesia has produced a sizable middle class, it has also introduced elements of civil society which are increasingly critical of the excesses of the Suharto regime. This has been matched in recent years by the expansion in Indonesia of home-grown NGOs.

Willy nilly, after more than a decade of silence, certain Indonesian intellectuals and others have broken ranks over the Indonesian consensus on East Timor and have been able to link repression of dissent in Indonesia with abuses inside East Timor. However, after two or three years of so-called *keterbukaan* (or openness), the Suharto regime has revealed to the world the limits of its concession to less authoritarian controls over society. Notable in this respect was the closing last year of three popular and mildly critical newsmagazines and the current crackdown on independent journalists.

How has Australia responded to this crisis? Instead of building bridges to democratic forces inside Indonesia, which would include moderate Islamic forces, Australia has struck out in a direction from which there seems no return. As with France in Algeria, it has sought to strengthen ties with the ruling regime, whatever the consequences.

While Australia has been careful to cultivate defense links with the Indonesia New Order from its inception, these links have until now been focussed upon such areas as officer training and the provision of equipment along the lines of better getting to know a testy neighbor. Of late, and very late, the defense relationship between Australia and the Suharto regime has undergone a qualitative shift to one of collaboration, not only with the airforce and navy, whose defense functions might be to a certain extent circumscribed (although that was not even the case in the invasion and occupation of East Timor), but to coddling the army whose repressive police role in the sprawling archipelago is well documented.

Indeed, a recent Australian Defence White Paper views Indonesia as strategic ally against "northern" threats.

Unthinkable in even the recent past, Indonesian Vice President General Try Sustrisno visited Canberra in September 1994. In March this year, the Dili massacre general, Sintong Panjaitan, was another guest of Canberra. The upcoming Indonesian Ambassador to Australia will be a military man. In March, Australia offered its highest award to the Indonesian foreign minister. But by entering into military exercises with the elite military unit named KOSTRAD, Australia seems to have crossed the Rubicon in its relations with the New Order regime. Just as the announcement in early 1995 that Australia will supply ammunition to the Indonesian armed forces affronts large numbers of Australians with any knowledge of recent Indonesian history, so the upcoming military exercises in northern Australia between Australian and Asian militaries including Indonesia— dubbed Kangaroo 95—has met with serious opposition as one would expect in an erstwhile democratic political culture.

Australia knows, just as Indonesia celebrates its fiftieth anniversary of its 1945 proclamation of independence [that is, its own unilateral declaration of independence against colonial power, much like that of Fretilin] that the ability of ABRI (the Indonesian armed forces) to invigilate against the Left and Islamic Right is the best guarantor of stability in the archipelago. But is it? By backing the wrong horse in the transition to a post-Suharto era, Australia may well find itself offsides with an increasingly restless population in this, the most populous Muslim country in the world.

Defense links lock in with business links, the hallmark of Australian Prime Minister Paul Keating's "Asia-links" policy and Australia's up front role in the APEC forum. But on the question of stressing business links ahead of other considerations like human rights, democratization, and fair play, Australia fails even by the self-set criteria that sets the country apart as a bolt hole for refugees from authoritarians gone wrong.

Appeasement of Domestic Lobby

But Australian political culture is also such as to oblige Canberra, or at least the government of the day, to periodically rethink or refine its foreign policy in line with popular sentiment or electoral backlash. Such a juncture seems to have arisen in early 1994. At this time even close relatives of the Indonesian President were mooting some kind of "special status" for East Timor, in what some observers have seen as a play by Suharto to parry the political strength of the armed forces. While such "concessions" have so often turned out to be illusory, it appears that Canberra was exposed as out of line with such "special autonomy" proposals for East Timor.

It can be no coincidence, then, that in July 1994, then Australian Foreign Minister Gareth Evans foreshadowed a subtle shift in policy by requesting Indonesia to downgrade its military presence in East Timor and to negotiate with the East Timorese. He also criticized Indonesia's attempts to stifle conferences on East Timor in Manila and Bangkok. Yet the limits of Canberra in standing up to Indonesia on East Timor are well-known. There is a sense that Evans is telling Jakarta to clean up its act to make it easier for his Party to manage domestic public opinion.

That Australian policy on East Timor is nothing but reactive is further highlighted by subsequent shifts in Labor Party policy on East Timor at the biennial Party conference in September which passed resolutions calling for a drawdown of Indonesian forces in East Timor, and the opening of the territory to news media and human rights groups. Even by recent UN standards or statements on East Timor, this revision of Australian policy is timorous. In any case, this new "tough line" resolution was approved only after a clause in the original resolution calling for East Timor independence was removed. Endorsement of the "new Evans line" can be seen in the call made in Dili in mid-March 1995 by the Australian Ambassador to Jakarta, Alan Taylor, for a reduction in military presence and more political autonomy for the "province," as East Timor is termed in Australian diplomatic language.

While the merits of the case might seem black-and-white to the reader, the fact of the matter is that a final ruling by the World Court will, to a large extent, turn upon procedural questions, international precedents, and determinations relating to Portugal's "standing" that otherwise may appear as obscure to lay persons. In June 1993, for example, action initiated in the High Court of Australia by José Ramos-Horta, José Gusmão, and Abel Guterres that Australia's entry into the Treaty was contrary to established norms of international law, failed.

A ruling by the World Court would go a long way in reaffirming Portugal as the administering power concerned with East Timor. It would give moral force to the rights of the East Timorese people in their quest for self-determination. It would strengthen the hand of the UN in its reengagement in the issue. A ruling by the Court against Portugal would give strength to the process in international law known as "historical consolidation" whereby, with the passage of time, a new reality is seen as in the world community's interest, even though the origins of the dispute may have been illegal.

Indonesia obviously, but also Australia, along with interested international oil companies, are counting on this kind of solution. But in any case, international momentum on the East Timor question, including the ongoing UN-mediated dialogue between Portugal and Indonesia, has gathered its own momentum. As former UN Secretary General Perez de Cuellar made it known in a public forum in Brunei Darussalam in September 1993 [see chapter 2], Australia's entry into the Timor Gap Treaty with Indonesia severely clouded a solution to the problem. Hopefully, justice at the World Court will lift the veil on the East Timor self-determination question once and for all.

Envoi

A footnote to the above might be the news to many in Australia, including even the inner circle of the then ruling Australian Labor Party, that then Prime Minister Paul Keating had flown to Jakarta on 13 December 1995 to sign a bilateral security pact with Jakarta. This secret diplomacy was met with major media comment in Australia and much feigned outrage on the part of the political opposition. Needless to say, with victory in the Australian federal elections of 1996, the incoming conservative government wasted no time in endorsing the pact and in continuing Canberra's hypocritical policy of being the only Western democracy to recognize—de jure and de facto— the Indonesian incorporation of East Timor.

6

In Memory of Denis Freney, East Timor Activist *Par Excellence*

The following message was placed on the electronic conference reg.easttimor on 21 October 1995. In so doing I sought to remind followers of this conference not only of the passing of one activist on behalf of East Timor, but of the decades-long struggle of the East Timorese for freedom. In the case of Denis Freney, as revealed below, his activism actually preceded the Indonesian invasion; indeed, preceded the birth of a second generation of Timorese activists who have rekindled the struggle for freedom both inside East Timor and in the diaspora.

Echoing the memorial piece on Denis Freney (1936–1995) published in *Matebian News* (Sydney) [Vol.3, No.5, September 1995], I think it important to flag the passing of this East Timor activist par excellence. As Mandy King and James Kesteven observe in their obituary piece, it was thanks to "Denis' inspiration, invaluable contacts, knowledge of the issue and committment" that made possible their jointly produced film on East Timor, entitled "The Shadow Over East Timor." Produced in 1986, the film was eventually shown on UK and Australian television. A revised version was shown on Australia's SBS Television within three weeks of the Dili massacre. On set in Darwin, as it were, or at least in an undisclosed location in the bush, it was Denis who made secret radio contact with Fretilin fighters in East Timor. It was via this radio link that the voice of Xanana

Gusmão was first heard in the outside world (18 May and 16 June 1988), albeit silenced by the Australian Labor government of Bob Hawke, just as the Fraser government had done before it apropos an earlier radio link.

But as the original East Timor campaigner, it would be fair to pass comment on Denis' earlier "career" in this respect. While personally unknown to myself, I would simply acknowledge Denis Freney's 1975 publication, *Timor: Freedom Caught between the Powers* (Spokesman Books, Nottingham, UK). Published around October 1975, the book also carries an appeal for humanitarian aid from the embattled Fretilin central committee in Dili, namely its first president, Francisco Xavier do Amaral, along with an interview with José Ramos-Horta. At that juncture, Fretilin comprised the *de facto* government in East Timor, the Portuguese flag was still flying in Dili, and Fretilin, in the words of do Amaral, "stressed its recognition of the Portuguese government as the only authority and the unique valid mouthpiece in the process of decolonization."

This 68-page work with preface by Ron Witton stands then as the first published book on East Timor. It was originally published in duplicated form by the Australian Campaign for Independent Timor, the pioneering support group which established branches in almost every state of Australia and of which Denis was a force.The table of contents reads as follows:

Chapter 1: The Background
Chapter 2: Behind the UDT Coup
Chapter 3: Portuguese Involvement
Chapter 4: America and the Coup
Chapter 5: Indonesia's Complicity
Chpater 6: The Australian Connection
Chapter 7: The Role of the Joint Intelligence Organisation
Chapter 8: Whitlam's Position
Chapter 9: Drawing the Threads Together

Writing of the danger of impending full scale Indonesian invasion, Freney wrote: "Such a blatant act of aggression would not 'restore order' or stabilize the region, but endanger the Indonesian military regime itself, which would face a long, Vietnam-type war in East Timor, and the explosive anger of its own people." "The issues in East Timor today are very clear cut", he continues, "Which side Australian workers and students take will be vital in the coming weeks, months and years."

Such prescience armed Denis Freney for the years ahead, as the virtual I.R. Stone of East Timor journalism in the pages of his *East Timor News*, for long years the single vital source of hard information on East Timor available in Australia. Notable was his, "A Reply to Prof. Arndt: An Apologist Who Can't Get His Facts Straight," *East Timor News*, Winter, 1982, pp.5-9 and "A Reply to Peter Hastings: A Sophisticated Apologist for Suharto's Genocide," *East Timor News*, Winter, 1982, pp.3-4.

Never disguising his support for Fretilin's righteous struggle or his own Australian working class links, Denis Freney also contributed to *Southeast Asian Chronicle* (No.94, 1984, pp.3-9), *Carpa Bulletin* (No.15, November 1983), among other left-wing and solidarity publications.

The best tribute for Denis Freney, then, is to recognize the courage of his convictions, the value of his disclosures, and the difficult times when he made them.

Envoi

*The Denis Freney story is also told with humility and verve in his **A Map of Days: Life on the Left**, William Heinemann Australia, Port Melbourne, 1991, two chapters of which are devoted to his activism on the East Timor question. These are chapter 18, "Dili and the Great Dismissal" and chapter 19, "Fretilin Calling."*

7

East Timor and the Japanese Media

Through 1995 and continuing into 1996, some hundreds of East Timorese "invaded" foreign Embassies and Missions in Jakarta as a way of gaining international attention for their cause. None, including those who entered the Japanese Embassy in mid-November 1995, succeeded in gaining political asylum overseas. With few exceptions, it was Portugal which accepted the repatriation of the Timorese otherwise mediated by the International Red Cross. Japan is no small player in the Indonesian economy. Japan, which has consistently supplied the lion's share of aid and investment to Indonesia since 1965, has also, ipso facto, provided the Suharto regime with the economic wherewithal to economically legitimize its rule. All this should confer special interest in East Timor on the part of Japan, especially as it aspires to a greater role in a reformed United Nations system. But has it? While an announcement by the Japanese Foreign Ministry on 28 March 1996 that it supports the mediating efforts of the UN Secretary General towards a "peaceful solution" and that it offered US$100,000 towards meeting the costs of the all-inclusive East Timorese dialogue is salutary, there is an overwhelming sense that, notwithstanding the efforts of the Japanese Diet Members' Forum on East Timor, for over twenty years Tokyo has willed East Timor at "peace" under Indonesian military stewardship. Hence, the heavy responsibility of the Japanese media on this question. The following appeared on reg.easttimor on 16 November 1995.

While the story of the twenty-one East Timorese asylum seekers who entered the Japanese Embassy in Jakarta on 14 November has now made the rounds, some of you out there—not least of all the asylum seekers themselves—might be wondering how this event has been portrayed in the Japanese media; indeed, how this "problem" has been handled by the Japanese bureaucracy?

Basically, over the last two days, the story has been carried in the three mass circulation dailies in Japan, the *Mainichi*, *Asahi*, and *Yomiuri*, along with their respective English language versions. There is an element of luck or good timing in this, as 13 November was a press "holiday," a virtual no-news day in Japan, and these papers did not appear on that day.

Perhaps the most prominent print media report on the event was "Seeking exile in Japan; 23 East Timorese in Embassy" in *Mainichi Shimbun* (15 November 1995). This article presented the basic facts of the matter while pointing out the timing of the Embassy occupation coinciding with the APEC summit. Alone among the print media reports, the *Mainichi* article also carried a photograph of the jubilant East Timorese inside the Embassy compound. The English-language *Mainichi Daily News* on the same day carried an AP report from Jakarta mentioning that an asylum request had been made to Japanese Ambassador Watanabe along with key points in the petition. It also carried the [erroneous] comment by a Japanese Embassy staffer that the Japanese government "has never given political asylum to anyone." This article was also accompanied by a photograph taken within the Embassy compound.

The same day the *Yomiuri Shimbun* carried a postage-stamp-size piece entitled "Japanese Embassy Exile Request, Jakarta, 21 East Timorese." This paper offered two follow-up stories on 16 November noting the meeting between Indonesian Foreign Minister Ali Alatas and his Japanese counterpart, Yohei Kono, in Osaka as to the "peaceful" management of the Embassy problem. No allusion was made in this article to any broader contextualization of the East Timor problem. The English language version of this paper (miniscule circulation and directed at foreigners in Japan) deemed the issue important enough to front-page two wire service reports (AP and Reuters, 15 November) and a single wire service report on 16 November, also on the front page. Parenthetically, *The Daily Yomiuri* is the paper that on 13 October 1994 published an infamous op ed piece on East Timor, entitled "What you don't know about East Timor, but should" by Irawan Abidin, then Indonesian Foreign Ministry spokesperson, which read with gross misrepresentation: "The tragic incident in Dili on Nov. 12, 1991, where four people lost their lives was indeed regrettable..."

Surprisingly, the *Asahi Shimbun* appeared to have passed over the question entirely on the 15th, although the bare facts were reported in a tiny column in that paper on the 16th. Parenthetically, the Nagasaki version of the *Asahi Shimbun* (17 October)—all the majors have regional versions—ran an interview with myself on conditions inside East Timor ("Be Informed about East Timor's Independence Struggle") along with photograph of Baucau market, linked with the [annual] East Timorese speaking tour [then] in Japan and the [then] upcoming visit to Nagasaki by Domingos Sarmento Alves, leader of the US Embassy occupation group at the time of the APEC conference in Bogor in November 1994.

While most of the above-mentioned Japanese language pieces fail to offer background on the East Timor problem in international context, a couple of recent articles in the Japanese press stand back from the tendency to marginalize the East Timor issue entirely. Noteworthy is the article by Fukuda, "Continuing Troubles in East Timor, Growing Antipathy Connected with the Nation, Religion... Suharto Government Taxing Its Brains for Counterplan" (*Asahi Shimbun*, 19 October 1995). This piece carries a map of East Timor (distinguished from Indonesia) as well as accurate background information on East Timor as a territory under Indonesian military occupation not recognised by the UN. This article also describes the Dili massacre as such, a massacre.

Also noteworthy is Ruriko Hatano, "Four Years Since the Massacre of the Inhabitants [of East Timor]. Intensification of Religious Confrontation. Occupation Army Aggravates Distrust" (*Yomiuri Shimbun*, 2 November 1995). A rare Japanese report filed from Dili, Hatano's prominently positioned article, along with map and two photographs (Bishop Belo and street scene in Dili), also comes with appropriate background and context.

Finally, the media *coup de grace*, as it were, for the group of twenty-one would have been two cameo performances played out on Japanese television, namely NHK Evening News, on the 14th and 15th of November, respectively. This was a rare media event, indeed, in Japan, possibly the first NHK news "feature" on East Timor since the visit of a delegation of Japanese MPs in mid-1994. Yet both of these reports, no longer than about thirty seconds, were relegated to the bottom of the news and neither offered any political context. The first, the dialogue of which I missed altogether, doubtless numbed by the preceding twenty minute analysis of the Aum Shinrykyo cult, offered panoramic shots of Dili. The second, coming between a report on dinosaur eggs and the weather report, showed graphic video of the group of twenty-one inside the Japanese Embassy compound with the banal comment that they were seeking independence for East Timor and that the Indonesian authorities would not object to their departure from Indonesia. To say that NHK skirts controversy and misses the point would be an understatement.

Finally, the *Japan Times* (15 November) appears not to have even rated the issue as newsworthy. But this should not surprise. In any case the value of the *Japan Times* [to the East Timor cause] is that it recycles interesting editorials from other newspapers. Such was "East Timor Needs All the Support It Can Get":

> The East Timorese are emerging as the Vietnamese of the South Pacific, people willing to take endless punishment to keep alive their dream of becoming a liberated country. And like the Vietnamese in their struggle against the French and the Americans, the East Timorese need all the help they can get from the rest of the world. *The Nation* [Bangkok] 12 November 1995.

Envoi

While the 1996 Nobel Peace Prize award was widely—and ritually—covered in the Japanese media, such attention was not reciprocated at an official level at the time of the visit to Japan in January 1997 of Nobel co-laureate José Ramos-Horta. Virtually snubbed by all but the most junior echelons of government, Ramos-Horta answered back that he would support claims from Japan on behalf of East Timor of unpaid war reparations money as compensation for Japan's highly destructive occupation of the half-island during the Pacific War, in addition to claims on behalf of "comfort women" or sex slaves of the Japanese Imperial Army.

While Japan has long retained its position as the Indonesian New Order's most consistent financial backer and political booster there is not a little irony that in 1996–97 the first strains in the relationship arose, not over East Timor or related issues of democratization and human rights in Indonesia, but over the Indonesian president's award to his youngest son of monopoly rights over the franchise on a so-called national car. Ingenuously dubbed the "Timor car," but actually manufactured in South Korea and imported duty free, this project severely damages the Japanese automobile industry's profile in Indonesia. Thus when in April 1997 Japan lodged a protest to the Geneva-based World Trade Organization, the action attracted a rare rebuke from the Indonesian president.

8

Chinese Maps?

*What follows is an exchange between myself and others on the electronic conference **reg.easttimor** apropos China and the East Timor question. This exchange commenced with my post, "China and East Timor" on 3 April 1996, and "concludes" with an interpretation in the Portuguese newspaper **Publico** on 11 April 1996.*

Friends of East Timor might take heart that at least one member of the Security Council, namely China, remains categorical as to its position on East Timor (just as it remains categorical on Taiwan, Hong Kong and Macau). From the *Administrative Division Atlas of the World*, China Geographical Services Press, Beijing, 1993, East Timor is listed as one of 101 administrative entities of Asia. The Republic of Indonesia is also listed as a country of 1,904,569 square kilometres comprising twenty-six (26) administrative divisions. In other words, according to this publication, China does not recognize Indonesia's claim to a 27th province. East Timor is not included in this publication as part of the Republic of Indonesia. There should be no doubt as to the official status of this publication, as nothing passes for publication in China that is not official. Thus the atlas includes Taiwan, Hong Kong, and Macau as administrative regions of China. Goa, for example, is recognized as part of India, Sikkim is not. Neither is the Turkish occupation of northern Cyprus recognized, nor the Moroccan occupation of Western Sahara. China is also consistent in its cartographic representation of East Timor's separate administrative status. All Chinese maps and globes recently inspected by this correspondent do not falsify on this question, but offer a correct delineation of East Timor right down to tennis-ball sized globes.

From *Administrative Division Atlas of the World*, East Timor is an administrative entity of 18,899 square kilometers with a population of 707,0000 (1989). The population of the capital Dilly/Dili is given at 60,000. East Timor comprises thirteen administrative subdivisions; Ailu, Ainaro, Baucau, Bobonaro, Cova Lima, Dilly, Ermera, Lautem (Lauten), Liquica, Manatuto, Ocussi (Oecusse), Same, Vikeke (Viqueque). All place names come supplied with Chinese character equivalents.

Date: 04 Apr 1996 22:38:44 -0500 (EST)
reg.easttimor@conf.igc.apc.org>
From: David Webster etantor@web.apc.org
Subject: Re: China and East Timor

Personally, I'd be happier if the government of China did not consider East Timor as a separate country, given its own genocidal occupation of Tibet and its apparent intention to use force against a small island neighbour (Taiwan). The governments of Indonesia and China have more in common than either would like to admit!

Date: 05 Apr 1996 16:06:12
reg.easttimor@conf.igc.apc.org>
Subject: Re: China and East Timor
From: Hugh Ekeberg <ekeberg@ozemail.com.au>
At 10:38 PM 04/04/1996 -0500, you wrote:

Not only Tibet, but Inner Mongolia and Xinjiang "province" which is Eastern Turkestan. The Uigyur, Kazak, and Kirgiz have suffered terribly from everything which afflicts the Tibetans and have risen up on occasions to free their home land only to suffer the consequences. Goes to show how colonialism flourishes in Asia.

Date: 06 Apr 1996 19:25:13
Conference "reg.easttimor"
From: Gunn
Subject: China and East Timor (Part II)

Gratified that my post on China and East Timor has provoked some healthy lateral thinking on China's own behavior towards the peoples it claims to be under Chinese administration. I suspect, however, the irony of the matter was carried in the original post and needed no amplification; witness Boutros Ghali in Beijing last week dismissing Taiwan as an "internal problem of China." But, let us not conflate questions of internal colonialism and fourth worldism with a classic Third World question like East Timor, which, as one of the last cases of aborted self-determination on the UN logbook, begs instrumental solutions. This is not to say that our concerns for so-called internationally unrecognized states and peoples should be *less* (West Irian), but that the East Timor case is delicately poised at a crucial juncture in the process of UN mediation towards an "internationally acceptable solution." While many of our concerns for East Timor, such as human rights abuses, status of women, militarization, etc., are Fourth World questions by definition and therefore link with our broader moral concerns for, say, the people of Tibet, etc, at the same time we should not dismiss the key question of East Timor's political status.

As Paula Escarameia has written in her aptly titled Harvard dissertation/monograph, *Formation of Concepts in International Law: Subsumption under Self-determination in the Case of East Timor* (Fundação Oriente, Lisboa, 1993), "By reversing the causality [of the East Timor case] Indonesia managed to imply the dismissal of the political instances from dealing with it and to allocate the issues to humanitarian organizations" (p.144). And so Escarameia shows how over the years the East Timor question was shuffled between various UN committees to the point where the self-determination question was virtually relegated to the status of a human right, not a political right. This was undoubtedly a small triumph of Indonesian (and probably Australian) diplomacy in the 1980s, but, to use Escarameia's language, it owes to the courage of the East Timor people in incredible adversity that they have once again reversed the causality of the case and recouped in the international arena their claims for both human and political rights. Fortunately, Boutros Ghali has not pronounced East Timor an internal problem of Indonesia. Quite the reverse.

It may also be misleading to infer from the *Administrative Division Atlas of the World* that China considers East Timor a separate country much less recognizes East Timor's independence. It is more the case that as a member of the UN Security Council China speaks the language of the UN Fourth Committee on Decolonization and treats East Timor accordingly. How politically correct are maps on East Timor in France, Russia, UK, and the US?

The notion that China should be dismissed because it is this or that regime is not one that occurs in UN councils. Neither is it a view shared by Portugal. In the context of the complex ongoing dialogue between Portugal and China over Macau, Portuguese Presidents, Prime Ministers, and Foreign Ministers are unfailing in their solicitations to China on the East Timor question at the highest levels. Rhetorically, at least, Chinese leaders have reciprocated concerns over East Timor to their Portuguese interlocuters. After all, China and Indonesia have a tiff over overlapping territorial waters [surrounding] the Natuna islands. [Remember Exxon's multi-billion investment in the Natuna oil deal is at stake here]. It would not be too far out to assert that some *quid pro quo* has been worked out between Portugal and China over East Timor in the course of the Portuguese-Chinese dialogue on Macau. On China, Macau (and Timor), read my book, or rather, get your local library to order *Encountering Macau: A Portuguese City-State on the Periphery of China, 1557-1999,* Westview Press, Boulder, 1996 ISBN 0-8133-8970-4 (US54.95)

Date: 08 Apr 1996 14:14:11 -0500 (EST)
Conference "reg.easttimor"
From: David Webster <etantor@web.apc.org
Subject: Re: China and East Timor (Part II)
RE: East Timor and Tibet

Gunn's comments are much appreciated. I should add that I don't intend any disrespect by disagreeing with one point in those comments. As before, I'm making my own comments personally, not presuming to tell the East Timorese what their strategy should be.

The international legal status of Tibet and Taiwan, it could be argued, is precisely the same as that of East Timor, despite what the UN says. That's why I mentioned those cases, and not any of China's multitudinous violations of the human rights of people it has colonized.

Tibet has functioned as an independent country for most of its history, even sacking the Chinese capital on occasion. With the coming of Buddhism, it stopped its warlike policy and retreated into isolation, but was no less independent for that. It was conquered by China under the Ming dynasty, but broke away. It was also part of the Manchu empire, and the Mongol empire—both of which also conquered China. The association of Tibet and China as part of a single empire, however, did not make them the same country any more than Australia and New Zealand are the same country because they were both colonized by Britain. Under these various foreign rulers, Tibet maintained its own forms of government.

Following the fall of the Qing dynasty early this century, Tibet again regained its independence, with its diplomatic representatives travelling on Tibetan passports around the world. China's invasion in 1950 was clearly illegal under international law. The only reason Tibet did not make it onto the UN agenda then—or in 1959 with the flight of the Dalai Lama—was that it had no UN member governments willing to plead its case.

Taiwan has a similar history, being incorporated into China only during the Ming dynasty, then ruled by a local kin, and finally becoming a Japanese colony before being handed to China in 1945. It was ruled from the mainland for just four years at this time. Taiwanese President Lee Teng-hui speaks better Japanese than Mandarin, and Taiwanese have their own language as well. The legal fiction perpetrated by its KMT government explains why Taiwan has not asserted its own strong claim to independence.

Both Tibet and Taiwan can boast distinctive cultures with an awareness of themselves as separate entities from China, common linguistic and historical traditions, and defined territories.

The difference between these two cases and East Timor lies solely in their status at the UN—which is, of course, a significant strength for those campaigning in support of East Timor. However, supporters of East Timor do themselves no favors by isolating themselves from those campaigning for self-determination and human rights in other colonized nations. In this context, I was very happy to see [that] José Ramos-Horta recently appeared on a joint platform in Geneva with advocates for Tibet and Western Sahara, and that East Timor holds membership in the "Fourth World" association UNPO. Let's use the UN advantage East Timor possesses, by all means, but never forget that its struggle and that of Tibet are in fact one and the same.

Date: 17 Apr 1996 20:33:22 +0000 (GMT)
Reply-To: Conference "reg.easttimor"
Subject: Timor Torture Photos
Source: **Publico**
Date: 11 April 1996
Dateline: Lisbon
Byline: Joaquim T. de Negreiros
Original Language: Portuguese
Headline:MORE EVIDENCE OF TORTURE IN TIMOR:
TIMORESE RESISTANCE DIVULGES PHOTOS OF THE RESULTS

OF THE INDONESIAN ARMY'S HANDIWORK: Chinese Atlas "separates" Timor (abridged)

An official atlas recently published in Peking includes East Timor on a list of 101 autonomous administrative territories in Asia. On the Chinese map, Indonesia is described as a country with an area of 1,904,569 sq. kms., consisting of 26 regions. According to the area and number of regions stated in the atlas, autonomous status has been attributed to East Timor, which Jakarta considers as being its 27th Province.

In addition, the same map does not recognize Moroccan sovereignty over Western Sahara, Turkish occupation of Northern Cyprus, or Indian authority over Sikkim. On the other hand, however, the territories of Macau and Hong Kong are presented as administrative regions directly subordinate to Peking, and Formosa also appears as an integral part of the People's Republic of China.

The atlas should not be seen as a statement reflecting the Peking authorities' support for the Timorese cause. Since the last UN General Assembly vote (in 1982, when China's vote helped to get a resolution adopted, against the wishes of Indonesia) it has been the question of human rights that has brought East Timor into the limelight at various international forums. On that very issue China (which shares with Indonesia an uncomfortably high position on the list of countries accused of serious violations, and which is often confronted with frequent comparisons between the cases of East Timor and Tibet), has appeared reluctant to subscribe to criticism of the Jakarta regime.

9

The "Blue Book" and East Timor

In July 1993, then Australian Foreign Minister Gareth Evans announced that senior officials of the Department of Foreign Affairs and Trade (DFAT) had been instructed to prepare a "Blue Book" relating to UN involvement in world peacekeeping operations. This was named after the now famous "Red Book" upon which the UN operation in Cambodia of 1992-93 was strongly modeled. The "Blue Book" is designed to cover everything from how and when the UN should intervene to the amount of force that should be used along with the kind of resources that would be required to contain the conflict. In 1994, with Jefferson Lee, I wrote that "it would be hypocritical in the extreme" if this ambitious plan on preventive diplomacy and peacekeeping, presented to the UN General Assembly in September 1993, actually diverted attention from the East Timor case, as was the case with Australian as much as Indonesian initiatives on UN intervention in Cambodia. We wrote, "It seems to us that to make good this nation's albeit highly compromised good faith, Gareth Evans could now instruct his Department to draw up a peace plan for East Timor along the lines of the Red Book on UN intervention in Cambodia. There is no time to be lost." [1] By way of developing this thesis, the following paper was presented to an international conference on "Peacekeeping Initiatives for East Timor" hosted by the Department of Political Science, Australian National University, Canberra, on 11–12 July 1995.

What is to be done or, rather, what can be done to achieve an "internationally accepted solution" to the East Timor "problem," given the operational mandates of UN peacekeeping operations and mindful of the progress of UN-sponsored talks on East Timor which seem— appropriately and optimistically—headed for a referendum in line with General Assembly resolution 37/30 of November 1982.

It is encouraging in this sense to observe that participants at the intra-East Timorese dialogue at Burg Schlaining, Austria, on 5 June 1995 affirmed (paragraph six of consensus statement) the importance of the ongoing negotiations between the governments of Portugal and Indonesia under the auspices of the Secretary-General aimed at finding a "just, comprehensive and internationally acceptable solution" to the East Timor question in line with resolution 37/30 of 23 November 1982 on the "Question of East Timor." [2]

Briefly, this resolution upholds the inalienable right of all people to self-determination and independence, confirms Portugal's role as administering power, calls for the UN Secretary-General to explore with all parties directly concerned ways to achieve a "comprehensive settlement of the problem", and, additionally, calls on the specialized agencies to assist the people of East Timor "in close cooperation with Portugal, as the administering power." This reiteration of resolution 37/30 at this UN-sponsored forum is important and, arguably, reverses the process of what some observers have called the "subsumption" of the self-determination issue on East Timor over the years. [3]

What I am arguing for in this chapter, then, is a specific "peace-building" role for the UN in East Timor. This concerns the reactivization of the UN in the East Timor problem, not just as distant arbiter between pro-independence and pro-integration East Timorese factions, and not just as facilitator of conversations between the foreign ministers of Indonesia and Portugal, but as prime mover in a peace-building process and even in the management of East Timor. While I am also concerned to see the UN open a permanent UN human rights office in Dili as a matter of high priority, I am arguing further for the creation of a UN Transitional Authority on East Timor or UNTAET that would serve as an umbrella organization for all the components of a UN mission in East Timor for a specified time in the run up to a referendum and the reconstitution of civil society. The sooner Australia states its bona fides in this peace process, the better. The sooner the East Timor question is regionalized the better.

I mean by "peace-building" the sense of the term used by Boutros Boutros-Ghali in his June 1992 report, *An Agenda for Peace: Preventive Diplomacy and Peacekeeping*. [4] Peace-building, as such, involves the disarming of warring parties and the restoration of order, the repatriation of refugees, the monitoring of elections, the protection of human rights, the meeting of humanitarian needs, and the rebuilding of civil society. It also links up with what Gareth Evans described in his 1993 book *Cooperating for Peace* [5] as "expanded peace keeping" or what often involves the "total reconstitution of broken and devastated societies." UN diplomatic efforts in Namibia, El Salvador, Mozambique, the Western Sahara and Angola have all involved peacekeeping operations with mandates that include conflict resolution beyond strictly peacekeeping and peace enforcement definitions or those that might strictly be defined as Article 6 and Article 7 missions. Peace-keeping, then, is what comes after the war, the conflict, or the civil strife and is designed to prevent lapse into war. In the case of East Timor, it comes after the UN body failed to act on its own resolutions, actions which may have prevented the tragedy which we discuss in dry academic terms today. Given the right political cues, then, the emphasis of peace-building is on the civilian rather than military aspects of the problem.

The failure by the UN to act upon its own resolutions as to involvement on the ground in East Timor is all the more surprising as even Resolution 37/30 (section 3) calls "....upon all specialized agencies and other organizations of the UN system, in particular the World Food Programme, the United Nations Children's Fund and the Office of the UNHCR, immediately to assist, within their respective fields of competence, the people of East Timor, in close cooperation with Portugal, the administering Power". The "evolutionary" shift in priorities on East Timor on the part of the UN "from self-determination to humanitarian issues to and procedural dismissal" has been well exposed by Paula Escarameia in her 1993 study, *Formation of Concepts of International Law: Subsumption under Self-determination in the Case of East Timor.* [6] But the "subsumption of facts" to an array of legal ideas described by Escarameia can work both ways. Today it is the flaunting of the humanitarian question in East Timor [the Dili massacres/Ninjas/Liquisa] that reimposes a reevaluation of the procedural logjam at the UN [the intra-Timorese dialogue alongside the foreign ministers conference] and which, for whatever reasons, has provoked a rethinking and reevaluation of such concepts as "integrasi," "special status" [Prabowo Subiato], "autonomy" or free association [some Timorese], and self-determination/independence [many Timorese].

As the Bosnia case starkly reveals, without a clarification of doctrine, a UN mission can find itself badly positioned. Configured for "peacekeeping" it may end up involved in the kind of "peace-enforcement" for which it is not equipped. By definition, however, the East

Timor case should be easier to handle than almost any recent UN mission. The military equation is so lop-sided in Indonesia's favor that a conflict or "civil-war" dimension (such as in Angola) is almost entirely lacking. To the extent that a conflict situation exists in Timor, as the Liquisa murders of January 1995 dramatize, then it is foremost between ABRI and the Timorese people. Elements of the situation in East Timor bear more resemblance to Cambodia post-1979 where the withdrawal of one army, that of Vietnam, was the *sine qua non* of a political solution as part of the UN involvement. The immediate problem in East Timor—as even Gareth Evans appears to have acknowledged of late—is the imperative for the demilitarization of East Timor through the drawdown of the Indonesian military presence. The tenor of reports such as those of the UN rapporteur on extrajudicial, summary, or arbitrary execution, Mr. Bacre Waly Ndiaye [see Documents], confirms the linkage between breakdown of civil society in East Timor and militarization.

At the time of writing, we await a signal from the Office of the UN Secretary-General as to an *in situ* UN presence in East Timor, but, to reiterate, I am arguing in terms of both what should be done and what can be done in line with generalized concepts of UN peacekeeping.

A UN presence could monitor and verify this withdrawal while, at the same time, assist in the de-mobilization of local Timorese adjuncts of ABRI. Falantil, or at least the surviving rump of the Fretilin armed forces, has already signalled its willingness for a cease-fire. It would not necessarily be the task of the UN to enforce the withdrawal of Indonesian military forces from East Timor. Rather, it would be the international legal obligation of Indonesia to take that step, just as the Vietnamese armed forces made their timely and largely verified exit from Cambodia during the start-up phase of the UN operation in that country.

In other words, the doctrine of UN involvement/intervention in East Timor must rest on a political solution, namely Indonesian acquiescence in a UN-brokered solution. Even, I repeat even, Indonesian Foreign Minister Ali Alatas is saying as much of late. As Indonesia knows, the militarization of East Timor is a legacy of the Indonesian occupation and its converse, the demilitarization of East Timor and its transfer to interim UN rule, depends upon Indonesian acquiescence. Necessarily, a UN presence in East Timor would be a graduated process, just as the character of a UNTAET mission would change, in line with new political realities engendered by each stage of the peace process. Broadly, the transition would be from the strictly humanitarian to the political, as electoral registration and other procedures necessary to hold a referendum on independence get under way, and as elements of a UN-designed civil administration are moved in to fill the void created by the departed Indonesian battalions.

There are numerous precedents and models upon which the UN could draw in its reinvolvement in the East Timor case. Of necessity, I will be selective in this exposition, but what should be apparent from a scrutiny of the UN peacekeeping record since its inception almost fifty years ago, beginning with the establishment of UNTSO on 29 May 1948 to oversee the peace in Palestine, is creativity or flexibility around certain principles.

There are no provisions in the Charter of the UN for peace-keeping operations as such. Rather, the legal basis for such operations is the mandate of each separate mission. Nevertheless, the Security Council has, by its actions, established a broad body of doctrine. It is the Secretary-General who has overall responsibility for providing direction to peace-keeping based on mandates defined for such operations by the Security Council and, in some exceptional circumstances, by the General Assembly. The way forward has been captured in the report of the then newly elected Secretary-General, Boutros Boutros-Ghali in June 1992, namely *An Agenda for Peace: Preventive Diplomacy and Peacekeeping*, notably his strictures on an active "peace-making," even though a more sober note is reflected in *Supplement to an Agenda for Peace* published in January 1995.

As no one international problem or conflict situation entirely replicates another, so the UN has demonstrated its ability to craft its *modus operandi* to local conditions and circumstances. It is also a truism that UN intervention in any one conflict has always proceeded out of a consensus or political will set by or with the endorsement of the Permanent Five. To be sure, the UN has engaged itself in much soul-searching as to various features of peace-keeping operations, not excluding budgetary considerations. As revealed by a UN report of 17 March 1995, special attention must be given to the so-called start-up phase of a potential operation. Of particular interest in this report are recommendations concerning an enhanced information component, an electoral component, a repatriation component (with UNHCR as "responsibility center"), and a human rights component, a civilian police component. The overall thrust of complex missions, then, is to enhance the humanitarian and civil administration aspects of peace-keeping operations. [7]

We observe, in the case of East Timor, that it is the Secretary-General who is the "responsibility center" and the taker of initiatives, assisted by secretaries answerable to a Secretariat. But as "facilitator" of the UN-sponsored talks on East Timor, the UN Secretary-General has also asserted that his role is very "limited," that any permanent resolution of the status of East Timor would require a decision of the UN General Assembly. [8] Given the pro-active role of the Secretary-General is other disputes, as discussed below, there is a certain ambiguity or circularity in these arguments.

Namibia: lessons from a former trusteeship

The example of the southwest African state of Namibia is also illustrative. Despite Namibia's status over long time as a mandate, first of the League of Nations and then of the United Nations, the South African government continued to rule the country as a *bantustan*. Trusteeships, like other non-self-governing territories, were bound in UN law to GA Resolution 637 (VII)–16 December 1952 on the right of peoples and nations to self-determination, and GA resolution 1514 (XV)–14 December 1960 on the granting of independence to colonial countries and peoples, the major international covenants underpinning the "age of decolonization."

In 1971, in a historic judgement, the International Court of Justice declared Namibia to be illegally ruled. South Africa's contempt of the UN Council for Namibian independence, set up in 1968, is well captured in the language of the 20 September 1986 General Assembly Resolution on the "Question of Namibia."

> Reaffirming that Namibia is the direct responsibility of the UN until genuine self-determination and national independence are achieved in terms of the relevant resolutions and decisions of the General Assembly....Gravely concerned that, twenty years after the termination by the General Assembly of the mandate of South Africa over Namibia, the racist regime continues its illegal occupation of the Territory in violation of the relevant resolutions and decisions of the UN....Declaring that the illegal occupation of Namibia by racist South Africa, its brutal repression of the Namibian people and its repeated acts of aggression and destabilization of neighbouring sovereign States, including from the Territory of Namibia, constitute a breach of international peace and security.

While the facts of the case are somewhat different, the analogy with the Indonesian annexation and plunder of East Timor is striking. The Resolution continued:

Reaffirms the inalienable right of the Namibean people to self-determination, freedom and national independence in an untruncated territory including Walvis Bay, the Penguin Islands and all adjacent offshore islands in accordance with the charter of the UN and General Assembly resolution 1514 (XV) of 14 December 1960, as well as the subsequent relevant resolutions and decisions of the Assembly and the security Council.....calls upon the UN Council for Namibia to take immediate practical measures to establish its Administration in Namibia....Commends the South West African People's Organization for their exemplary leadership by it to the Namibian people for over a quarter of a century and for sacrifices in the field of battle....condemns the plunder by South Africa and other foreign economic interests of the natural resources of Namibia.

From April 1989 to March 1990, UNTAG oversaw the transition of Namibia from South African control to independence. As such, it performed traditional peace keeping roles as in monitoring the cease-fire between the South Africa Defence Forces and SWAPO and it also took part in "peace-building" activities such as in monitoring elections for a constituent assembly. According to Heininger, the UN Transition Assistance Group (UNTAG), formed to implement this Resolution, was "the first UN operation to combine traditional peacekeeping with peace-building. [9]

We recall that Nauru (independent in 1968) and New Guinea (which became independent as PNG in 1975) were Australian trust territories. The last of the eleven trust territories under the UN system administered by the Trusteeship Council, Palau, ended on 1 October 1994, after Palau was deemed to have exercised its right to self-determination through "free association" with the US. This transpired after various UN-monitored plebiscites. Henceforth, the Trusteeship Council will meet only if the need arises.

Thomas G. Weiss has also observed that with the last UN trust territory becoming independent, the Trusteeship Council, one of six primary organs of the UN, is left with no *raison d'être*. He asks, "Could not this council be transformed to handle temporarily the problems of states that have ceased to function, and to provide breathing space for civil society to be reconstituted?" [10] East Timor, of course, remains one of the principal items on the agenda of the UN Committee on Decolonization. The Special Committee of 24 or the Special Committee on the Situation with Regard to the Implementation of the Declaration on the Granting of Independence to Colonial Countries and Peoples which meets annually in New York in July takes petitions and reports to the General Assembly [see Documents].

The Cambodia Analogy

While one could certainly enter reservations, there is much evidence that the UN-brokered peace in Cambodia is more of a success than a failure. It would, accordingly, be appropriate to dwell upon Australia's and Indonesia's pro-active involvement in the Cambodia problem. For a second opinion one would not have to go further than Gareth Evans' and Bruce Grant's 1991 assessment of the matter. [11]

But we have provided our own analysis. [12] The "Evans Plan" or Australian Peace Proposal for Cambodia was first made explicit by Senator Evans in a statement before the Australian Senate on 24 November 1989. As outlined in the DFAT "Red Book" actually prepared for the informal meeting on Cambodia in Jakarta held between 26 and 28 February 1990, the plan consisted of four elements, each matched by a "working paper" and each pertaining to a transitional period. These were: the overall structure of government, civil administration, the electoral organization, and security questions linked with neutrality and post-war reconstruction. Additionally, four annexes concerned a draft UN mandate, a "framework" negotiating text, an implementation timetable, and a resources timetable. [13] Following the precedent of the UN role in brokering Namibia's independence, the Evans Plan called for the Vietnamese-installed government in Phnom Penh to "step back" from its role as *de facto* government while at the same time holding back the resistance factions in the transitional period. The Plan also proposed that the UN be directly involved in the civil administration of Cambodia during a transition period leading up to the elections that the UN would organize and conduct.

In the event, intense diplomatic moves (and rivalry) by countries like France, Indonesia, and Australia abided by the willingness of the Permanent Five to see a solution through, led to the landmark Comprehensive Political Settlement of the Cambodia Conflict signed in Paris on 23 October 1991. The UN was involved with this process from the outset. So was ASEAN, the leading regional organization. Notably, the UN backed the seat of the ousted Democratic Kampuchea faction and, in so doing, upheld the principle of defending state sovereignty against aggression, a reference to the invasion of Cambodia by Vietnam in 1979 and the installation of the puppet PRK regime.

At the risk of attracting major flak from a coterie of Australian

Cambodianists, we supported this position. But just as we supported the principle of state sovereignty in Cambodia *vis-à-vis* Vietnamese ambitions, so we fall in line with the UN principle of defending state sovereignty on East Timor. On 9 September 1993, I heard the arguments of former UN Secretary General Perez de Cuellar, during a public address in Brunei Darussalam, in favor of UN involvement in Cambodia as vindication of the "impartiality principle" of the world body with respect to UN resolutions [see chapter 2]. When questioned as to whether this principle applied to Indonesia over its invasion of East Timor, he answered in the affirmative.

How, then, did the UN mission in Cambodia work? According to the author of one study on the question, Janet E. Heininger:

> Unlike Namibia, where it oversaw the transition to independence and supervised elections held by the South African authorities, the UN was mandated to assume the actual management of Cambodia and take it through the transition from civil war through free elections to the establishment of a democratically elected government. In Cambodia, the UN ran the elections, rather than merely monitoring them. More than any previous or subsequent UN mission, UNTAC stretched the concept of peace-building to the limit. [14]

Heininger also described the Evans proposal of an erstwhile UN takeover of Cambodia as a "radical departure" for the international organization that had long shed itself of "trusteeship" responsibilities.[15]

In fact, established by the UN Security Council on 28 February 1992, the mandated functions of UNTAC ended only on 24 September 1993, following the promulgation of a new Constitution and the installation of the Government following the UN-monitored elections. In the interim transitional period, the UN worked through a Supreme National Council of Cambodia (SNC) in which the "sovereignty, independence and unity" of Cambodia were enshrined. This Council comprised the four major factions and was chaired by Prince Sihanouk. Prior to the deployment of UNTAC, the UN deployed a small advance mission to assist the Cambodian parties maintain a cease-fire.

Headed by a special representative of the Secretary-General (Yasashi Akashi), and based in Phnom Penh, UNTAC at maximum strength comprised some 22,000 international civilian and military personnel deployed throughout the country supplemented by locally recruited staff. UNTAC comprised six distinct components: human rights, electoral, civil administration, civilian police, repatriation, and rehabilitation. Voter registration that was set at over 4.6 million (or some 96 per cent of the estimated eligible population, including returning refugees) commenced on 5 October 1992, in the face of cease-fire violations. Twenty political parties officially registered. The elections were held from 23 to 28 May 1993 in all 21 provinces of Cambodia. To be sure, on the one hand the PDK boycotted the elections and, on the other, UNTAC did not entirely dismantle the Phnom Penh (PRK) administrative/military structure as required under the terms of the Paris Agreement.

The duly elected Constituent Assembly began work on 14 June 1993. Although not foreseen under the Paris Agreements, UNTAC provided logistical and operational assistance and technical advice to the Assembly. UNTAC began the complex withdrawal process, nevertheless delegating a range of activities to various agencies of the UN system, promoting development, providing humanitarian assistance, and fostering human rights. On the day that the UNTAC mandate was declared ended (24 September 1993), Sihanouk, as head of state, formally promulgated the new constitution which the Constituent Assembly had formally adopted. Sihanouk was elected King of Cambodia by a royal council and the Constituent Assembly transformed itself into a legislative assembly. Cambodia became an independent, sovereign state.

While numerous commentators have highlighted the contradiction in the West's support for Kuwait against Iraq, sanctions against the South African apartheid regime, and operational support for Indonesia notwithstanding the invasion and occupation of East Timor, we have taken pains to expose the contradiction between the West's—particularly Australia's—support for the Cambodia Peace package and its inaction on East Timor. We further argued that Australian and Indonesian action on Cambodia was the smokescreen behind which for long years Indonesia—with the West's connivance—could get on with the task of devouring East Timor, its resources and people together. Very early Vietnam reached an understanding with Indonesia not to raise the East Timor self-determination issue. There is a sense that Indonesia has never felt comfortable about the concurrent raising of genocide issues in both Cambodia and East Timor that would have been implied when Australia, notably Foreign Minister Bill Hayden, pushed that idea. In any case, mutual back-slapping by Australia and Indonesia over a durable peace in Cambodia brings little cheer to East Timorese.

The lessons of Cambodia for East Timor, then, are that aggression and violation of sovereignty must not be rewarded. It simply sends the wrong signals.

There are also many lessons from UNTAC for a future UNTAET. I would simply highlight the human rights component, the repatriation component, the electoral component, the rehabilitation component, and the civilian police component. All would be necessary on the ground in East Timor to oversee a transition. Obviously there is no king or king-maker in East Timor in the form of a Sihanouk, all of which is to suggest that the question of leadership and loyalties in a revived East Timorese state should be given much attention.

But, as the Cambodia case again points up, there is a need for a clear concept of state-building and constitution-building as part of any "peace package" for East Timor. As with the People's Republic of Kampuchea in Cambodia prior to the UN intervention, so the Republic of Indonesia has built a complex web of overlapping governmental and military structures inside East Timor, in my view even more penetrating and totalistic than its Marxist-Leninist analogues in Indochina. It will be small solace for the East Timorese if such structures and individuals remain in place even after a UN-supervised transition.

Western Sahara: the lesson of voter registration

The case of Western Sahara, a Spanish colony since 1884, also bears scrutiny, especially given the parallels with East Timor, namely major cases of aborted decolonization in the face of invasion and annexation. Sandwiched between Morocco, Mauritania and Algeria this arid land fronting the Atlantic coast supports a mixed Arab-Berber population of little over 210,000.

The similarities between the plight of the Saharan Arabs and the East Timorese were also noted by David Pontes, writing in the Portuguese newspaper *Publico* of 26 August 1995. "In both territories," the paper observed,

> the new occupiers have exercised brutal repression, isolated them from the international community, created police states, and carried out a colonisation policy of transferring foreign populations into the territories (a reference to the Moroccan invasion of Western Sahara in November 1975).

Further, the paper continued:

> In the cases of these former colonies, whose peoples are clamouring for independence, there are third countries exploiting their economic resources. In Timor it is Australia. In the Sahara, the Germans (Krupp) are after phosphates and the Spanish and Portuguese are busy fishing the Sahara's rich coastal waters. [16]

In brief, after much delay, Spain agreed in 1975 to hold a referendum on self-determination for the territory under UN auspices. King Hassan of Morocco, however, claimed it for Morocco on the basis of "historic title" predating Spain's colonization. The Republic of Mauritania made a similar overlapping claim. Both claims were rejected in an ICJ advisory opinion in 1975 which supported the claim for self-determination. One day later, Hassan called for a peaceful invasion of Western Sahara. In November 1975, Morocco invaded Western Sahara, after agreement with Spain, and in December of the same year the full-scale invasion of East Timor commenced after Portugal abandonned Dili to Fretilin and withdrew to offshore Atauro island. *Publico* newspaper also finds it more than just coincidence that one man, former US Secretary of State Henry Kissinger, had been in both Rabat and Jakarta at the exact time of these respective invasions. [17]

The author was also present in Casablanca when one of these so-called Green Marches was launched by Morocco's King Hassan II with the aim of demographically flooding the territory. But when the Security Council failed to condemn Morocco, Spain ceded the territory to Morocco and Mauritania. This act was resisted by Polisario, the independent movement of the Saharans, supported by Algeria. In February 1976, Polosario formally proclaimed a government-in-exile of the Sahrawai Arab Democratic Republic (SADR). Meanwhile, Mauritania, under pressure from Polisario guerrillas abandoned all claims to its portion of the territory in August 1979, a void largely filled by Morocco. In 1984 Polisario's government-in-exile won formal membership in the Organization of African Unity (OAU). Resolutions in defense of Western Sahara in the UN General Assembly have consistently won support.

As a UN public relations document makes clear, in 1985 the UN Secretary-General, in cooperation with the OAU, initiated a joint mission of good will for a solution to the question of Western Sahara. In this mission, the two parties to the conflict, the government of Morocco and the Frente Popular para la Liberacion de Saguia el-Hamra y de Rio de Oro (Frente Polisario), were presented with proposals to settle the conflict in conformity with the 1960 General Assembly Resolution 1514 (XV), namely, the declaration on the granting of independence to colonial countries and peoples. This was to be accomplished by means of a cease-fire and the holding of a referendum to enable the people of Western Sahara to exercise their right to self-determination, to choose between independence and integration with Morocco.

According to the Secretary-General's plan, sanctioned by the Security Council on 27 June 1990, there would be a transitional period during which the Special Representative of the Secretary-General would have sole and exclusive responsibility over all matters relating to the referendum, including its organization and conduct. He would be assisted by MINURSO (UN Mission for the Referendum in Western Sahara).

According to the plan, the transitional period would begin with the taking effect of a cease-fire and end with the proclamation of the results of the referendum. Following the announcement of a cease-fire, MINURSO would verify the reduction of Moroccan troops in the Territory, monitor the confinement of Moroccan and Polisario troops to designated locations, take steps with the parties to ensure the release of all Western Saharan political prisoners or detainees, oversee the exchange of prisoners of war (ICRC), implement the repatriation programme (UNHCR), identify and register qualified voters, and organize and ensure a free referendum and proclaim the results. The civilian component of MINURSO would range from 800 to 1000, while the military component would consist of around 1,700 armed forces personnel along with 300 police.

MINURSO was set up on 29 April 1991, a cease-fire was proclaimed by the Secretary General on 6 September. While the government of both Morocco and Polosario have reiterated their confidence in the UN, they continue to have divergent views on key elements of the plan. A major sticking point as far as Polosario is concerned are criteria for voter eligibility. Given the policies of the Moroccan government to demographically flood Spanish Sahara, it is natural that Polosario would wish that the Spanish census of 1974 be the exclusive basis of defining the electorate rather than criteria set down in 1991. To help break the impasse over this question, the Secretary-General decided in May 1991 to establish an Identification Commission for the referendum. In 1993 a compromise proposal was put forward based on the albeit imperfect 1974 census, but providing the only demographic and tribal data about the territory. Both sides still expressed reservations, however, thus derailing the timetable for the referendum scheduled for late 1993.

It is notable that, in the compromise formula on voting criteria, the revised lists of the 1974 census, together with the supplement listing the names of additional persons expected to reach the age of 18 years by 31 December 1993 were accepted. It is also notable that application forms were distributed in refugee camps in the Tindouf area of Algeria, as well as in certain locations outside the Territory where numbers of Western Saharans were known to be living. In other words, thousands of individuals foreign to the Territory were to be included in the electorate. On 4 November 1994 the Secretary-General reported that because of the complexity of tribal subgroups the registration process was far more difficult than expected. In fact, the Secretary-General travelled to the region on 25–29 November 1994, meeting the major parties concerned, including Algerian authorities in Algiers. The Secretary-General recommended 1 June 1995 as the start of the transitional period leading to a referendum in October 1995. MINURSO envisaged a full-strength force of 1,700 military observers and troops, 300 police, and around 1,000 civilian personnel, although current strength is about one-tenth of the above.

There are analogies and differences here with respect to the East Timor case. Unlike Fretilin/East Timor, Polosario took the step of forming a government-in-exile which, notably, attracted the backing of the leading regional organization. Contrariwise, the role of ASEAN in conspiring with Indonesia to bury East Timor is well known. There are some analogies also in Morocco's and Indonesia's claims to "historical title," although, for well-known reasons, Indonesia has not notably pushed this argument of late.

There are also lessons in the Western Sahara case for East Timor, especially in the eventuality of a voter-registration exercise. With the hindsight of the so-called Act of Free Choice for the people of West Irian in mind, East Timor should be particularly vigilant to ensure a voter registration that guarantees some firm concept of *jus soli*, that guarantees rights for refugees and that does not reward immigrants from outside East Timor. This is a very important issue to consider in any Peace Plan for East Timor. [18]

In a lucid discussion on this issue, Sasha Stepan has observed that, unlike the East Timor case, and unlike Fretilin, Polosario and its cause enjoyed both diplomatic and military support from one state (Algeria), and the broader endorsement and engagement of the Organization for African Unity (OAU), in the interests of regional order. It also owed to the hands-on efforts of then UN Secretary-General Perez de Cuellar, notably in obtaining in principle agreement in August 1988 between Morocco and Polosario as to UN involvement in seeking a cease-fire and referendum. To the extent that East Timor has gained support, Stepan argues, it has been from NGOs, distant states such as Angola, and, for a time, Mozambique and Portugal, not Australia and not ASEAN. [19]

In fact, the situation is analogous to the case of the West African state of Liberia, where civil anarchy ensued in the wake of the overthrow of the government headed by President Samuel Doe in 1990, and where UNOMIL (UN Observer Mission in Liberia) is the first UN peace-keeping mission undertaken in cooperation with a peace-keeping operation set up by another organization. This is a reference to the initiative of the Economic Community of West African States (ECOWAS), a sub-regional organization, in assisting the Liberians to establish peace in the country. Nevertheless, the UN only agreed to send a small force in the latter stages of conflict, and after ECOWAS was accused of taking sides in the conflict.

To repeat, while Australia's role in the making of the East Timor tragedy is now well known, the ASEAN countries, obviously, but also the South Pacific Forum, and the Asia-Pacific Economic Cooperation (APEC) have equally stood back from engagement in the issue. Should these organizations continue to abrogate their responsibilities in the face of diplomatic and other blusters (Indonesian pressure on the Philippines to abort the June 1994 Manila Conference on East Timor is a good case in point), then there seems to be no alternative but to issue a call to action by interested NGOs within and without the UN process on East Timor.

El Salvador: lessons from the Cold War

As the *New York Times* for 5 May 1995 editorialized on the central American country of El Salvador:

> With the April 28 departure of its peacekeeping mission from El Salvador, the UN can celebrate a quiet victory. Three years after the initial peace agreement was signed between the Salvadoran government and guerrilla insurgents, a divided society has begun to heal. Lawlessness, human right abuses, and bitter mistrust have given way to the beginnings of a civil society.
>
> For the US, the UN mission in El Salvador has been a bargain. American taxpayers underwrote a misguided proxy war there during the 1980s to the tune of $6 billion....But the UN provided much more than needed funds for El Salvador. It served as a trusted mediator in a place where trust was in short supply. It presided over elections in which the FMLN, the party of the guerrilla insurgents,

participated for the first time as a legitimate political organization. It supervised the demobilization of the guerrilla forces and the hated National Police and the training of a new civilian police force.

As the editorial concluded: "In a time when the role of the UN is being questioned, El Salvador stands a heartening example of success." Success, to be sure, but only if the root causes of the civil conflict have been eliminated in the process. *The Times* of course is referring to the country that Ronald Reagan (and this newspaper) compared favorably to Marxist Nicaragua that fairly might be described, after Noam Chomsky, as a "death squad democracy," a reference to the murder of Archbishop Oscar Romero, acts of terror against the church and universities, intimidation of journalists and liberals, not by the erstwhile Marxist guerrillas but by the US-backed Duarte regime. [20]

The UN presence in El Salvador [UN Observer Mission in El Salvador or ONUSAL], a country of some 5,750,000 people, took form in 1991 as a result of a complex negotiating process, initiated by the Government of El Salvador and the Frente Farabundo Marti para la Liberacion Nacional (FMLN) and conducted under the auspices of the UN Secretary General. Following a preliminary agreement (the San Jose agreement) between the two sides on 26 July 1990 relating to a UN observer mission to monitor human rights and freedoms, the UN Security Council, *following the Secretary-General's recommendation*, decided, on 20 May 1991, to establish ONUSAL as an integrated peace-keeping operation. All up, a 1,000 military and police, 170 international civilian staff, and 187 local staff oversaw the verification of a cease-fire and the signing of a Peace Agreement (New York, 25 September 1991) in a two-phase operation that saw the military component of the operation replaced by police. Following the end of armed conflict, (declared on 23 December 1992), ONUSAL's mandate was further enlarged (8 January 1993) to oversee national and local elections. The FMLN was legalized accordingly (UN public relations document).

As two students of the UN role in El Salvador have written, this was the first time that the UN has attempted to broker the end of an internal conflict and the first peacekeeping mission to incorporate the concept of *post-conflict peace-keeping*. A notable feature of ONUSAL, these authors underscore, was its special role in preventing or dissuading further human rights violations. "Early UN deployment of human rights monitors helped to create a climate more conducive to a negotiated end to the conflict, and contributed to a reduced incidence of violence against civilians." [21]

While the East Timor situation is not one of pure internal conflict, there are plenty of parallels here with the El Salvador case, both as to the role of international actors and as to what the UN can accomplish under its newly defined role in peace-building.

The lessons for East Timor from El Salvador should be obvious; demilitarization, respect for human rights, and rebuilding civil society. But to achieve this breakthrough, El Salvador required a critical stepping back by the US from its role in support of the Duarte regime and a corollary spirit of reconciliation by the guerrillas. But just as central America might be said to have achieved a peace dividend from the end of the Cold War, so, one hopes, the same be achieved in East Timor, unfortunate victim of the same kind of logic or, at least, Cold War phobias.

Eritrea: lessons from history

On 27 April 1993, following a fifty-year struggle, the new nation of Eritrea came into being following an internationally supervised election. Eritrea is a small country of about 3.5 million people in the Horn of Africa. Colonized by Italy from 1889, Eritrea was under British rule for ten years from April 1941, following Eritrea's capture by Commonwealth forces. In 1952, following a UN vote, and although more than 50 per cent of the male-only electorate had voted for parties advocating independence, Eritrea was federated with neighboring Ethiopia [the comparison with the UN role in brokering Libya's independence is apposite here]. In 1962 Haile Selasie formally annexed Eritrea as the fourteenth province of the empire (sound familiar?). The armed struggle against Addis Ababa's US-Israeli backed rule in Eritrea commenced apace, two-thirds "liberated" during my visit in 1972. Until the victory of the "Marxist" Mengistu regime in Addis Ababa in 1974, the US had maintained a major communication base in Asmara, capital of Eritrea, and a naval installation in the Red Sea port of Massawa. But like the Haile Selasie regime before it, the Soviet (and Israeli)-backed Dergue also fell into what one writer has called the "Eritrean trap." [22]

From 1978 until May 1991 when their tactical ally, the Tigrean People's Liberation Front, overwhelmed the Mengistu regime and took over the government in Addis Ababa, the Eritrean People's Liberation Front (EPLF) and the Eritrean Liberation Front (ELF) successively fought both a guerrilla warfare campaign and conventional campaigns against the Dergue. To a significant degree, the two major fronts settled their differences in the interest of victory. Meanwhile, the EPLF occupied the Eritrean capital, Asmara, ending the 30-year war that saw both Asmara and Massawa, the Red Sea port, fought over several times in horrific battle scenes costing the lives of 60,000 Eritrean fighters and 40,000 civilians, not to mention Ethiopian casualties.

On 29 May 1991 the EPLF announced the formation of a Provisional Government of Eritrea in preparation for the 23–25 April referendum on independence (not from Italy, of course, but from the new transitional government in Ethiopia). The result was a landslide vote for independence, announced on 27 April 1993.

One Western observer of the election process has written, there was nothing to stop the EPLF from evolving into a centralized dictatorship, but in fact as a guerrilla party EPLF rule was fairly democratic. In the event, one of the first actions the Eritrean government took after the referendum was to begin drafting a constitution. A multiparty system had, meanwhile, quickly evolved, by appearances, not based on race or religion. While Eritrea maintains one of the best-trained and supplied armies in the region, it has built on its fund of goodwill with the new order in Addis Ababa and maintains good relations with all neighbors. [23]

Clearly, there are lessons here for despots of both the obscurantist and authoritarian-militarist varieties, just as there are lessons for former "freedom fighters." The Eritrea victory, then, should give hope to "secessionists" and national liberation fronts around the world just as it should concern "fragile" states held together by degrees of coercion. While there may be specific lessons in the Eritrea case for Acehnese and Irianese (and lessons in the Haile Selasie and Mengistu cases for Indonesia), the East Timor case, as I have reminded certain newspaper editors, is not a simple secession issue, but one concerning the right to self-determination. The long slumbering Eritrea "rebellion," then, even in the face of the 1952 UN federal "solution," demonstrates the possibilities for liberationist struggles in the post–Cold War era. [24] The lessons from Ethiopia/Eritrea for the East Timor resistance also suggest that taking the long view may not altogether be hopeless, that timing or taking advantage of a changing international situation can be decisive, and that unity and constitutional preparedness in the lead-up to and in the aftermath of an internationally-supervised election/referendum could be imperative.

Mozambique: lessons from Frelimo

Even prior to the 1974 April revolution in Lisbon, the Front for the Liberation of Mozambique (Frelimo) had secured for itself a liberated zone in the country along with elements of a state apparatus. Frelimo assumed power in 1975 without either a referendum or elections. Full independence was granted by Portugal on 25 June 1975 with Frelimo leader Samora Machel as president and Frelimo as the only legal party. Portuguese was chosen as an official language and the legal and administrative system adopted is derivative of Portuguese norms. In 1976–77 Rhodesia countered Mozambique's support of UN sanctions against that country by launching Renamo. When, in turn, Rhodesia became independent Zimbabwe, the South African government sowed the seeds of a devastating civil war in Mozambique through its support for Renamo. But, by 1984, erstwhile Marxist Frelimo moved closer to the West, rewarded by membership in the World Bank and IMF, and transformed itself into a multiparty state. One early supporter of Maputo, we may take note, was the Thatcher government. Devasted by war and drought, the peace process between Renamo and Frelimo began in earnest in 1992. A solution brokered in Rome was quickly verified by the UN Security Council that established UN Operation for Mozambique (UNOMOZ) and a Supervisory and Monitoring Commission to oversee implementation of the peace accord. One major innovation in the Mozambique operation was that an arm of the UN—the World Bank—kept the country afloat financially.

The last act for UNOMOZ, and the most daunting, was the organization of elections. Approximately 2,500 international election monitors helped guarantee the integrity of elections by verifying, monitoring, and evaluating electoral registration and other procedures. Nearly 88 percent of the 6.1 million registered voters in a country of some 17,400,000 people of different ethnic and sub-ethnic groups cast ballots. Among the twelve candidates running for president, the incumbent President Chissano and his ruling Frelimo party won, with over 53 per cent of the vote, with the Renamo leader Dhlakama coming in second with 34 percent. Frelimo also won a narrow majority in the National Assembly out of fourteen parties contesting.

As Lloyd has written of Mozambique, although the UN military presence was crucial to the implementation of the peace process, the necessary condition was the prior political agreement between the parties. To oversimplify, he states, "the World Bank provided financial security and the UN provided military protection." To a great extent, the lessons of Angola, where the political process broke down amid appalling civilian loss of life, was well learned. [25]

The point is that the electoral process in Mozambique was vastly more complex than in East Timor and the scale of human suffering of far greater dimensions than even East Timor. Building upon UN experience and "institutional memory" in Mozambique, the UN have their role cut out from themselves in East Timor. We note the role of Japanese election monitors in Mozambique (and Haiti) under the UN umbrella and their participation in a future UNTAET would be more than welcome. We may also note the significant role played by the contingent of Uraguayan peacekeepers in Mozambique (and Cambodia), now currently on mission in Angola with UNAVEMIII. While Indonesian peacekeepers formed an important contingent in Cambodia, it is of more than passing interest that the Luanda government in Angola—with East Timor in mind—has rejected a UN proposal that Indonesian troops join that mission.

Recommendations

1. Potential UN involvement in East Timor requires conceptual clarity from the outset (the so-called "start-up phase"). As the UN body has itself recognized in a recent review, [26] this must involve clear definition of:

- overall direction and coordination
- preparation during the negotiation phase
- allocation of responsibility for support functions
- information component
- electoral component
- repatriation component
- human rights component
- civilian police component
- military component

But just as the UN at 50 seeks to clarify its doctrinal approach to peace-keeping and peace-building, so the East Timor case will provide a model case to world-order outcomes if this body is to be respected into the next millennium.

2. As a corollary to the above I would argue that a great deal more

conceptual clarity by independence-seeking Timorese is also required. This applies not only to the contingency of a referendum in East Timor like a Spanish Sahara, but also with reference to future state structures, including representative institutions, leadership, and especially the need for a constitutional convention (of which lessons could be learned from the experience of Eritrea). This is not to deprecate the vision or energy of Timorese in the diaspora, just to remind them of the urgency. I merely note that the resistance has held back from taking the step of proclaiming a government-in-exile.

3. To single out the problematical electoral component, and bearing in mind the experience of Spanish Sahara, great care should be taken in voter registration, with special reference to Portuguese and Church census figures, to the needs and rights of East Timorese born since 1975 and now of voting age (18?), as well as to the needs of Timorese in the diaspora. Such an exercise would also be mindful of the tens of thousands of Indonesian immigrants who have entered East Timor since 1975, whose eligibility to participate in any electoral exercise would have to be carefully screened.

4. The scale of potential UN operation (electoral component, humanitarian component, or whatever) must be commensurate with East Timor's size. The negative lessons of UNTAC are apposite here. East Timor would not welcome a second (UN) invasion on top of the havoc wreaked by the present occupier. This not only concerns the threats imposed upon East Timorese society by large numbers of outsiders but also the problems of absorption of aid, corruption, and aid dependency entailed by large-scale international operations. The multinational character of any future UN-component operation in East Timor must be carefully chosen, Lusophone instead of the kind of cacophony of languages imposed upon Cambodia where the triumph of English-as-second language serves to rupture part of that country's history.

5. It seems to me that the creation of a national Timorese army in any UN-mediated peace is not a solution to the profound militarization of Timorese society that has occurred since 1974, and, for that matter, during its experience of Portuguese colonialism. Taking the cue here from Haiti's President Jean-Bertrand Aristide's decision in April 1995 to dissolve the army would be a necessary step. As he stated on this occasion, "The Haitian army did not do anything good for us. It was an occupying force." [27] But while the Caribbean nations talk of demilitarization, the reverse is the case in this part of the world. The point is that a future independent East Timor simply could not defend itself against predatory neighbors. While a future independent

East Timor must, necessarily, invigilate its borders, just as Macau (and Hong Kong) defend their borders against illegal immigrants with the cooperation of China, it is different from saying that East Timor should support an armed force beyond a civilian-led police force. East Timor's future security as a neutral, non-aligned state serving as a model of disarmament must be underwritten by international consent and that state should never again be allowed to become a victim or pawn.

From each of these case studies in UN peacekeeping, it is obvious that each situation is specific and so, in turn, have been the specifics of UN deployment. The success or failure of the mission concerned has more often than not turned on the prior establishment of political will as much as on careful preparation for the operation. In certain cases, the precondition for peace was the end of the Cold War and the end of proxy conflict (Cambodia/Namibia/Mozambique/Eritrea/El Salvador); in other cases, the role of regional organizations (Spanish Sahara/El Salvador/Liberia/Cambodia). In one case (Eritrea), astute military and diplomatic prowess coupled with the fortuitous collapse of a tyranny. In other cases, special initiatives by the UN Secretary-General (Spanish Sahara) and, in still others I have not discussed, the dominating role of big powers (the US role in Haiti). Any or all of these "'Blue Book' solutions" could be relevant and welcome to the East Timor case.

Notes

1.   Geoffrey C. Gunn and Jefferson Lee, *A Critical View of Western Journalism and Scholarship on East Timor* (Manila: Journal of Contemporary Asia Publishers, 1994), pp.250-1.

2.   The importance of the affirmation contained in paragraph six is, perversely, confirmed by Indonesia's predictable rejection of its inclusion. See "Improve Timor Scene: Alatas," *Jakarta Post*, 22 June 1995. See Declaração de Burg Schlaining, Austria, 5 de Junho de 1995.

3.   Paula Escarameia, *Formation of Concepts in International Law: Subsumption under Self-determination in the Case of East Timor* (Lisbon: Fundacão Oriente, 1993).

4.   Boutros Boutros-Ghali, *An Agenda for Peace: Preventive Diplomacy and Peacekeeping*, Report of the Secretary-General, UN General Assembly and Security Council, A/47/277, S/24111, June 17, 1992.

5.   Gareth Evans, *Cooperating for Peace: The Global Agenda for the 1990s and Beyond* (Sydney: Allen and Unwin, 1993), p.55.

6.   Escarameia, op.cit.

7.   Final report on the in-depth evaluation of peace-keeping operations:

start-up phase. Report of the Office of Internal Oversight Services. United Nations Economic and Social Council. E/AC.51/1995/2 17 March 1995.

8. See, e.g. "UN chief believes E Timor talks making progress" (Agence France Presse), [Bandung], 24 April 1995.

9. UN document A/RES/S-14/1.

10. Thomas G. Weiss, "The United Nations at Fifty," *Current History*, May 1995, pp.227.

11. Gareth Evans and Bruce Grant, *Australia's Foreign Relations in the World of the 1990s* (Melbourne: Melbourne University Press, 1991).

12. Geoffrey C. Gunn and Jefferson Lee, *Cambodia Watching Down Under*, (Bangkok: Institute of Asian Studies, Chulalongkorn University, IAS Monograph, No. 047, 1991). See "Epilogue: The Evans Plan on Cambodia (1990): An Australian Solution?," pp.273-306.

13. *Cambodia: An Australian Peace Proposal* (Working Papers prepared for the Informal Meeting on Cambodia, Jakarta, 26-28 February 1990), AGPS, Canberra, 1990.

14. See Janet E. Heininger, *Peacekeeping in Transition: The United Nations in Cambodia* (New York: The Twentieth Century Fund Press, New York, 1994), p.9.

15. Ibid., pp.15-16.

16. David Pontes, "En Route to war," [original in Portuguese] *Publico*, 26 August 1995.

17. Ibid.

18. Pontes observes that when Deputy Director of census control services Frank Rudy resigned, he presented a controversial report to the US House of Represetatives denouncing "Morocco's prepotency in the face of Minurso's passivity," a reference to various irregularities committed by Morocco. Also pointing a finger at the UN, Rudy claimed that "it was no longer possible to salvage Minurso as an institution with any credibility."

19. Sasha Stepan, *Credibility Gap: Australia and Timor Gap Treaty*, Development Dossier No. 28 (Canberra: Australian Council for Overseas Aid, 1990), pp.29-32.

20. Noam Chomsky, *Necessary Illusions: Thought Control in Democratic Societies* (London: Pluto Press,1989), chap. 4.

21. David Holiday and William Stanley, "Building the Peace: Preliminary Lessons from El Salvador," *Journal of International Affairs*, 46, No. 2 (Winter, 1993).

22. René Lefort, *Ethiopia: An Heretical Revolution?* (London: Zed Press, 1983), pp.39-41.

23. Roy Patemen, "Eritrea Takes the World Stage," *Current History*, May 1994, pp.228-31.

24. Bereket Habte Selassie, *Eritrea and the United Nations and Other Essays* (Trenton, N.J.: The Red Sea Press, 1989).

25. Robert B. Lloyd, "Mozambique: The Terror of War, the Tensions of Peace," *Current History*, April 1995, p.154.

26. Final report, op.cit.

27. "Aristide disbands Haitian army," *Daily Yomiuri*, 30 April 1995.

Documents

Document 1

G.A. RESOLUTION 3485 (XXX) – 12 DECEMBER 1975

Res. 3485 (XXX). Question of Timor

The General Assembly,

Recognizing the inalienable right of all peoples to self-determination and independence in accordance with the principles of the Charter of the United Nations and of the Declaration on the Granting of Independence to Colonial Countries and Peoples, contained in its resolution 1514 (XV) of 14 December 1960,

Having examined the chapter of the report of the Special Committee on the Situation with regard to the Implementation of the Declaration on the Granting of Independence to Colonial Countries and Peoples relating to the question of Timor, [1]

Having heard the statements of the representatives of Portugal, as the administering Power, [2] concerning developments in Portuguese Timor and the implementation with regard to that territory of the relevant provisions of the Charter and the Declaration, as well as those of General Assembly resolution 1541 (XV) of 15 December 1960,

Bearing in mind the respon-sibility of the administering Power to undertake all efforts to create conditions enabling the people of Portuguese Timor to exercise freely their right to self-determination, freedom and independence and to determine their future political status in accordance with the principles of the Charter and the Declaration, in an atmosphere of peace and order,

Mindful that all States should, in conformity with Article 2, paragraph 4, of the Charter, refrain in their international relations from the threat or use of force against the territorial integrity or national independence of any State, or from taking any action inconsistent with the purposes and principles of the Charter;

Deeply concerned at the critical situation resulting from the military intervention of the armed forces of Indonesia in Portuguese Timor,

1. Calls upon all States to respect the inalienable right of the people of Portuguese Timor to self-determination, freedom and independence and to determine their future political status in accordance with the principles of the Charter of the United Nations and the Declaration on the Granting of Independence to Colonial and Peoples;

2. Calls upon the administering Power to continue to make every effort to find a solution by peaceful means through talks between the Government of Portugal and the political parties representing the people of Portuguese Timor;

3. *Appeals* to all the parties in Portuguese Timor to respond positively to efforts to find a peaceful solution through talks between them and the Government of Portugal in the hope that such talks will bring an end to the strife in that Territory and lead towards the orderly exercise of the right of self-determination by the people of Portuguese Timor;

4. *Strongly deplores* the military intervention of the armed forces of Indonesia in Portuguese Timor;

5. *Calls upon* the Government of Indonesia to desist from further violation of the territorial integrity of Portuguese Timor aad to withdraw without delay its armed forces from the Territory in order to enable the people of the Territory freely to exercise their right to self-determination and independence;

6. *Draws the attention* of the Security Council, in conformity with Article 11, paragraph 3, of the Charter, to the critical situation in the Territory of Portuguese Timor and recommends that it take urgent action to protect the territorial integrity of Portuguese Timor and the inalienable right of its people to self-determination;

7. *Calls upon* all States to respect the unity and territorial integrity of Portuguese Timor;

8. *Requests* the Government of Portugal to continue its co-operation with the Special Committee on the Situation with regard to the Implementation of the Declaration on the granting of Independence to Colonial peoples and requests the Committee to send a fact-finding mission to the Territory as soon as possible, in consultation with the political parties in Portuguese Timor and the Government of Portugal.

2439th plenary meeting
12 December 1975

Document 2

S.C. RESOLUTION 384 (1975)–22 DECEMBER 1975

Resolution 384 (1975), as proposed following consultations among Council members, S/11915, adopted unanimously by Council on 22 December 1975, meeting 1869.

The Security Council,

Having noted the contents of the letter of the Permanent Representative of Portugal (S/11899),

Having heard the statements of the representatives of Portugal and Indonesia,

Having heard representatives of the people of East Timor,

Recognizing the inalienable right of the people of East Timor to self-determination and independence in accordance with the principles of the Charter of the United Nations and the Declarations on the Granting of Independence to Colonial Countries and Peoples, contained in General Assembly resolution 1514 (XV) of 14 December 1960,

Noting that General Assembly resolution 3485 (XXX) of 12 December 1975, *inter alia,* requested the Special Committee on the Situation with regard to the implementation of the Declaration on the Granting of Independence to Colonial Countries and Peoples to send a fact-finding mission to East Timor,

Gravely concerned at the deterioration of the situation in East Timor,

Gravely concerned also at the loss of life and conscious of the urgent need to avoid further bloodshed in East Timor,

Deploring the intervention of the armed forces of Indonesia in East Timor,

Regretting that the Government of Portugal did not discharge fully its responsibilities as administering Power in the Territory under Chapter XI of the Charter,

1. Calls upon all States to respect the territorial integrity of East Timor as well as the inalienable right of its people to self-determination in accordance with General Assembly resolution 1514 (XV);

2. Calls upon the Government of Indonesia to withdraw without delay all its forces from the Territory;

3. Calls upon the Government of Portugal as administering Power to co-operate fully with the United Nations so as to enable the people of East Timor to exercise freely their right to self-determination;

4. Urges all States and other parties concerned to co-operate fully with the efforts of the United Nations to achieve a peaceful solution to the existing situation and to facilitate the decolonization of the Territory;

5. *Requests* the Secretary-General to send urgently a special representative to East Timor for the purpose of making an on-the-spot assessment of the existing situation and of establishing contact with all the parties in the Territory and all States concerned in order to ensure the implementation of the present resolution;

6. *Further requests* the Secretary-General to follow the implementation of the resolution and, taking into account the report of his special representative, to submit recommendations to the Security Council as soon as possible;

7. *Decides* to remain seized of the situation.

S/11922. Letter of 24 December 1975 from Portugal.

S/11923 (A/31/42). Letter of 22 December 1975 from Indonesia (transmitting Declaration on Establishment of Provisional Government of Territory of East Timor, done at Dili, 17 December 1975).

Document 3

S.C. RESOLUTION 389 (1976)–22 APRIL 1976

Resolution 389 (1976), as proposed by 3 powers, S/12056, adopted by Security Council on 22 April 1976, meeting 1914, by 12 votes to 0, with 2 abstentions (Japan, United States) (Benin did not participate in voting)

The Security Council,

Recalling its resolution 384 (1974) of 22 December 1975,

Having considered the report of the Secretary-General of 12 March 1976,

Having heard the statements of the representatives of Portugal and Indonesia,

Having heard the statements of representatives of people of East Timor,

Reaffirming the inalienable right of the people of East Timor to self-determination and independence in accordance with the principles of the Charter of the United Nations and the Declaration on the Granting of Independence to Colonial Countries and Peoples, contained in General Assembly resolution 1514 (XV) of 14 December 1960,

Believing that all efforts should be made to create conditions that will enable the people of East Timor to exercise freely their right to self-determination,

Noting that the question of East Timor is before the General Assembly,

Conscious of the urgent need to bring to an end the continued situation of tension in East Timor,

Taking note of the statement by the representative of Indonesia,

1. *Calls upon* all States to respect the territorial integrity of East Timor as well as the inalienable right of its people to self-determination in accordance with General Assembly resolution 1514 (XV);

2. *Calls upon* the Government of Indonesia to withdraw without delay all its forces from the Territory;

3. *Requests* the Secretary-General to have his Special Representative continue the assignment entrusted to him under paragraph 5 of Security Council resolution 384 (1975) and pursue consultations with the parties concerned;

4. *Further requests* the Secretary-General to follow the implementation of the present resolution and submit a report to the Security Council as soon as possible;

5. *Calls upon* all States and other parties concerned to cooperate fully with the the United Nations to achieve a peaceful solution to the existing situation and to facilitate the decolonization of the Territory;

6. *Decides* to remain seized of the situation.

Document 4

G.A. RESOLUTION 37/30 –23 NOVEMBER 1982

Res. 37/30. Question of East Timor

The General Assembly,

Recognizing the inalienable right of all peoples to self-determination and independence in accordance with the principles of the Charter of the United Nations and of the Declaration on the Granting of Independence to Colonial Countries and Peoples, contained in its resolution 1514 (XV) of 14 December 1960, and other relevant United Nations resolutions,

Having examined the chapter of the report of the Special Committee on the Situation with regard to the Implementation of the Declaration on the Granting of Independence to Colonial Countries and Peoples relating to East Timor [1] and other relevant documents,

Taking note of the report of the Secretary-General on the question of East Timor, [2]

Taking note of resolution 1982/20 [3] adopted on 8 September 1982 by the Sub-Commission on Prevention of Discrimination and Protection of Minorities,

Having heard the statement of the representative of Portugal, [4] as the administering Power,

Having heard the statement of the representative of Indonesia, [5]

Having heard the statements of the representative of the Frente Revolucionaria de Timor Leste Independente and of various petitioners, as well as of the representatives of non-governmental organizations, [6]

Bearing in mind that Portugal, the administering Power, has stated its full and solemn commitment to uphold the right of the people of East Timor to self-determination and independence,

Bearing in mind also its resolutions 3485 (XXX) of 12 December 1975, 31/53 of 1 December 1976, 32/34 of 28 November 1977, 33/39 of 13 December 1978, 34/40 of 21 November 1979, 35/27 of 11 November 1980 and 36/50 of 24 November 1981.

Concerned at the humanitarian situation prevailing in the Territory and believing that all efforts should be made by the international community to improve the living conditions of the people of East Timor and to guarantee to them the effective enjoyment of their fundamental human rights,

1. *Requests* the Secretary-General to initiate consultations with all parties directly concerned, with a view to exploring avenues for achieving a comprehensive settlement of the problem and to report thereon to the General Assembly at its thirty-eighth

session;

2. *Requests* the Special Committee on the Situation with regard to the Implementation of the Declaration on the Granting of Independence to Colonial Countries and Peoples to keep the situation in the Territory under active consideration and to render all assistance to the Secretary-General with a view to facilitating the implementation of he present resolution;

3. *Calls upon* all specialized agencies and other organizations of the United Nations system, in particular the World Food Programme, the United Nations Children's Fund and the Office of the United Nations High Commissioner for Refugees, immediately to assist, within their respective fields of competence, the people of East Timor, in close consultation with Portugal, as the administering Power;

4. *Decides* to include in the provisional agenda of its thirty-eighth session the item entitled "Question of East Timor".

77th plenary session
23 Novembr 1992

---

1. Official Records of the General Assembly, Thirty-seventh Session, Supplement No.23 (A/37/23/Rev.1), chap.X.

2. A/37/538.

3. See E/CN, 4/1983/4-E/CN.4/Sub 2/1982/43 and Corr. 1 chap.XXI

4. Official Reords of the General Assembly. Thirty-seventh Session. Fourth Committee. 14th meeting, paras.17-19.

5. Ibid. 23rd meeting, paras 22-37.

6. Ibid. 15th-18th meetings.

Document 5

A/46/694
S/23235
ANNEX

Joint statement issued by the Permanent Representatives of the People's Republic of Angola, the Republic of Cape Verde, the Republic of Guinea-Bissau, the Republic of Mozambique and the Democratic Republic of São Tome and Principe to the United Nations on 18 November 1991

On the 12th of the current month of November the world was shocked by a press report about a barbarian massacre perpetrated against the defenceless population of East Timor by the occupation forces of Indonesia.

In accordance with press accounts of different sources, confirmed by the Indonesian official press, this action of violence took place when the armed forces of Indonesia shot at a group of people of 1,000 East Timorese and foreigners who were paying their last respect, in the cemetery of Santa Cruz to Sebastiao Rangel and Afonso Henriques, two young East Timorese who were also assassinated by Indonesian soldiers in an incident that took place earlier on the 28th of October last.

The tragic and unjustifiable result of this outrageous act of violence translated into scores of dead and many wounded people. Such an incident is a challenge to our universal conscience on the untenable situation in which the East Timorese people found themselves and whose exercise of the sacred and inalienable right to self-determination as well as their fundamental human rights are being denied through the use of force and repression.

Deeply concerned by the above-mentioned situation, the Permanent Representatives of the People's Republic of Angola, the Republic of Cape Verde, the Republic of Guinea-Bissau, the Republic of Mozambique and the Democratic Republic of São Tome, acting on behalf of their respective Governments:

1. Repudiate and condemn most vehemently the massacre of 12 November perpetrated by the repressive forces of Indonesia in their unsuccessful attempt to silence the East Timorese people whose long-lasting resistance to oppression is a clear evidence of their attachment to freedom and of their indomitable willingness to exercise their fundamental and inalienable right to self-determination.

2. Call on the Indonesian Government to put an immediate end to the violence against the

East Timorese population and co-operate with the United Nations in its efforts to promote a just and lasting solution for the question of East Timor, in conformity with the United Nations principles and relevant resolutions in the field of decolonization.

3. Invite the Human Rights Commission to take the necessary steps to undertake as soon as possible an inquiry into the facts with a view to establishing the responsibilities.

Reaffirm their common position that East Timor is a question of decolonization and emphasize the United Nations responsibility in the creation of conditions and mechanisms to ensure to the East Timor people the free choice of their right to self-determination and independence.

Request the United Nations Secretary-General to renew his efforts view to finding a peaceful solution to the conflict.

(Signed) Afonso VAN-DUNEM "MBINDA"
Permanent Representative of the People's Republic of Angola to the United Nation.

(Signed) José Luis JESUS
Permanent Representative of the Republic of Cape Verde to the United Nations

(Signed) Boubacar TOURE
Permanent Representative of the Republic of Guinea-Bissau to the United Nations

(Signed) Pedro Comissario AFONSO
Permanent Representative of the Republic of Mozambique to the United Nations

(Signed) Joaquim Rafael BRANCO
Permanent Representative of the Democratic Republic of São Tome and Principe to the United Nations

Document 6

A/46/747
ANNEX

Declaration on the situation in East Timor issued at Brussels on 3 December 1991 by the European Community

(Informal meeting of Ministers of Foreign Affairs, Egmont Palace, Brussels, 2 and 3 December 1991)

The Community and its member States reviewed the situation in East Timor in the light of the latest reporting available as well as the decisions of Government of Indonesia to set up a commission to investigate the violent incidents of Dili that cost the life of many innocent and defenceless citizens.

They reiterate their condemnation of these unjustifiable actions by the armed forces of Indonesia.

The Community and its member States stressed once again the paramount importance they attached to the full repect of human rights as expressed, in particular, in the declaration of the European Council of Luxembourg on 25-26 June 1991.

They also stress, in this respect, the importance of the resolution of the regulation adopted by the Development Council on human rights, democracy and development of 28 November 1991.

They call upon the Indonesian authorities to respond to the serious concerns expressed by the international community. They support the demands for a thorough and credible investigation by impartial and independent authorities.

The Community and its member States will review the cooperation between the European Community and Indonesia in the light of the above-mentioned orientations and regulations and taking into account the response of the Indonesian authorities.

The Community and its member States stress their support for a just, comprehensive and internationally acceptable settlement of the East Timor issue, respecting the principles of the Charter of the United Nations, and taking into account the need to defend human rights and fundamental freedoms and the full respect of the legitimate interests and aspirations of the population of this territory.

Document 7

UNITED NATIONS

Economic and Social Council

Distr. GENERAL
E/CN.4/1993/49
10 February 1993
Original:ENGLISH/FRENCH

COMMISSION ON HUMAN RIGHTS
Fifty-ninth session Agenda item 12

QUESTION OF THE VIOLATION OF HUMAN RIGHTS AND FUNDAMENTAL FREEDOMS IN ANY PART OF THE WORLD, WITH PARTICULAR REFERENCE TO COLONIAL AND OTHER DEPENDENT COUNTRIES AND TERRITORIES

Situation in East Timor
Report of the Secretary-General

CONTENTS

Introduction
I. UPDATE ON THE GOOD OFFICES ACTIVITIES OF THE SECRETARY-GENERAL CONCERNING THE QUESTION OF EAST TIMOR
II. ACTIONS TAKEN BY

SPECIAL RAPPORTEURS AND WORKING GROUPS OF THE COMMISSION ON HUMAN RIGHTS CONCERNING EAST TIMOR
A. Action taken by the Working Group on Enforced or Involuntary Disappearance,
B. Action taken by the Special Rapporteur on Extrajudicial, Summary or Arbitrary Executions,
C. Action taken by the Special Rapporteur on the question of torture,
Introduction

1. At the-forty-eighth session of the Commission on Human Rights, the Chairman made a statement on 4 March 1992 announcing what had been agreed by consensus on the situation of human rights in East Timor (see E/CN.4/1992/84 para. 457). By that statement, the Commission, inter alia, encouraged the Secretary-General to continue his good offices for achieving a just, comprehensive and internationally acceptable settlement of the question of East Timor. The Commission also requested the Secretary-General to continue to follow closely the human rights situation in East Timor and to keep the commission informed at its forty-ninth session. The present report has been prepared in response to the requests contained in the above-mentioned statement.

I. UPDATE ON THE GOOD OFFICES ACTIVITIES OF THE SECRETARY-GENERAL CONCERNING THE QUESTION OF EAST TIMOR

2. Following the appointment of Mr. S. Amos Wako in early February 1992 as the Personal Envoy of the Secretary-General to consult with the Government of Indonesia and to obtain clarifications on the tragic incident which occurred in Dili, East Timor, on 12 November 1991, Mr. Wako visited Indonesia and East Timor from 9 to 14 February 1992. He submitted his report to the Secretary-General on 19 February 1992. On 24 March 1992, the conclusions and recommendations contained in Mr. Wako's report were transmitted to the Government of Indonesia.

3. Between February and December 1992, the Secretary-General met with the Indonesian Foreign Minister, Mr. Ali Alatas, on five occasions (New York in February, September and December, Beijing in April, Jakarta in September). At every opportunity the Secretary-General discussed the human rights situation in East Timor, with particular reference to the violent and tragic incident at the Santa Cruz cemetery in Dili and its aftermath, and more recently the situation of the detained leader of FRETILIN, Mr. Jose (Xanana) Gusmao.

4. Mr. Alatas has kept the Secretary-General informed at thes meetings and through letters in which he conveyed on different occasions of the reaction of his Government to the conclusions and recommendations made in the report of Mr. Wako and the steps taken by the Government vis-à-vis the 12 November 1991 incident. He has transmitted, inter alia, the full report of the National Commission of Inquiry on the Dili incident, and a copy of a statement of the Army Chief of Staff on the findings of a Military Council of Honour and on the actions taken against some members of the armed forces in connection with that incident. He has also kept the Secretary-General up-to-date on the progress made in locating persons reported missing as a consequence of the shootings at the Santa Cruz cemetery and on the trial of the civilians indicted in connection with that incident.

5. The Secretary-General has repeatedly discussed with the Indonesian Foreign Minister the possibility of dispatching a follow-up mission to Mr. Wako's first visit. While a date for such a visit has not yet been set, Indonesia in principle has accepted the idea and has promised to propose a date.

6. Since the arrest of Mr. Xanana Gusmao near Dili, on 20 November 1992, the Secretary-General has been following the situation of the detained FRETILIN leader. Soon after his arrest, he asked the Indonesian

authorities to ensure that the International Committee of the Red Cross was given immediate access to the prisoner. He further discussed the matter with the Foreign Minister at their meeting in New York in December.

7. With respect to the search for an overall solution to the question of East Timor, the Secretary-General decided, as a result of his consultations at the highest level with the Governments of Indonesia and Portugal as well the discussions conducted over several months in New York between senior United Nations officials and the respective ambassadors of the two countries, to invite the Foreign Ministers of the two countries to hold informal consultations under his auspices and without preconditions. Those informal discussions were held in New York on 26 September; they dealt with issues of format and modalities for the resumption of the talks aimed at finding a lasting solution to the question of East Timor. The first formal meeting of the two Foreign Ministers and the Secretary-General was held again in New York on 17 December 1992, at which frank and substantive discussions were held. The parties have agreed to continue their talks on 20 April 1993 in Rome under the auspices of the Secretary-General. While there has not as yet been any significant progress in these talks, the Secretary-General once again reiterates his commitment to continue to conduct his good offices in the search for a comprehensive and internationally acceptable solution to the question of East Timor.

II. ACTIONS TAKEN BY SPECIAL RAPPORTEURS AND WORKING GROUPS OF THE COMMISSION ON HUMAN RIGHTS CONCERNING EAST TIMOR

A. Action taken by the Working Group on Enforced or Involuntary Disappearance.

8. Information regarding the action taken by te Working Group on Enforced or Involuntary Disappearances with regard to East Timor is described in detail in chapter II of the Working Group's report to the Commission (see E/CN.4/1993/25, paras. 278-290). The Working Group transmitted to the Government of Indonesia a total of 224 cases of disappearances related to the incident at the Santa Cruz cemetery in Dili, East Timor. Among those cases, 17 were transmitted on 10 December 1991 under the Working Group's urgent action procedure. The remaining 207 cases were transmitted by the Working Group on 15 December 1992. The Government of Indonesia informed the Working Group that 8 of the 17 persons whose cases had been transmitted on 10 December 1991 were alive and well and were

residing at their respective addresses. In accordance with its methods of work, the Working Group considered these cases clarified since, after having communicated the reply of the Government to the sources, they did not contest the reply within a period of six months.

B. Action taken by the Special Rapporteur on Extrajudicial, Summary or Arbitrary Execution.

9. Information regarding the action taken by the Special Rapporteur on extrajudicial, summary or arbitrary executions with regard to East Timor is described in detail in chapter IV of the report of the Special Rapporteur to the Commission (see E/CN.4/1993/46, para. 348-353). Paragraph 348 of the report describes the contents of the cables sent by the Special Rapporteur to the Government following the Dili incidents, calling on the authorities to investigate them, in conformity with the Principles on the Effective Prevention and Investigation of Extra-legal, Arbitrary and Summary Executions and to ensure that those identified as responsible for extrajudicial killings and other abuses would promptly be brought to justice. The Special Rapporteur also requested information about allegations to the effect that an additional number of persons, including witnesses to the events of 12

November 1991, had subsequently been executed by members of the 700 and 744 Battalions of the Hasanuddin Division of the Indonesian Army. The Government communicated to the Special Rapporteur the findings of the National Commission of Inquiry and information on the subsequent prosecution of 10 members of the armed forces. The report of the Special Rapporteur reproduces in full the conclusions of the National Commission of Inquiry.

10. The Special Rapporteur further communicated to the Government his continuing concern with regard to allegations received, according to which the composition procedures and working methods of the National Commission of Inquiry were incompatible with the above-mentioned Principles in a number of important respects, and that the nature of the criminal charges brought against those tried for their part in these killings and the length of sentence imposed could be interpreted as contributing to a climate of impunity.

C. Action taken by the Special Rapporteur on the question of torture

11. Information regarding the action taken by the Special Rapporteu on the question of torture with regard to East Timor is described in detail in chapter II

of the report of the Special Rapporteur to the Commission (see E/CN.4/1993/26, paras. 270-274). Attention is also drawn in this connection to the report of the Special Rapporteur, on his visit to Indonesia and East Timor in November 1991, (E/CN.4/1992/17/ Add.1), and in particular to chapter III of the report, entitled Visit to East Timor".

12. During 1992, the Special Rapporteur transmitted to the Government information concerning several persons who were allegedly subjected to torture in East Timor following the Dili incidents. In its reply, the Government affirmed that some of the persons mentioned had never been detained or tortured, and others had been detained and later released, but had not been tortured. The Special Rapporteur also sent to the Government two urgent appeals on behalf of Xanana Gusmão who was arrested on 20 November 1992, and on behalf of several other people arrested during November 1992 and kept in incommunicado detention since their arrest. With regard to Xanana Gusmão, the Government replied that he had been treated in a manner consistent with humanitarian considerations in accordance with Indonesian law. With regard to the second urgent appeal, no reply had been received.

ANNEXES

Annex 1

INFORMATION PROVIDED BY THE INDONESIAN GOVERNMENT

Note Verbale dated 29 May 1992 from the Permanent Representative of Indonesia to the United Nations addressed to the Secretary General

The above-mentioned note verbale, including, inter-alia, annexes concerning the advance report of the National Commission of Inquiry into the 12 November 1991 incident in Dili, the follow-up to that report and the findings of the Military Honour Council on that incident, and action taken, is contained in General Assembly document A/47/240, dated 3 June 1992, which is available for consultation.

Note verbale dated 30 June 1992 from the Permanent Mission of the Republic of Indonesia to the United Nations Office at Geneva addressed to the Centre for Human Rights communicating information concerning the trials of a number of military personnel in connection with the incident of 12 November 1991 in Dili

1. Following the findings and recommendations of the Military Honorary Council (MHC) announced by the Army Chief of

Staff, 10 military personnel were brought before the Military Court in Denpasar, Bali, from 29 May to 5 June 1992. They were charged under the Military Penal law for committing grave infringements of military ethics and violating military discipline, in particular disobeying orders. All of the 10 persons were found guilty as charged and sentenced to imprisonment ranging from 8 to 18 months. The relevant part of the Press Statement of the Army Chief of Staff dated 26 February 1992 announcing the result of the MHC as contained in document E/CN.4/1992/79, the list of the military personnel who were brought to trials and their respective sentences are enclosed herewith.

2. The trials took place in Denpasar instead of Dili due to the fact that all of the defendants had been transferred to the Udayana Military Command, Bali.

3. From the beginning, as in the case of the trials of the civilians in the incident, the military trial proceedings were open to the public and have been attended by foreign observers.

LIST OF 10 MILITARY PERSONNEL BEING TRIED FROM 29 MAY TO 5 JUNE 1992

1. First Corpral L.P. Martin Alau: Sentenced to 17 months imprisonment;
2. Private Second Class Alfonso de Jesus: Sentenced to 8 months of imprisonment;
3. Private Second Class Matheu Maya: Sentenced,to 8 months of imprisonment;
4. Master Sergeant Udin Syukur: Sentenced to 18 months of imprisonment;
5. Master Sergeant P. Saul Meda: Sentenced to 12 months of imprisonment;
6. Master Sergeant Aluysius Rani: Sentenced to 14 months of imprisonment;
7. Second Lieutenant Mursanib: Sentenced to 14 months of imprisonment;
8. Second Lieutenant John H. Aritonang: Sentenced to 12 months of imprisonment;
9. Second Lieutenant Edi Sunryo: Sentenced to 12 months of imprisonment;
10. Second Lieutenant Johanes A. Penpada: Sentenced to 8 months of imprisonment."

Letter dated 4 January 1993 from the Permanent Representative of the Republic of Indonesia to the United Nations addressed to the Secretary-General transmitting to him a letter dated 28 November 1992 addressed to him by the Foreign Minister of Indonesia

Thank you for your letter of 20 November 1992, in which you inquired about the recent arrest of Mr. Xanana Gusmão by the Indonesian security forces.

I should like to confirm that

Mr. Xanana Gusmão was indeed apprehended in Dili on the morning of 20 November by the Indonesian security apparatus who were aided by information and cooperation from the local population.

At the present moment he is in safe custody and is being questioned in preparation for his court trial on the basis of the Indonesian criminal code and law in criminal procedures. I should like to assure you that he will be tried in strict accordance with those laws, i.e. in open, public court, and he will be provided with full legal assistance. I should also like to personally assure you of his good health and that he is not being ill-treated in any way.

As regards access to him by the International Committee of the Red Cross, I am pleased to inform you that such access will be granted in due time in accordance with existing regulations.

(Signed): Ali Alatas

(Foreign Minister)

Annex II

INFORMATION PROVIDED BY THE PORTUGUESE GOVERNMENT

Note verbale dated 5 June 1992 from the Permanent Representative of Portugal to the United Nations addressed to the Secretary-General transmitting a statement of the Portuguese Government issued in Lisbon on 27 May 1992 on the sentencing of East Timorese in Jakarta and Dili

The Portuguese Government draws the attention of the international community to the trials of East Timorese arrested during the Santa Cruz massacre, on November 1991. These trials are taking place without the minimum requirements of impartiality and legal defence. Two of the defendants have already been sentenced with heavy prison terms. There is a sharp contrast between the sentencing of the victims - who have been accused of engaging in non-violent political activity in favour of the internationally recognised rights of the East Timorese people - and the fact that there was no significant punishment at all for the officers responsible for the terrible violence.

Indonesia is accused of bad faith as it has acted in flagrant violation of the provisions of the declaration adopted by the United Nations commission on Human Rights in March 1992, which it had accepted and subscribed to. In this, Indonesia has shown an arrogant disrespect for the universal condemnation that followed the massacre.

Letter dated 26 June 1992 from the Permanent Representative of Portugal to the United Nations addressed to the Secretary-General transmitting a statement the Portuguese Government on East Timor, issued in Lisbon on 23 June 1992

Recent sentences against East Timorese civilians strike again ominous contrast with the leniency shown towards the Indonesian military brought to trial for their involvement in the 12 November massacre.

Two more East Timorese civilians, whose trials in Dili have now finished, have been given heavy prison sentences for nonviolent activities in connection with the massacre committed on 12 November 1991 by the Indonesian military in the capital of the Non-Self-Governing Territory of East Timor, illegally occupied by Indonesia.

Juvencio de Jesus Martins and Felismino da Silva Pereira were condemned respectively to six years and five years and eight months in prison, for their alleged participation in organizing the demonstration that was, on that occasion, barbarously repressed by Indonesian troops, causing heavy human losses, as was widely reported. In-the meantime, and according to what has been publicly disclosed, several low-ranking Indonesian military (two second lieutenants, one sergeant and three privates) - these three, curiously enough, all of East Timorese origin, were court-

martialled and given sentences of between 8 and 18 months, imprisonment. The charges brought against them (disobeying orders and inflicting wounds with a bayonet) are clear indicators that a serious investigation into those actually responsible for an atrocity that prompted worldwide indignation is still far from sight. Who ordered the shooting at Santa Cruz cemetery? Who are those accountable for many killed and wounded? These questions remain unanswered in spite of all the promises subsequently made by the Indonesian authorities.

"Indonesia committed itself to identifying and punishing all those deemed responsible for that tragedy. So far its understanding of that commitment has led it to inflict heavy penalties such as those referred to above upon East Timorese, indicted not for any violent activities, but for organizing peaceful demonstrations. There is a shocking and unacceptable discrepancy between these penalties and those imposed on the military (small fry as they may be) who took part in that terrible brutality.

"Indonesia continues to blatantly disregard the commitments it gave in subscribing to the consensus agreed upon by the United Nations Commission on Human Rights, as announced in the declaration of its Chairman on 4 March 1992.

"Not only has the punishment

of the authors of that carnage been translated into ludicrous measures: those civilians, whose release without delay was requested by the Commission on Human Rights, have been sentenced.

"This shows that the Indonesian Government acted with complete cynicism in the Commission's dealings with this issue. It also shows Indonesia's contempt for human rights.

"Portugal expresses its firmest condemnation of these actions and hopes that the international community will draw from them the appropriate conclusions. Portugal affirms also its full solidarity with all those East Timorese who have been sentenced to unjust and illegitimate penalties aimed at repressing their struggle to ensure that the people of East Timor have the freedom to choose their political future."

Letter dated 21 July 1992 from the Permanent Representative of Portugal to the United Nations addressed to the Secretary-General transmitting a statement by the spokesman of the Ministry of Foreign Affairs of Portugal on the sentencing to life imprisonment of a Timorese in Dili, issued in Lisbon on 2 July 1992

"Portugal has repeatedly denounced the steady cynicism and contempt with which Indonesia defies international criticism and demarches. The Jakarta authorities continue to offer a deplorable image in the trials and sentencing of the Timorese civilians arrested in the wake of the massacre committed on 12 November 1992 in Santa Cruz cemetery.

"It has now been the turn of Gregorio da Cunha Saldanha to be sentenced to life imprisonment, accused of having been the main instigator and organizer of the demonstration held on that day. A few days ago Francisco Miranda Branco was given 15 years. Neither of them was charged with violence, and both should therefore, like the other civilian demonstrators who have received long prison sentences, have been released without delay in accordance with the United Nations High Commissioner for Refugees consensus statement to which Indonesia subscribed.

"The iniquitous and unlawful sentence handed down to Gregoria da Cunha Saldanha holds Indonesia's growing contempt for the international community. It is clear proof that the promises it made with the aim of lessening the indignation caused by the massacre cannot be trusted, and that the Indonesian authorities have no intention whatsoever of respecting the commitments they gave before the Commission on Human Rights.

Indonesian repression of the survivors of the Santa Cruz massacre remains merciless, whilst the soldiers actually responsible for the shooting have been given token sentences mainly on charges of disobeying orders. The promised investigations into the circumstances surrounding the massacre, and punishment of those responsible, have produced this grotesque result, which reveals a total lack of good faith.

Indonesian willingnes to go back on its own word cannot be ignored by those who hitherto have sought to justify their own acceptance of the Jakarta Government's promises and the cooperative attitude it has been demonstrating since the Santa Cruz massacre.

Note Verbale dated 20 November 1992 from the Permanent Mission of Portugal to the United Nations Office at Geneva addressed to the Centre for Human Rights transmitting a communique from the Portuguese Government on the occasion of the anniversary of the Santa Cruz massacre of 12 November 1991

The brutal massacre of Timorese civilians at the hands of Indonesian troops exactly one year ago today represented in so far as the outside world was able to judge, a new development concerning the question of East Timor.

"As from 12 November all that could be maintained by the illegal occupants of the Territory was that the denunciations that

had been regularly made–not only by Portugal but also by other countries, organizations and authorities–concerning the unbearable situation in the Territory were pure calumny and groundless acusations. Finally, at the end of more than 15 years' occupation, during which everything was done to erect a wall of isolation and silence, the stark reality of unbridled repression revealed its true face in the light of day.

The occupation of East Timor, with the thousands of victims that it has brought in its wake, has not prevented or frightened the Timorese, especially the youngest of them, from demonstrating in support of their rights and basic freedoms. With the passing of time, the occupation has not acquired a firmer basis or come to be accepted; on the contrary, the determination of those subjected to it has but grown stronger. Santa Cruz may be said to have alerted the international community to the continuing tragedy of a small people, invaded and subjugated by force, against whom an intolerable act has been committed which denies all the major principles considered mandatory and universal in these last years of the twentieth century.

"The tragic sacrifice of so great a number of young people has then not been in vain. It has stirred many sluggish consciences, revealed inconsistencies and hypocrisies and created the conditions for setting in train a whole series of political and diplomatic actions that have unquestionably placed the question of East Timor in a different perspective. The new positions adopted by the European Communities on the question, the interruption of United States military aid to Indonesia, the deliberations within the United Nations Commission on Human Rights and the spontaneous demonstrations of solidarity witnessed in many countries show that the matter is now at last coming to the attention of world public opinion in a context conducive to ensuring respect for the fundamental rights of the Timorese people, which must be given practical repression.

Unfortunately, it must also be realized that this growing awareness on the part of the international community regarding the tragic question of East Timor has not had satisfactory repercussions on the situation persisting in the Territory.

It must be stressed that Indonesia has still not shown the slightest intention to put an end to the persistent violations of human rights in East Timor, as is demonstrated by the following facts: the grotesque contrast between the token penalties imposed on those responsible for the killings at Santa Cruz cemetery and the heavy prison sentences, including a sentence of life imprisonment, meted out to the surviving Timorese civilians, who were not charged with acts of violence; the prohibitions on access to the Territory by human rights organisations that have requested to go there; the scandalous statement by a so-called "governor" who has said that it would have been desirable for all the demonstrators to have been killed; and the recent news concerning a wave of arrests affecting hundreds of people.

The Portuguese Government once again draws the attention of the international community to this persistent situation which is a real challenge to purportedly universal values and principles, with regard to both peoples' rights and human rights. Meaures must be taken to avert at all costs any repetition of the violence that occurred on 12 November 1991 in East Timor, attesting to a confrontation which has its roots in the denial of such rights. Recent history proves that with time, illegitimate situations imposed by force become not more firmly established but, on the contrary, more precarious.

It is therefore imperative for a negotiated, peaceful solution to be found that can lead to the conclusion of the process of decolonisation of the Territory with full respect for its cultural and religious identity and the legitimate rights of its people, including the right of political self-determination, in accordance with the Charter of the United Nations and the resolution, already adopted by the General Assembly and the Security Council on the problem.

Note Verbale dated 25 November 1992 from the Permanent Mission of Portugal to the United Nations Office at Geneva addressed to the Centre for Human Rights transmitting a communique of 20 November 1992 on the detention of Xanana Gusmão.

According to very recent news, the Indonesian authorities, which are illegally occupying the Territory of East Timor, captured the leader of the Timorese resistance, Xanana Gusmão in Dili this morning.

Xanana Gusmão, by virtue of his courage and steadfastness in the constant struggle waged in defiance of great dangers and in adverse circumstances, symbolizes the determination of the people of East Timor to oppose the brutal occupation of Indonesia.

The Portuguese Government calls on the international community to act as swiftly as possible to secure the release of Xanana Gusmão and obtain guarantees as to his physical well-being, while ensuring that his rights as a human being are fully respected by the Indonesian authorities.

Portugal reaffirms its determination to continue its action to defend the rights and freedoms of the people of East Timor, including the right of political self-determination, which has always been refused it and without which it will not be possible to put an end to the intolerable situation that persists in East Timor.

Letter dated 2 December 1992 from the Permanent Representative of Portugal to the United Nations addressed to the Secretary-General transmitting a statement by the spokesman for the Ministry of Foreign Affairs of Portugal following the appearance of Xanana Gusmão in a film broadcast by Indonesian television

In view of the gross inconsistency of the recent remarks made on Indonesian television by Xanana Gusmão taking into account the positions he had assumed over many years of resistance to the occupation of East Timor, we regard with the utmost concern his current situation as everything points to the belief that he is surely being the victim of threats and aggression to his person, his family and his companions.

The Portuguese Government, therefore, appeals to the United Nations, the international community and, in particular, to the International Committee of the Red Cross that they seek to bring about an immediate end to a situation that represents a violation of the most basic human rights".

Note verbale dated 1 February 1992 from the Permanent Representative of Portugal to the United Nations Office at Geneva, addressed to the Centre for Human Rights, transmitting an Aide-memoire on the situation in East Timor, dated 11 August 1992

The contents of the above-mentioned aide-memoire are summarised in document E/CN.4/Sub.2/1992/SR.19 of 21 August 1992, paragraphs 72 to 77, which is available for consultation.

Note verbale dated 2 February 1992 from the Permanent Mission of Portugal to the United Nations Office at Geneva addressed to the Centre for-Human Rights transmitting a communique of 30 January 1993 on the trial of Xanana Gusmão leader of the Timorese resistance:

Various Indonesian authorities, have issued a number of ambiguous and inconsistent statements, regarding the trial of Xanana Gusmão, the leader of the Timorese resistance. It has now been announced that trial will begin on 1 February in Dili, capital of East Timor, a Non-Self-Governing Territory under Portuguese administration, under illegal occupation by Indonesia.

The Portuguese Government draws attention to the fact that Xanana Gusmão is to be tried by an occupying power which, since its military invasion of the Territory, has used brutal repression and massive violation of the most fundamental human rights in its attempts to suppress all opposition to its illegal rule. That rule has been imposed in defiance not only of the principles and fundamentals of international law and the Charter of the United Nations but also in direct breach of resolutions in East Timor adopted by the General Assembly and the Security Council.

Xanana Gusmão is now on trial for resisting this forcible imposition of a political situation, which ignores entirely the right to self-determination of the people of East Timor. It is the Indonesian regime which, in putting Xanana Gusmão on trial, is acting outside international law since it lacks the legal, political and moral authority to do so.

East Timor is a Territory under military occupation, and Indonesia is not recognized internationally as having any lawful authority there. Under these circumstances the trial of Xanana Gusmão, and should they be brought to trial, of any other Timorese currently held by the authorities, fall fully within the relevant provisions of international humanitarian law, in particular the Geneva Convention of 12 August 1949 relative to the protection of civilian persons in time of war. Indonesia is formally bound by this Convention.

The Convention applies irrespective of the legality or otherwise of Indonesia's. occupation of the Territory. Under the terms of the Geneva Convention relative to the protection of civilian persons in time of war (which applies to East Timor by virtue of its article 2), Xanana Gusmão is in particular entitled to be tried in accordance with the law in force at the moment of occupation; the accused is entitled to be judged impartially and after a fair trial, to be represented by the advocate of his choice who may act without hindrance in the preparation and presentation of the defence (including the freedom to visit the accused); the accused is entitled to be informed immediately of the charges he face; he is entitled to the services of an interpreter; he must not be subjected to physical or psychological pressure and he is not obliged to confess his guilt. These are just some of his more pertinent rights, apart from the respect of human life and physical integrity, his personal honour and personal dignity, his right not to be subjected to torture, ill-treatment, degrading treatment or any other form of physical or psychological coercion.

It has nevertheless become apparent that Indonesia intends to apply its own penal laws including its catch-all anti-subversion laws which Indonesia agreed before the United Nations Commission on Human Rights to repeal. The prisoner has been kept incommunicado, except for a single visit by the International Committee of the Red Cross and a number of interviews in front of television camera. for propaganda purposes. It seems that he has not been allowed a free choice of advocate: an official defence attorney has been appointed, who is unable to speak any language familiar to the prisoner and is reputed to have had professional dealings with the police. The authorities have produced number of conflicting statements on the charges the prisoner may face, although no one has been allowed to communicate with Xanana Gusmão, he has already been forced to make public confession under circumstances degrading to his personal honor and dignity.

Portugal protests vehemently against the trial of Xanana Gusmão which, apart from being unlawful, is clearly going to be carried out under circumstances offering no guarantees of impartiality and objectivity. There is a risk that the trial will develop into a sombre farce whose aim is to persuade world opinion that Indonesia's forcible annexation of East Timor is not a fait accompli, sacrificing the legitimate right to self-determination of the Timorese people".

Annex III

MATERIAL PROVIDED BY NON-GOVERNMENTAL SOURCES

During the period covered by the present report (March 1992 to January 1993) the Secretariat continued to receive a large amount of material concerning the situation in East Timor. Such material as provided by international non-governmental organizations, Indonesian human rights groups and groups concerned specifically with human rights in East Timor, based in most cases in Portugal. The Secretariat also received dozens of petitions from people in different countries, calling for the release of political prisoners in East Timor, and in particular the release of Xanana Gusmão.

The following is a summary of the allegations contained in the above-mentioned information relating to the period covered by the present report. It should be noted that, among the above-mentioned organizations and groups which have provided the Secretariat with pertinent material during that period, Amnesty International is the only organization to have done so in a consistent and regular manner. The summary was therefore prepared principally on the basis of material provided by that organization. Nevertheless, to the extent that other organizations or groups provided material which is not mentioned in any of the Amnesty International publications, it is reflected in parts B and C of the summary.

A. Information received from Amnesty International, a non-governmental organization in consultative status (category II)

Amnesty International provided, during the period covered by the present report, the following documents: Indonesia/East Timor: Fernando de Araujo Prisoner of Conscience, May 1992 ; Indonesia/East Timor: The Suppression of Dissent, July 1992 and East Timor: In Accordance with the Law - Statement before the United Nations Special Committee on Decolonization, July 1992. In addition, between 23 November and 18 December 1992, the Secretariat received nine publications entitled Amnesty International–Urgent Action", containing a list of people who were allegedly arrested and/or disappeared in the wake of the arrest of Xanana Gusmão. The following summary was prepared on the basis of information contained in the above-mentioned reports and publications.

It was reported in the statement made by Amnesty International to the United Nations Special Committee on Decolonization in July 1992 that in the aftermath of the Dili incidents, military intimidation of the East Timorse population increased; many suspected political activists including young people and Catholic priests, were subjected to imprisonment death threats and beatings. Households suspected of harbouring pro-independence activists were subjected to searches and their members were threatened with violence by the military. By way of example, it was reported that in March 1992, three persons, Felismina dos Santos Conceicao, Alfonso Rangel and Amarao de Araujo were convicted under Article 122 of the Criminal Code of acting against the national interest and were sentenced to prison terms of between two and five years. The three were accused of stealing four secret military documents which were, according to Amnesty International, reports of human rights violations - and "sending them to members of the resistance movement overseas (who, according to the source, were members of a Portuguese parliamentary delegation.

In May 1992, more details were given by Amnesty International on some of the East Timorese civilians arrested following the Dili incidents:

– on 25 May 1992, Fernando de Araujo was sentenced to nine years, imprisonment for undermining the Indonesian Government and disgracing the nation in the eyes of the international community." Araujo described was described as a founder member and leader of Renetil, a student organization which, according to the source, peacefully opposes the integration East Timor with Indonesia. He was charged with organizing a protest demonstration in Jakarta, on 19 November 1991, against the killings and beatings at the Santa Cruz Cemetery in Dili;

– on 26 May 1992, João Freitas da Canara was convicted, by a court in Jakarta, of subversion and sentencd to 10 years' imprisonment, for organizing a protest against the Santa Cruz killings;

– Domingos Barreto and Vingito da Silva Guterres, accused of publicly insulting the Indonesian Government during the protest in Jakarta, were also convicted in May and sentenced to prison terms of six months and four and a half years, respectively. They had been charged under article. 154 and 155 of the Criminal Code, which define "expressing feelings of hostility, hatred or contempt toward the Indonesian Government as a criminal offence; in addition to the four persons mentioned above, who were convicted of subversion or of other offenses in connection with the Santa Cruz killings, the source provided a list of persons still detained in Jakarta and in East Timor, in connection with the same incidents. In Jakarta, one person was charged with publicly expressing hostility toward the Government and as still being tried, and 17 others were listed as "conditionally released but current circumstances unclear. In East Timor, two were charged with subversion and six with publicly expressing hostility toward the Government. Their verdict and sentence were not known at the time of the publication (May 1992). Twenty-four others were listed as reportedly confined outside Dili and receiving mental guidance.

According to Amnesty International, reports received from East Timor in June 1992 indicated that the military investigation into the fate of those who remained disappeared after the Santa Cruz killings, made little progress in locating the 90 officially acknowledged victims of disappearance. It was further reported that residents had said that the bodies of some persons were buried outside Dili, and that they believed the army was, reluctant to open the graves because the number of dead was much higher than that officially announced.

As regards the practice of torture and ill-treatment of alleged political opponents, Amnesty International reported in July 1992 that a pattern of short-term detention, torture and ill-treatment of such persons continued to be reported in East Timor. Suspected political activists, including Catholic priests, had allegedly been made to strip naked and were beaten and kicked; many had al-

legedly been subjected to death threats.

In June 1992 Francisco Miranda Branco and Gregorio da Cunha Saldanha, who had been charged in Dili with subversion for organizing the funeral procession which preceded the Santa Cruz killings, were sentenced to 15 years imprisonment and for life imprisonment, respectively. It was further reported that by June 1992 three of the persons detained and charged with public expression of hatred of the Government had been sentenced to prison terms ranging from six months to almost seven years.

On 23 November 1992, Amnesty International issued two "Urgent Action" publications. One of these documents listed 14 persons who were allegedly among hundreds of East Timorese detained by Indonesian military and police forces during the period preceding the issuing of the document. It as reported that many of those arrested and suspected opponents of Indonesian rule prior to the anniversary of the November 1991 Santa Cruz killings were released after interrogation, but that the 14 people named in the document, and possibly many others, were reported to remain in custody and the source expressed fear that they may be subjected to torture and ill-treatment. According to Amnesty International such fears were based on reports that Indonesian security forces routinely denied political detainees access to a lawyer, in contravention of Indonesia's own Code of Criminal Procedure (KUHAP, articles 54 and 55), and that representatives of the International Committee of the Red Cross (ICRC,) were consistently denied access to detention centres until interrogation had been completed.

The other Urgent Actions publication issued on 23 November 1992 as well as five consecutive Urgent Action publications issued on 24, 26 and 30 November and 4 and 10 December 1992, dealt with the arrest of Xanana Gusmão and of several other people arrested at the same time or shortly afterwards. Those arrested were still denied visits by the ICRC and close relatives of Xanana Gusmão, including his sister, her husband and two of their children and members of the Araujo family, in whose residence Gusmão had been arrested on 4 December 1992, Amnesty International alleged that Gusmão and at least 20 of his close associates and relatives arrested since 20 November 1992 (the day of his arrest) remained in incommunicado detention and that at least one of those detained, Jorge Manuel Araujo Serrano, was reported to have been tortured to death while in custody. The source therefore reiterated its fears that Gusmão and the ther detainees had also been tortured or

ill-treated while under interrogation. It was also alleged that at least two of the women held in Dili, possibly Ligia de Araujo, aged 22, and Regina Conceicao Araujo Serrano, aged 18, had been raped by Indonesian officers in front of their relatives on 29 November. It was further reported that according to unnamed sources within the police headquarters (in Denpasar, Bali), Xanana Gusmão has been beaten and tortured with electrical shocks and subjected to severe psychological pressure while under interrogation .

On 10 December 1992 it was reported that the Indonesian Government had permitted representatives of the ICRC to visit Xanana Gusmão at an unspecified location in Jakarta on 7 December 1992; but that at least 39 others, and possibly many more, detained in East Timor since early November 1992, were still denied visits by the ICRC and are being held in incommunicado detention.

On 4 December 1992 Amnesty International published a list of 14 persons who were reported to have "disappeared" after being arrested by Indonesian security forces in early November 1992. Five others, also arrested in mid-November, were believed to be detained in Dili, but their exact whereabouts remained unknown and there were fears that they may have "disappeared" .

On 18 December 1992, Amnesty International published a list of 25 people arrested since early November 1992 in Manatuto and Same Districts and in Dili. Their precise whereabouts were not known, but they were believed to be detained in military detention centres in the towns of Baucau, Same and Dili. It was alleged that they were at risk of torture and ill-treatment The source added that here had also been unconfirmed reports that 17 relatives of an East Timorese activist living in Portugal were arrested on 25 November 1992 in Dili, and fears were expressed that they too may be at risk of torture.

B. Information received from the International Commission of Juristst (ICJ), a non-governmental organisation in consultative status (category II)

The International Comission of Jurists (ICJ) provided the Secretariat with a detailed report on the trials in Dili and Jakarta, entitled "Tragedy in East Timor", dated October 1992. The ICJ sent observers to the trials in Dili and Jakarta. As regards the trials in Jakarta, the ICJ observer concluded that they were basically conducted in an appropriate manner and, with one critical exception, in accordance with the due process provisions of the KUHAP. "There as no direct evidence of governmental or military interference in the proceeding... It is dif-

ficult, therefore to assess the impartiality of the judges"... The patina of judicial due process cannot, however, be used to obscure the grim reality of the conseqences of raising a voice in dissent in Indonesia with respect to the sensitive matter of East Timor. It must be emphasised that the very existence of the subversion and so-called hate-sowing law, both of which are relics from the days of colonial oppression and less politically stable times, represents a serious violation of basic human rights... The trials and the guilty verdicts, taken together, however, reveal Indonesia's compulsion to eliminate dissent with respect to East Timor, whether that dissent is expressed to other Indonesians or to the outside world, even at the expense of the basic rights of its own citizens".

With regard to the Dili trials, the ICJ reported that one of their observers had difficulty in obtaining permission to travel to East Timor, and that another observer had his visa application denied on the basis that by the time the authorities had dealt with it, the trials would have concluded. The ICJ concluded that, in the experience of its two observers, the Government of Indonesia had not complied with the spirit or the letter of the statement made at the United Nations Commission of Human Rights by the Chairman on 5 March 1992 which, inter alia, urged the Indonesian authorities to "facilitate access to East Timor for additional humanitaran organisations and for human rights organisations". After comparing the sentences meted out to members of the military forces involved in the killings, on the one hand, and the East Timorese citizens on the other, the report noted that the charges brought against the military officers and personnel subseqent to the 12 November incident are patently inappropriate to the crimes involved. Moreover, the relative lack of seriousness of the charges, not to mention the sentences, does not bear any comparison with the charges and sentences brought against the demonstrators and those who organised the demonstration. It may fairly be said that justice, has been turned on its head in this case".

In conclusion, the report noted the following:

"Indonesia, as a Member State of the United Nations, has pledged to achieve in cooperation ith the United Nations, the promotion of universal respect and observance of human rights and fundamental freedoms.

"Indonesia has breached article 19 of the Universal Declaration of Human Rights in permitting prosecutions under the Anti-Subversion Law against defend-

ants whose crimes involved no eleent of violence, but who held opinions and sought to express those opinions as well as to receive and impart information and ideas in relation to the self-determination of East Timor.

"Indonesia has also breached article 20 of the Universal Declaration of Human Rights in permitting prosecutions under the Anti-Subversion Law against persons who ought to arrange a peaceful demonstration and who engaged in meeting and planning for those demonstrations. The fact that the demonstration. produced some element of violence (in Dili, the violence was clearly, on the evidence available, offered on the part of the military) does not appear to have been the fault nor the intention of the defendants".

C. Information received from their non-governmental sources.

Asia Watch published a report entitled "East Timor: the Court. Martial", dated 23 June 1992, which described in detail the trials of nine soldiers and one policeman, by military or police courts in Bali, for their role in the killings at the Santa Cruz, Cemetery. In its conclusions, the Report offered, inter alia, the following: "The courts martial help give the Indonesian Government an appearance of evenhandedness ... But justice is not the same as even-handedness. The fact that any investigation and any courts martial at all took place is a step forward for the Indonesian Government and should be recognised as such, but there has been no real accounting for the death. and disappearance that took place on 12 November 1992. None of those convicted in late May and early June started the shooting: none organized the disposal of bodies or planned the cover-up, which stressed the factor of spontaneity. It is difficult to avoid the conclusion that the courts martial were stage-managed for international consumption, particularly when documents which might shed further light on events in Dili, such as the full report of the National Commission of Inquiry and the full report of the Council of Military Honour, have been kept under wraps. The report contained two appendices. The first lists the military personnel who were put on trial and their sentences, ranging from 8 to 18 months' imprisonment; and the second lists East Timorese civilians who were put on trial and the sentence requested by the prosecution (then available) and the sentences given to those already sentenced (7 out of 18), ranging in most of the cases from two and a half years to life imprisonment (only in one case was the defendant given a prison sentence of less than one year).

The Indonesian Human Rights Forum, a newsletter prepared by the Indonesian Legal Aid Foundation (YLBHI), reported in its No. 4/1992, issue of April – June 1992, about the trials in Dili of eight youths charged with subversion for having masterminded the demonstration in Santa Cruz Cemetery on 12 November 1991, and the trials in Jakarta of Joao de Freitas Camara and Fernando de Araujo. Some of the accused were represented by a team of lawyers of the Legal Aid Foundation and the Indonesian National Bar Association (YLBHI-IKADIN). The newsletter reported the following: "...All lawyers on the legal team hold positions of senior advocates which allow them each to practice in any Indonesian province. Despite the legitimacy of the legal team to present the eight East Timorese charged with subversion in a Dili court, the Dili judge claimed the YLBHI-IKADIN team did not have the authority based on their procedural failure to secure permission from the High Court of the Eastern Provinces in Kupang, West Timor, to practice in Dili. ... The Dili judge refused to allow the team to represent the defendants on grounds of procedural flaws and instead appointed a Dili lawyer ... to represent the defendants. The defendants were not in agreement with ths directive of the Dili judge. By Indonesian Criminal Procedural Code, a defendant has the right to choose his representation. However, given that the Dili judge refused to allow the YLBHI-IKADIN team to practice, the judge claimed that by law a substitute lawyer must be appointed whether or not the defendants agreed with the appointed lawyer. Clearly, the refusal of the Dili judge to allow the YLBHI-IKADIN team to represent the defendants violate the rights of the defendants by Criminal Procedural Code, article No. 55 (KUHAP) which states, "... the defendant has the right to choose his legal advisor". In protest at the decision of the judge which violated the rights of the defendent, the Director of YLBHI requested that the Indonesian Supreme Court correct the error of the Dili judge. The Supreme Court received the reqest of YLBHI and sent a telegram directing the judge of the Dili Court to honor the YLBHI-IKADIN team and allow them to represent the defendants in Dili court in East Timor ..."

On 16 May 1992 an organization called Peace is possible in East Timor Oecumenical Association, based in Lisbon, Portugal, provided the Secretariat with a list of 234 persons who have allegedly disappeared following the November 1991 Santa Cruz killings. With regard to 52 of these people, the source reported that there were contradictory indications as to whether they were dead or disappeared.

Document 8

Report by the Special Rapporteur, Mr. Bacre Waly Ndiaye, on his mission to Indonesia and East Timor from 3 to 13 July 1994 (E/CN.4/1995/61)

A. Framework of the invitation by the Government of Indonesia

1. In a letter dated 19 November 1993, the Special Rapporteur on extrajudicial, summary or arbitrary executions expressed to the Government of Indonesia his interest in carrying out a visit to East Timor. In this context, he referred to Commission on Human Rights resolution 1993/71, "Extrajudicial, summary or arbitrary executions" and resolution 1993/47; "Human rights and thematic procedures", in which the Commission encouraged Governments to invite special rapporteurs to visit their countries, and 1993/97, "Situation in East Timor", in which the Commission urged the Government of Indonesia to invite the Special Rapporteur to visit East Timor and to facilitate the discharge of his mandate.

2. In its reply, the Government of Indonesia drew the Special Rapporteur's attention to the fact that the Commission members had adopted resolution 1993/97 by a vote; Indonesia and many other member countries had rejected the resolution. Therefore, Indonesia did not feel compelled to abide by its provisions. It was further stated that the Government of Indonesia would give due consideration to a request for a visit to Indonesia, including East Timor, of any special rapporteur, as long as it was based on United Nations consensus resolutions.

3. In a letter dated 24 January 1994, the Government of Indonesia extended to the Special Rapporteur an invitation to visit Indonesia (Jakarta and East Timor) in accordance with resolutions 1993/71 and 1993/47.

4. During a meeting with the Indonesian delegation at the fiftieth session of the Commission on Human Rights, the Special Rapporteur expressed the wish not to limit his mission to East Timor, but also to visit some regions of Indonesia, such as Aceh and Irian Jaya, where, according to the reports brought to his attention, grave violations of the right to life, continued to occur. This request was not accepted by the representatives of the Indonesian Government.

B. Purpose of the mission

5. The purpose of the Special

Rapporteur's visit should be seen in the framework of the mandate entrusted to him by the Commission on Human Rights (see E/CN.4/1994/7. paras. 5-12) and in the light of the Chairman's statement on the situation of human rights in East Timor, agreed upon by consensus by the Commission on Human Rights at its fiftieth session (E/1994/24-E/(CN.4/1994/132. para. 482). In this statement, the Chairman declared that the Commission noted with concern continuing allegations of human rights violations in East Timor and that a matter of preoccupation to the Commission was the *incomplete information* (emphasis added) concerning the number of people killed and the persons still unaccounted for as a result of the Dili violent incident of 12 November 1991. While acknowledging the efforts made to account for those persons, the Commission called upon the Government of Indonesia to continue its investigation on those still missing in the circumstances surrounding the matter.

6. The objectives of the Special Rapporteur were therefore the following:

(a) To collect more information about the tragic events that occurred at the Santa Cruz Cemetery in Dili on 12 November 1991 (see below, paras. 16-23 and E/CN.4/1992/30, paras. 279-286), and in particular to assess the Government's fulfilment of the standards under international law concerning the use of force by law-enforcement officials and its obligation to investigate all allegations of summary executions, to bring to justice their perpetrators, to provide compensation to the families of the victims and to prevent their occurrence. The Special Rapporteur based his analysis on several international instruments falling within his mandate (see E/CN.4/1994/7, paras. 9-10), and in particular the Principles on the Effective Prevention and Investigation of Extra-legal, Arbitrary and Summary Executions, endorsed by the General Assembly in its resolution 44/162, adopted by consensus on 15 December 1989. Given the particularities of the situation of the right to life in East Timor, the Special Rapporteur also took into account the Declaration on the Protection of All Persons from Enforced Disappearance, endorsed by the General Assembly in resolution 47/133 of 18 December 1992;

(b) To gather reliable information about the situation of the right to life in East Timor since the Dili killings.

7. During his visit, the Special Rapporteur clearly indicated to all the Indonesian authorities and the members of the security forces he met with, that, as mentioned in the Chairman's statement, the information so far provided to the Commission on Hu-

man Rights was insufficient, and that since the Indonesian Government had extended an invitation to him, he expected to receive new elements of information during his visit.

8. The Special Rapporteur wishes to emphasize here that his mission in no way aimed at an analysis of the political status of the territory of East Timor or at its level of economic development. The Special Rapporteur stresses that his only purpose is always to examine the respect for the right to life, irrespective of any other considerations including those mentioned above. Furthermore, such elements can in no way be invoked as grounds for any weakening of or derogation from the absolute character of the right to life.

C. Programme of the visit

9. The Special Rapporteur spent 4 1/2 days in Jakarta, 1 in Denpasar and 4 1/2 in East Timor (including a visit to Viqueque and Ossu, southern East Timor).

10. During his visit, the Special Rapporteur met with the following officials of the Indonesian Government (in chronological order): Minister for Foreign Affairs a.i. and high level officials of the Foreign Ministry, Jakarta Raya Military Commander, Minister for Home Affairs, Chief of National Police, Secretary-General of the Department of Defence and Security, Chief of General Staff of the Armed Forces, Military Commander of Zone IX (which includes East Timor), Governor of East Timor, East Timor District Attorney, Chief of the Court of East Timor Province. Members of the East Timor Local House of Representatives, Chief of East Timor Police, East Timor traditional leaders, Military Resort Commander of East Timor, members of the National Commission of Human Rights, members of the Human Rights Commission of the People's Consultative Assembly, Minister of Justice, Attorney-General.

11. In addition, the Special Rapporteur interviewed Xanana Gusmão (former leader of the Timorese clandestine resistance) at Cipinang Prison (Jakarta), one prisoner at Becora Prison and four at Balide Prison (both in Dili, East Timor). He had also expressed the wish to meet with six persons convicted by an Indonesian court of having organized the Dili demonstration of 12 November 1991. However, since those prisoners had been abruptly transferred from Becora Prison (Dili) to Semarang Prison (Central Java) on 12 June 1994, and taking into account his already full schedule, the Special Rapporteur decided, with the consent of the Indonesian authorities, to send his assistant

to Semarang to interview the six prisoners on his behalf.

12. The Special Rapporteur also met representatives of nongovernmental human rights organizations in Jakarta, members of the clergy in East Timor (including Bishop Belo) and witnesses of violations of the right to life in East Timor— including a number of eyewitnesses of the Dili killings. The Special Rapporteur also met with the Ambassador of the United States of America and the Ambassador of the Netherlands. On 12 July he held a press conference in Jakarta.

13. The Indonesian authorities cooperated fully with the Special Rapporteur during his visit. He was granted freedom of movement in East Timor, and he was able to talk to all the individuals he wished to meet.

14. The Special Rapporteur takes this opportunity to express his gratitude for the warm hospitality of the Indonesian authorities as well as for the full access to places and persons granted to him and his delegation.

D. East Timor and the thematic mechanisms of the Commission on Human Rights

15. In recent years, several of the thematic mechanisms of the Commission on Human Rights have received, and acted upon, allegations of human rights violations by members of the Indonesian security forces in East Timor and, in connection with events in East Timor, in Indonesia. The Special Rapporteur on extrajudicial, summary or arbitrary executions repeatedly expressed concern at reports of shortcomings in the investigations into the Santa Cruz killings. The Special Rapporteur on the question of torture transmitted to the Government of Indonesia information concerning several persons who were allegedly subjected to torture while in detention. Some of them were said to have been detained in connection with the events of 12 November 1991. The Working Group on Arbitrary Detention investigated the case of one person accused and convicted of masterminding a demonstration in Jakarta to protest against the Santa Cruz killings. The Working Group decided that his arrest and continued detention upon conviction were arbitrary. In the case of another person serving a prison sentence of nine years for his involvement in the demonstration on 12 November 1991 in Dili, the Working Group on Arbitrary Detention transmitted to the Government of Indonesia an urgent appeal after receiving reports that he had been subjected to ill treatment putting his life at risk. The Working Group on Enforced or Involuntary Disappearances also examined the situation

of disappearances in Indonesia and East Timor. At the time of its most recent report, there were still 375 outstanding cases (see also below, para.22). More detailed information on the activities of the thematic mechanisms may be found in their respective reports to the Commission on Human Rights.

E. Violations of the right to life in East Timor: background and context

16. East Timor was a colony of Portugal for more than 455 years. On 7 December 1975, a full-scale invasion of East Timor by the Indonesian armed forces put an end to a decolonization process which had started with the April 1974 coup d'etat in Portugal. On 17 July 1976 East Timor was declared Indonesia's twenty-seventh province. The United Nations has never recognized Indonesia's sovereignty over the territory. Armed and peaceful underground opposition to the integration with Indonesia has continued since the invasion, in spite of the heavy Indonesian military presence in East Timor and the tight control of the population.

17. There have been repeated allegations according to which between 1975 and 1980, an estimated 100,000 Timorese out of a population of 700,000 were killed by the Indonesian armed forces. Between 1980 and 1984, it has been further alleged that another 100,000 were killed or died of starvation or disease.

18. The most serious and notorious case of extrajudicial killings since then took place on 12 November 1991 at the Santa Cruz Cemetery, in Dili. On that date, unarmed civilians participated in a peaceful pro-independence march to the grave of Sebastiao Gomes, a young man killed on 28 October during an attack by Indonesian security forces on the Motael church, where he and a number of other Timorese political activists had taken refuge.

19. The procession, in which an estimated 3,000 to 4,000 people (mainly students and other young people) participated, started after the early memorial mass for Sebastiao Gomes. Banners and slogans hostile to the integration of East Timor with Indonesia were displayed during the march. Along the route (approximately 1 km from the cemetery), a major and a private in civilian dress were reportedly injured by demonstrators. The killings started in front of the entrance to the cemetery when soldiers opened fire on the crowd, minutes after it had arrived. The walls of the cemetery and the large number of people made it difficult to escape. The shooting continued for between 5 and 15 minutes /2/ and was followed by further shooting,

beating and stabbing inside the perimeter of the cemetery. Moreover, according to eye-witness testimonies gathered by the special Rapporteur, a number of wounded demonstrators transported in trucks to the military hospital were ill-treated or deliberately killed during the journey or at the hospitals morgue.

20. It was reported that on that same day, and on the following days, road-blocks were set up and operations carried out in Dili and in neighbouring villages to round up survivors of the killings who had managed to escape, andallegedly to kill some of them.

21. During his visit, the Special Rapporteur was told by the Indonesian authorities that 19 persons had been killed on 12 November 1991, although the National Commission of Inquiry (see para. 28 and annex, para. 7) had affirmed that "there were sufficiently strong grounds to conclude that the death casualties totalled about 50". According to the testimonies gathered in East Timor by the Special Rapporteur, the total number of persons killed was estimated to be between 150 and 270, although some estimated it to be around 400. It was alleged that the bodies of the victims had been buried in unmarked mass graves or dumped in the sea.

22. There exist large discrepancies between the assessments of the number of cases of disappearances subsequent to the Santa Cruz killings. This is true for the figures reported by non-governmental entities, as well as for those given by the Indonesian authorities, which acknowledged only 66 cases of disappearances but whose lists of names contained anomalies. /3/ The Working Group on Enforced or Involuntary Disappearances transmitted to the Government of Indonesia a total of 224 cases of disappearances alleged to have occurred in connection with the Santa Cruz killings.

23. The Indonesian Government and military authorities expressed regret for the Santa Cruz killings, which they consider as a tragic accident that arose out of a provocative action by anti-integration elements.

F. The Indonesian Government's actions regarding cases of extrajudicial, summary or arbitrary executions in the light of international standards: the example of the Santa Cruz killings

24. During his mission to Jakarta and East Timor, the Special Rapporteur examined, in the light of international standards, the way in which the Indonesian authorties had acted regarding the killings of unarmed civilians by members of the security forces on 12 November 1991 at the Santa Cruz Cemetery, as well as regarding allegations of alleged subse-

quent killings. /4/ In so doing, the Special Rapporteur focused on the following main aspects:

(a) The investigations carried out to establish the facts, to identify the perpetrators, to assess the responsibilities for the killings, to determine the number and identity of the victims and missing persons and to locate them;

(b) The actions taken to bring to justice the perpetrators of the killings and disappearances;

(c) The measures aimed at compensating the victims or their families;

(d) The endeavours to prevent the recurrence of such tragedies.

25. A brief description of those actions follows. An analysis can be made in the section containing the Special rapporteur's conclusions.

G. The investigations

26. The investigative steps taken subsequent to the killings included an internal military investigation immediately after the killings, appointing by presidential decree a National Commission of Inquiry, and actions by the police aimed at identifying the corpses of the victims and determining the whereabouts of the missing persons. Those steps are described below. The Special Rapporteur will comment on them in his conclusions.

27. An internal military investigation, headed by the Deputy Chief of Strategic Intelligence, began in November 1991, before the arrival of the National Commission of Inquiry in Dili. During his visit, the Special Rapporteur requested, both orally and by a letter dated 11 July 1994, that the report of this investigation be made available to him. At the time of the completion of the present report, this request had not been satisfied.

28. A National Commission of Inquiry (NCI), established by Presidential Decree No. 53, commenced its work on 21 November 1991. Its activities covered the preparatory gathering of information in Jakarta from 21 to 27 November, followed by an investigation in East Timor from 28 November to 14 December 1991. The NCI met with a variety of representatives of the local authorities, members of the Church, members of the armed forces, private individuals and eye-witnesses; visited hospitals and police detention centres; inspected Santa Cruz Cemetery; exhumed one grave at Hera Cemetery and carried out unsuccessful inspections and excavations at locations at Pasir Putih, Tasi Tolu and Tibar in response to information received from the local people alleging that those were places of mass burial of victims. During his visit, the Special Rapporteur requested, both orally and in his

letter of 11 July 1994, that the full report of this investigation be made available to him. At the time of the completion of the present report, this request had not been satisfied. The Special Rapporteur therefore had to rely on the preliminary report of the NCI, dated 26 December 1991, the conclusions of which are reproduce in the annex.

29. The Chief of the East Timor Police explained to the Special Rapporteur the steps taken by the local security forces to identify the bodies of the 19 acknowledged victims: one of them, a foreigner, could be identified because he was carrying identification documents. The remaining 18 corpses were buried the day after the killings (13 November 1991), as the morgue of the hospital could accommodate only three to four bodies. This was done after appeals had been made unsuccessfully over the radio, on television and in newspapers for the families to come and identify the bodies. The fingerprints of the victims had been taken but, due to the fact that the police were very busy interrogating the 308 suspects arrested at the cemetery, photographs of the bodies had not been taken. Identification had been impossible because of the lack of dental records and other technology. The Chief of Police also told the Special Rapporteur that medical certificates had been issued by the hospital concerning the 19 bodies.

30. As regards the investigations carried out concerning the fate and whereabouts of the missing persons, the Chief of Police informed the Special Rapporteur that a public appeal had been made on 7 December 1991 to encourage the relatives of missing persons to report the cases. Many people had lodged complaints with the police regarding missing relatives (the last of those reports was made in early 1992); records had been established and communicated to the Commander. The police had tried to locate the missing persons according to the relevant police guidelines. Orders were issued to police sub-offices in East Timor and to provincial police chiefs throughout Indonesia to collect data on newcomers to their area. However, there was no special investigative team dealing with disappearance cases.

31. The Special Rapporteur was informed that the number of persons still missing had been reduced from 66 to 56 as a result of the investigations carried out by the Government of Indonesia: one son had been found in his house, two others had come forward, had fled the country, two were in Jakarta; four bodies were found outside Dili, but it could not be ascertained if these were the remains of persons considered missing (see para. 57 below).

32. During his visit, the Special Rapporteur requested, both orally and in his letter of 11 July 1994, that the medical files of the 18 unidentified bodies, copies of the above-mentioned appeals to the public, the files of the persons whose disappearance had been reported by their family, and the police guidelines for the investigations of disappearances be made available to him. At the time of the completion of the present report, none of those requests had been satisfied.

H. Prosecution of the perpetrators

33. The Honorary Military Council, which was established after the NCI submitted its preliminary report to the President, began its work in January 1992. By a letter dated 27 February 1992 from the Permanent Representative of Indonesia to the United Nations Office at Geneva addressed to the Chairman of the Commission on Human Rights (E/CN.4/1992/79), the salient parts of the announcement made by the Indonesian Chief of Staff of the Army on the results of the investigation conducted by the Honorary Military Council were communicaed as follows:

"1. After thoroughly studying the report of the Council, the Chief of Staff of the army came to the conclusion that there were three categories of offences/misconduct committed by the Local Commander of the army and his subordinates in the handling of the 12 November incident. It is deemed necessary, therefore, to take the following actions:

Six officers who were found guilty of misconduct will be punished: three officers will be dismissed from military service, two officers will not be given any post within the organizational structure of the Army although [they remain] still on active duty, and one officer temporarily will not be given any post within the organizational structure of the Army.

"2. The field commander and members of the military who acted without command and beyond acceptable norms will be brought before the Military Court in accordance with the laws and regulations. The number of persons to be brought to the Military Courts is: four officers, three sub-officers and one private.

"3. Further investigations will be pursued concerning five officers who failed to take appropriate actions during the incident".

34. The court martial set up by the Indonesian military as a response to the matters arising out of the 12 November killings took place at Denpasar, Bali, from 26 May to 6 June 1992. Ten low-

ranking members of the security forces were convicted under article 103, paragraph 1, of the Military Criminal Code for disobeying orders. Only one of them was found guilty of assault, in violation of article 351 of the Criminal Code, for cutting off the ears of a demonstrator. The others received disciplinary sentences. That is to say that none of the military personnel was charged with murder or manslaughter.

The Commander of the Armed Forces explained to the Special Rapporteur that the reason for this was that "there was no evidence on who killed who. The sentences ranged from 8 to 18 months.

35. The Special Rapporteur was told that the six senior officers mentioned above were responsible for intelligence and security in East Timor and it was therefore their responsibility to take action to forestall the demonstration; they were punished because they were commanding the troops that participated in the incident, but had given no order to open fire on the demonstrators. The Special Rapporteur was given no further information on the grounds for punishing those officers.

36. Four Timorese were convicted of subversion and nine were tried on felony, incitement to hatred or sedition charges in trials in Dili and Jakarta. They were charged in connection with either the Dili demonstration or the demonstration in Jakarta to protest the killings. The sentences were extremely harsh (many were condemned to 9, 10 and 15 years' imprisonment), and one Timorese accused of having organized the demonstration was sentenced to life imprisonment.

I. Compensation of the relatives

37. The Special Rapporteur was told that the practice in the event of a death caused by soldiers is to give a bag of rice and a piece of cloth to the family of the victim. According to the military commander of East Timor, it is rather 3 million rupiahs and 50 kg of rice. However, the Indonesian officials met by the Special Rapporteur declared that no compensation had been granted to the families of the persons killed or disappeared.

J. Prevention

38. The Minister of Defence and Security declared that the rules concerning riot control, as well as the equipment, had been improved. Furthermore, a bill on demonstrations was being drafted. However, the Commander-in-Chief of the Armed Forces informed the Special Rapporteur that no changes had been made in the teaching programme of the

soldiers, because the present one was in accordance with the needs. The essence of the problem had been the insubordination of irresponsible officers in the field. The Chief of the National Police informed the Special Rapporteur that the use of firearms by the police was very selective. Arms were not issued to policemen below the rank of sergeant and were used only in field operations. Warning shots should be fired, and the last resort should be non-lethal shots.

K. Violations of the right to life since 12 November 1991

39. The Secretary-General of the Department of Defence and Security told the Special Rapporteur that there had been no further deaths since the Dili incident and no combat against the armed resistance. The Chief of General Staff of the Armed Forces declared that no one had been killed in demonstrations, but that it was possible that deaths had occurred during armed clashes in the countryside.

40. While the number of cases of human rights violations seems to have substantially decreased in East Timor since 1991, the testimonies and reports gathered by the Special Rapporteur clearly show that violations of the right to freedom of expression, association and peaceful assembly, arbitrary arrests, disappearances, torture and extrajudicial executions continue to occur. Information on the cases received will be processed and transmitted to the Government of Indonesia, in accordance with the Special Rapporteur's methods of work. A summary will be included in the annual report to the Commission. Information of relevance to other mechanisms of the Commission on Human Rights will be passed on to those mechanisms.

II. CONCLUSIONS

41. The Special Rapporteur based the following conclusions on the information given to him during the meetings he held in Jakarta and in East Timor, on documentary evidence brought to his attention before and during his mission, and on the various reliable testimonies he gathered. It should be noted once again that during his visit the Special Rapporteur requested, both orally and by a letter dated 11 July 1994, that some important official documents referred to by the Indonesian authorities, mostly reports regarding the Santa Cruz killings, be made available to him. At the time of the completion of the present report, this request had not been satisfied.

42. The Special Rapporteur

believes that, in examining the situation of the right to life in East Timor, other grave human rights violations attributed to the Indonesian armed forces in Indonesia itself (for instance in Aceh and Irian Jaya), as described in his previous reports to the Commission, should be borne in mind. In particular, the patterns of dealing violently with political dissent and the virtual impunity enjoyed by members of the security forces responsible for human rights violations should be recalled.

A. The Government's responsibility in the killings

43. The Basic Principles on the Use of Force and Firearms by Law Enforcement officials adopted by the Eighth United Nations Congress on the Prevention of Crime and the Treatment of Offenders held at Havana, Cuba, from 27 August to 7 September 1990, provide that law enforcement officials, in carrying out their duties, shall as far as possible apply non-violent means and shall only use force in exceptional cases including self-defence or defence of others against the imminent threat of death or serious injury. Such force must be proportional to these objectives and the seriousness of the crime, and must minimize damage and injury.

Force may only be used when less extreme mean are insufficient. Of particular relevance in the context the Santa Cruz killings are principles 12 to 14, which prohibit the use of force against participants in lawful and peaceful assemblies. Force may only be used to the minimum extent necessary in the dispersal of unlawful assemblies.

44. The Code of Conduct for Law Enforcement Officials, adopted by the General Assembly in its resolution 34/169 of 17 December 1979. provides in article 3, that "law enforcement officials may use force only when strictly necessary and to the extent required for the performance of their duty".

45. The Special Rapporteur received reports indicating that the security forces were fully aware days in advance of the preparations for the demonstration. For example, it was reported that on 11 November members of the security forces had tried to dissuade people to take part in the demonstration. It was also reported by some sources that trenches had been dug with road-building machines during the days preceding the demonstration, allegedly to be used subsequently as mass graves. Furthermore, taking into account the number of security personnel and informers present in Dili, the Special Rapporteur is of the opinion that the authorities could

not possibly have been unaware of the preparations for the 12 November demonstration.

46. The report of the NCI makes references to "an uncontrollable group of security personnel, who were not in proper formation nor in proper uniform and obviously in a highly-charged emotional state (...) a group of unorganized security personnel, acting outside any control or command, also fired shots and committed beatings, causing more casualty. The Chief of General Staff of the Army told the Special Rapporteur that those men were not irregular forces but troops out of uniform who had their weapons but who had no time to go back to their barracks for their uniforms.

47. It becomes clear from all the testimonies gathered by the Special Rapporteur–apart from those of some Indonesian officials, who claimed that the demonstrators were armed with knives and grenades and had tried to seize firearms from the soldiers –that the demonstrators carried no firearms. The Special Rapporteur is unaware of any evidence, in the trial documents or elsewhere, to the contrary. According to witnesses met by the Special Rapporteur, the sticks produced in court at the Dili trials were in fact used to hold up the banners, not as weapons. The only acts of violence reported, namely the stabbing of a major in plain clothes and the beating of a

private, took place almost one hour before, and more than one kilometre away from Santa Cruz Cemetery. The Special Rapporteur asked all the officials he met with whether members of the security forces had been killed on 12 November 1991. The answers were invariably negative. Furthermore, the film footage taken by foreign journalists within the cemetery viewed by the Special Rapporteur shows soldiers moving around the cemetery, apparently without any fear or constraint, while others are beating 12 people on the ground. But even if the claims that the demonstrators were threatening the lives of members of the security forces had been supported by the available evidence, it would not explain why the demon-strators who were trying to flee the scene of the killings were shot in the back; why, after the shooting had stopped, soldiers went on stabbing, kicking and beating the survivors (including the wounded) inside the cemetery, on the way to the hospital, and allegedly also at the hospital itself: or why sporadic shooting was heard throughout the city and in neighbouring villages during the rest of the day, and possibly during several days. The violence of the security forces towards the demonstrators was illustrated by the information concerning the 91 wounded obtained by NCI at the "Wire Husada" Military Hospital and reflected in its report: 42 persons suffered gunshot wounds, 14 stab wounds and 35 wounds caused by blunt instruments.

48. The Special Rapporteur, after careful consideration of the available evidence, including the numerous eye-witness testimonies he gathered, reached the following conclusions:

(a) A proper crowd control operation could have been set up beforehand to deal with the demonstration, thus avoiding the killings;

(b) The forces that perpetrated the killings on 12 November 1991 were regular members of the armed forces;

(c) The procession that took place in Dili on 12 November 1991 was a peaceful demonstration of political dissent by unarmed civilians; the claims of some officials that the security forces had fired in self-defence and had respected the principles of the necessity and the proportionality of the use of lethal force are unsubstantiated;

(d) There are, therefore, reasons to believe that the actions of the security forces were not a spontaneous reaction to a riotous mob, but rather a planned military operation designed to deal with a public expression of political dissent in a way not in accordance with international human rights standards.

B. Analysis of the investigations

49. The following paragraphs contain the Special Rapporteur's analysis, in the light of the pertinent international standards, of the measures taken by the Government of Indonesia.

50. The Principles on the Effective Prevention and investigation of Extra-legal, Arbitrary and Summary Executions, endorsed by the General Assembly in its resolution 44/162 of 15 December 1989 spell out, inter alia, the following principles regarding investigations on allegations of extrajudicial, summary or arbitrary executions.

51. Principle 9 states: "There shall be thorough, prompt and impartial investigation of all suspected cases of extra-legal, arbitrry and summary execution ... The purpose of the investigation shall be to determine the cause, manner and time of death, the person responsible, and any pattern or practice which may have brought that death. It shall include an adequate autopsy, collection and analysis of all physical and documentary evidence and statements from witnesses..." Principle 10 states, inter alia, that "those persons conducting the investigation shall have at their disposal all the necessary budgetary and technical resources for effective investigation".

52. From the information he

gathered during meetings with the representative of the East Timor judiciary and law enforcement authorities, the Special Rapporteur concluded the following:

(a) The investigation carried out by the police forces was not thorough, as will be shown below;

(b) Given that the police is itself a part of the armed forces and the grave allegations concerning the adverse role of the police in the Santa Cruz killings and subsequent incidents, the conditions for an independent and impartial investigation were not present;

(c) The forensic examination was inadequate. Although a medical examination was carried out by the hospital on the 19 acknowledged corpses, no adequate autopsies were performed. The Chief of Police told the Special Rapporteur that the necessary technological means were not available in East Timor, and that no forensic expert was sent from Jakarta. Likewise, no ballistic examination was conducted to connect the bullets fired with the weapons of the members of the security forces present at the cemetery, even though such an analysis could have been conducted later in the capital;

(d) The criminal investigation was inadequate, failing to clarify either the identity of the perpetrators or the victims, nor even the number of the latter. It did not determine the fate and whereabouts of the missing persons. In fact, it appears that the witnesses interrogated by the police were questioned on their involvement in the organization of the demonstrations rather than on possible unlawful acts carried out by members of the security forces, or the identity of the killed and disappeared.

53. Principle 11 states that "in cases in which the established procedures are inadequate because of lack of expertise or impartiality, because of the importance of the matter or because of the apparent existence of a pattern of abuse ... Governments shall pursue investigations through an independent commission of inquiry or similar procedure. Members of such a commission shall be chosen for their recognized impartiality, competence and independence as individuals. In particular, they shall be independent of any institution, agency or person that may be the subject of the inquiry. The Commission shall have the authority to obtain all information necessary to the inquiry and shall conduct the inquiry as provided for under these Principles.

54. The Special Rapporteur feels that the creation of the National Commission of Enquiry was an encouraging initiative. As regards the work of the NCI, he reached the following conclusions:

(a) The NCI was created by presidential decree and its composition was widely criticized, for it did not include any member totally independent of the Government. Most of the East Timorese met by the Special Rapporteur declared that the NCI had not been trusted by the population;

(b) None of the members of the NCI had the necessary technical expertise to corrct the shortcomings found in the investigations carried out by the police. For instance, the Commission should have conducted a thorough search for alleged mass burial sites, carried out full exhumations of known graves, performed proper autopsies and examined ballistic evidence. As regards the last point, the only finding NCI reported was that there were 70 bullet marks in Santa Cruz Cemetery. Another example of a lack of competence is shown by the unprofessional manner in which the only exhumation was carried out, and by the irrelevance of the conclusions drawn therefrom (see below, para. 57 (d)).

(c) The Special Rapporteur welcomes the creation of the National Human Rights Commission (NHRC), established by presidential decree in June 1993, as a very positive step towards improved respect for human rights. However, it has so far not dealt with human rights violations in East Timor, and in particular the Santa Cruz killings. Moreover, most observers met by the Special Rapporteur were of the opinion that the NHRC had neither the mandate /5/ nor the means to deal efficiently with this case. /6/

55. Principle 12 states: "The body of the deceased person shall not be disposed of until an adequate autopsy is conducted by a physician, who shall, if possible, be an expert in forensic pathology... If the body has been buried and it later appears that an investigation is required, the body shall be promptlyand competently exhumed for an autopsy. If skeletal remains are discovered, they should be carefully exhumed and studied according to systematic anthropological techniques." Principle 13 states that "[t]he autopsy shall, at a minimum, attempt to establish the identity of the deceased and the cause and manner of death... Detailed colour photographs of the deceased shall be included in the autopsy report ... "

56. As regards the way in which the investigations dealt with the bodies of the victims, the Special Rapporteur concluded the following: According to the Chief of the East Timor Police, the bodies of the acknowledged 19 victims were buried at Hera on 13 November, one day after the killings. No adequate autopsy had been performed, no pictures of the corpses had been taken and, to date, 18 of the bodies remain unidentified. It is not known

what measures were taken as regards the bodies of victims allegedly buried in mass graves. The Special Rapporteur therefore reached the same conclusion as the NCI, which reported that "there was careless handling of those who died, because although the visum et repertums were performed the deceased were not properly identified. Little opportunity was given to the families/friends of the victims to identify the bodies".

57. As regards the information provided by the Government according to which 10 of the 66 missing persons had been found, the Special Rapporteur notes the following:

(a) The four bodies found in July 1992 outside Dili could not be identified nor could their remains be linked to persons reported missing after the Santa Cruz killings. However, the Government considered that they could constitute a clarification of the fate of four individuals included in its list of 66 missing persons;

(b) Only two persons out of the 10 whom the Government had reported as having been found were in fact included in the list of 66 names;

(c) According to all the witnesses met by the Special Rapporteur and contrary to the declarations made by the Chef of the East Timor Police, no appeal was made on 12 or 13 November 1991 for relatives of missing persons to come to the hospital to identify the bodies of the 19 victims:

(d) The Chief of Police told the Special Rapporteur that a tractor had been used by the NCI to excavate graves. The Special Rapporteur cannot help being surprised that such an indiscriminate means of digging, contrary to the basic methodology of any expert exhumation and likely to be detrimental to the outcome of any subsequent forensic analysis, was used. The conclusions drawn from this exhumation were irrelevant: the victim was buried in a coffin, completely dressed, and there was only one corpse in the grave. No autopsy was conducted on the body, and therefore no pertinent information, such as the identity of the corpse or the cause of death, was given. However, the Military Commander of East Timor told the Special Rapporteur that the normal procedure to deal with a case of a civilian killed was to conduct a forensic analysis, and that a ballistics expert was usually brought from Jakarta. The Special Rapporteur was also informed that four graves were found in July 1992, but that forensic tests could not conclusively tie the remains to the Santa Cruz killings, and that the identity of the deceased could not be determined.

58. Principle 15 states: "Com-

plainants, witnesses, those conducting the investigation and their families shall be protected from violence, threats of violence or any other form of intimidation. Those potentially implicated in extra-legal arbitrary or summary executions shall be removed from any position of control or power, whether direct or indirect, over complainants, witnesses and their families, as well as over those conducting investigations."

59. As regards the atmosphere in which the investigations were carried out, the Special Rapporteur concluded the following: Most of the eye-witnesses interviewed by the NCI were held in prison or military hospital and th meetings are therefore believed to have been monitored by the security forces, i.e. not conducted confidentially. In fact, NCI itself concluded that it had "...faced obstacles because a number of prospective witnesses had not been willing to give their account of the event because of doubt and concern that they would be directly incriminated in the 12 November 1991 incident in Dili, or out of fear that they would be regarded as belonging to the anti-integration group."

60. Principle 17 states: "A written report shall be made within a reasonable period of time on the methods and findings of such investigations. The report shall be made public immediately and shall include the scope of the inquiry, procedures and methods used to evaluate evidence as well as conclusion and recommendations based on findings of facts and on applicable law. The report shall also describe in detail specific events that were found to have occurred and the evidence upon which such findings were based, and list the names of witnesses who testified, with the exception of those whose identities have been withheld for their own protection. The Government shall, within a reasonable period of time, either reply to the report of the investigation, or indicate the steps to be taken in response to it." To the knowledge of the Special Rapporteur, the only public report of the investigations carried out concerning the Santa Cruz killings is the preliminary report of the NCI. Neither the report of the internal military investigations nor that of the Honorary Military Council has been made public.

61. As regards the fate of the so far undetermined number of persons missing as a consequence of the Santa Cruz killings, the Special Rapporteur wishes to recall here article 13 of the Declaration on the Protection of All Persons from Enforced Disappearance, adopted by the General Assembly in its resolutio 47/133 of 18 December 1992. which provides that:

"1. Each State shall ensure that any person having knowledge or a legitimate interest who alleges that a person has been subjected to enforced disappearance has the right to complain to a competent and independent State authority and to have that complaint promptly, thoroughly and impartially investigated by that authority. Whenever there are reasonable grounds to believe that an enforced disappearance has been committed, the State shall promptly refer the matter to that authority for such an investigation, even if there has been no formal complaint. No measure shall be taken to curtail or impede the investigation.

"2. Each State shall ensure that the competent authority shall have the necessary powers and resources to conduct the investigation effectively, including powers to compel attendance of witnesses and production of relevant documents and to make immediate on-site visits.

"3. Steps shall be taken to ensure that all involved in the investigation, including the complainant, counsel, witnesses and those conducting the investigation, are protected against ill-treatment, intimidation or reprisal.

"4. The findings of such an investigation shall be made available upor request to all persons concerned, unless doing so would jeopardize an ongoing criminal investigation.

"5. Steps shall be taken to ensure that any ill-treatment, intimidation or reprisal or any other form of interference on the occasion of the lodging of a complaint or during the investigation procedure is appropriately punished.

"6. An investigation, in accordance with the procedures described above, should be able to be conducted for as long as the fate of the victim of enforced disappearance remains unclarified.

62. As regard the implementation of these provisions, the Special Rapporteur reached the following conclusions:

(a) As noted earlier by the Special Rapporteur, there is no independent State authority capable of investigating cases of disappearances in East Timor;

(b) Apart from the above-mentioned measures taken by the police to try to locate the 66 persons reported missing, there is no information on efforts made to investigate the alleged hundreds of cases of disappearances that have not been formally brought up with the authorities;

(c) As noted above, and according to the declarations of the Chief of Police himself, the necessary resources and technology have not been made available so as to allow a meaningful investigation to be conducted;

(d) The families are afraid of reporting the death or disappearance of their relatives, because they think they will be brought to court for having links with the clandestine resistance or for having supported the demonstration. Indeed, the Special Rapporteur was indeed told that anyone who presents a complaint is automatically considered to be subversive. It was reported, for example, that some of the victims had died of their wounds at home, but that the families had declared that they had died of malaria or diarrhoea. Most were too afrad even to report to the Bishop.

63. The East Timor District Attorney explained to the Special Rapporteur that his office was not competent in offences involving military personnel.

He further said that if a family complains about the disappearance of a relative, his office had no investigative power; he would informlly ask the police to pay special attention to that case. But the complaint would have to be given directly to the police, and there were no avenues for civilians to force them to carry out an investigation. He further stated that his office had no files about the Santa Cruz incident and had not participated in the NCI. Likewise, there was no investigation under way to identify the 18 bodies buried at Hera. The only actions taken by the District Attorney were related to the prosecution of participants in the demonstration.

64. With respect to the cases of disappearances:

(a) The Special Rapporteur feels that there is no ongoing investigation regarding the cases of the persons who remain missing;

(b) The Special Rapporteur was surprised when the Chief of the East Timor Police declared that no cases had been received from the Working Group on Enforced or Involuntary Disappearances:

(c) The Special Rapporteur is of the opinion that the dispute over the actual numbers of the dead and missing clearly indicates the need for further investigations. This controversy should, however, in no way obscure the need and the obligation to identify the dead and reveal the whereabouts of their remains, to identify and bring the perpetrators to justice and to compensate the families of the victims;

(d) The Special Rapporteur reached the conclusion that since the NCI completed its investigation, no institutionalized or organized effort has been made by the Indonesian authorities to account for the fate of the dead and disappeared.

Furthermore, the authorities did not allow independent human rights organizations, either domestic or international, to carry out human rights monitoring.

C. Analysis of the prosecution of the members of the security forces responsible for the killings and disappearances

65. The following paragraphs contain the Special Rapporteur's analysis, in the light of the pertinent international standards, of the measures taken by the Government of Indonesia.

66. The consensus statement made by the Chairman of the Commission on Human Rights on 4 March 1992 called for "the Indonesian Government to bring to trial and punish all those [members of the armed forces] found responsible (E/1992/22-E/CN4/1992/84. para. 457)".

67. Point 18 of the Principles on the Effective Prevention and Investigation of Extra-legal, Arbitrary and Summary Executions states that "Governments shall ensure that persons identified by the investigation as having participated in extra-legal, summary or arbitrary executions in any territory under their jurisdiction are brought to justice... This principle shall apply irrespective of who and where the perpetrators or the victims are, their nationalities or where the offence was committed." Point 19 states that Superiors, officers or other public officials may be held responsible for acts committed by officials under their authority if they had a reasonable opportunity to prevent such acts. In no circumstances, including a state of war, siege or other public emergency, shall blanket immunity from prosecution be granted to any person allegedly involved in extra-legal, summary or arbitrary executions."

68. The Basic Principles on the Use of Force and Firearms by Law Enforcement Officials, provide that arbitrary or abusive use of force and firearms by law enforcement officials is to be punished as a criminal offence under national law.

69. As regards the fate of the so far undetermined number of persons missing as a consequence of the Santa Cruz killings, the Special Rapporteur wishes to recall article 1 of the Declaration on the Protection of All Persons from Enforced Disappearance, which reads as follows:

"1. Any act of enforced disappearance is an offence to human dignity.

It is condemned as a denial of the purposes of the Charter of the United Nations and as a grave and flagrant violation of the human rights and fundamental freedoms proclaimed in the Universal Declaration of Human Rights and reaffirmed and developed in international instruments in this field.

"2. Any act of enforced disappearance places the person subjected thereto outside the protection of the law and inflicts severe suffering on them and their families. It constitutes a violation of the rules of international law guaranteeing, inter alia, the right to recognition as a person before the law, the right to liberty and security of the person and the right not to be subjected to torture and other cruel, inhuman or degrading treatment or punishment. It also violates or constitutes a grave threat to the right to life."

Moreover, article 4. paragraph 1, of the Declaration states: "All acts of enforced disappearance shall be offences under criminal law punishable by appropriate penalties which shall take into account their extreme seriousness." Article 16. paragraph 2. further states: "(Persons alleged to have committed any of the acts referred to in article 4, paragraph 1) shall be tried only by the competent ordinary court in each State, and not by any other special tribunal, inparticular military courts." Article 17, paragraph 1. states: "Acts constituting enforced disappearance shall be considered a continuing offence as long as the perpetrators continue to conceal the fate and the whereabouts of persons who have disappeared and these facts remain unclarified."

70. As regards the prosecution of the perpetrators of the Santa Cruz killing and connected grave human rights violations, the Special Rapporteur reached the following conclusions:

(a) According to the information brought to the attention of the Special Rapporteur, torture, murder and kidnapping are criminal offences under Indonesian law. They are also prohibited by the Military Criminal Code and b] variety of ministerial regulations. other provisions of the Military Criminal Code are designed to curtail the abuse of authority by members of the security forces and to ensure that commanding officers take responsibility for crimes committed by their subordinates. Thus, the minimum instruments allowing for the prosecution of the perpetrators exist. However, members of the armed forces, including the police, who have committed crimes or have abused their authority can stand trial only before military courts, even in cases where the victims are civilians;

(b) In spite of the recommendations formulated by the Special Rapporteur on the question of torture subsequent to his visit to Indonesia and East Timor in November 1991 (E/CN.4/1992/17/Add.1, para. 80), victims of human rights violations or their relatives still do not have direct access to the judicial system in cases of abuses perpetrated by members of the security forces. Consequently, such complaints have to be filed with the police, which belongs to the armed forces. In practice, investigations are, therefore, rarely concluded. This can hardly be called an effective remedy. The Special Rapporteur is not aware of any provision entitling a civilian to bring such a complaint before a judicial or other authority if the police have rejected the complaint or refused to carry out an investigation. Even the proesecutor has no authority to order the police to carry out an investigation if the police find a complaint filed by a civilian to be well founded, the file can be transmitted to the office of the Military Attorney-General, since the suspect would have to stand trial before a military court. This means that no civilian authority is involved in any way in dealing with a complaint filed by a civilian of an alleged encroachment on his fundamental rights. The Special Rapporteur feels that a system which places the task of correcting and suppressing abuses of authority by members of the army in that same institution will not easily inspire confidence. The Special Rapporteur believes that there is no reason why persons belonging to the military should be tried by military courts for offences committed against civilians during the essentially civil task of maintaining law and order.

Despite the fundamental shortcomings of its investigation, the NCI reached conclusions that engaged the responsibility of the security forces to a greater extent than was admitted by the police during the Special Rapporteurs's visit:

"according to information received from the Military Operational Command, the death toll reached 19 but according to the account of other eye-witnesses and sources, the death toll exceeded 19 and their figures varied from 50, 60 to over 100. Although the casualty toll until now was set at 19 dead and 91 wounded, the Commission feels that there are sufficiently strong grounds to conclude that the death casualties totalled about 50 while the wounded exceeded 91"

NCI, however, gave no indication as to why the figure of "about 50" had been retained. During his visit, the Special Rapporteur was told by all the officials he met that only 19 persons had died as a result of the 12 November 1991 event. The Chief of the East Timor Police declared that 6 persons had died at the hospital on that same day, in the afternoon, and 13 at the site of the incident. The Special Rapporteur reiterates his view that the dispute over the actual number of the dead and missing should not obscure the need and the obligation to identify the dead and reveal the whereabouts of their remains, to bring the perpetrators to justice and to compensate the families of the victims;

(d) The report of NCI concluded that "action must be taken against all those involved in the 12 November 1991 incident in Dili and suspected of having violated the law, and they must be brought to trial in accordance with the rule of law, Pancasila /7/ and the 1945 Constitution". However, this statement does not specify or recommend who should be brought to justice;

(e) The Special Rapporteur feels that the court martial set up as a response to the Santa Cruz killings was an encouraging first step towards the accountability of members of the armed forces for violations of human rights.

However, as mentioned above, the Court examined only the cases of 10 low-ranking members of the security forces, who were accused of having acted "without command and beyond acceptable norms", They were charged under article 103. paragraph 1. of the Military Criminal Code for disobeying orders. Only one of them was charged with assault, in violation of article 351 of the Code, for cutting off the ears of a demonstrator. That is to say that none of the few military personnel accused was charged with homicide, serious assault, or for having committed enforced disappearances. Likewise, there did not seen to have een any attempts made by the prosecution, for example by using ballistic evidence, to attribute to the accused the shots which caused deaths or wounds.

The sentences meted out by the military tribunal ranged from 8 to 18 months, which, considering the seriousness of the human rights violations that were committed on 12 November 1991 and possibly subsequently, seem to the Special Rapporteur to be inappropriately light penalties. Furthermore, the fate of the missing persons continues to be unknown;

(f) The Honorary Military Council appointed by the President dealt with the cases of six senior officers and found them guilty of misconduct. This procedure was not public and did not involve the participation of the families or of independent observers. Many elements about it therefore remain obscure; for instance, the exact grounds for punishing those officers is not known, and in any event they were never brought to justice;

(g) The Special Rapporteur is of the opinion that the inadequacy of the charges and the inappropriately light sentences imposed by the court martial on the few members of the armed forces accused of having been implicated in the 12 November 1991 incident are in no way a fulfilment of the obligation to punish perpetrators, and thus to provide a deterrent for the recurrence of a similar tragedy in the future. On the contrary, he feels that they illustrate that little importance is given to the respect of the right to life by Indonesian law enforcement officials in East Timor. On the other hand, the 13 civilians involved in peaceful protest during and after 12 November 1991 were sentenced to terms of up to life imprisonment. In paragraph 4 of its resolution 1993/97, the Commission regretted "the disparity in the severity of sentenes imposed on those civilians not indicted for violent activities - who should have been released without delay on the one hand, and to the military involved in the violent incident, of the other" The Special Rapporteur is also of the opinion that there was an unreasonable disparity between the sentences passed upon the perpetrators and upon the victims; the latter were, in fact, those really blamed for the killings. He believes that this disparity is much more illustrative of an implacable determination to suppress political dissent than a genuine commitment to protect the right to life and prevent extrajudicial executions.

D. Compensation of the families and dependents of the victims

71. Principle 20 states: "The families and dependents of victims of extra-legal, summary or arbitrary executions shall be entitled to fair and adequate compensation within a reasonable period of time."

72. Article 19 of the Declaration states: "The victims of acts of enforced disappearance and their families shall obtain redress and shall have the rig to adequate compensation, including the means for as complete a rehabilitation as possible. In the event of the death of the victim as a result of an act of enforced disappearance, their dependents shall also be entitled to compensation."

73. With respect to the above:

(a) According to the information brought to the attention of the Special Rapporteur, existing procedures for the redress and compensation of victims and relatives are ineffective and cumbersome. Members of the public with a human rights grievance face the daunting prospect of complaining to the armed forces, the very authority they believe to be responsible;

(b) According to the information gathered by the Special Rapporteur, the judiciary are largely shackled by the executive branch and the military, and the legal system suffers widespread corruption. The Special Rapporteur is concerned that there is no real right to defence in Indonesian courts. The few lawyers practising in East Timor are reportedly not trusted by the population, because they are considered to be linked to the Indonesian authorities;

(c) In the case of the Santa Cruz killings, no compensation has been granted, and no special mechanism has been created for that purpose. The Special Rapporteur believes that the first step towards compensation should be the identification of the dead and disappeared, which, in turn, requires the recognition by the Government of its responsibility.

E. Prevention

74. The Special Rapporteur believes that lessons regarding the behaviour of the security forces should have been drawn by the Indonesian authorities after the Santa Cruz killings, so as to take decisive action with a view to rendering the recurrence of such a tragedy impossible in the future. Unfortunately, the information gathered during meetings with Indonesian officials, both civilian and military, lead the Special Rapporteur to conclude that the conditions that allowed the Santa Cruz killings to occur are still present. In particular, the members of the security forces responsible for the abuses have not been held accountable and continue to enjoy virtual impunity

75. The Special Rapporteur welcomes the drafting of a bill on demonstrations and hopes that it will include provisions on the control of the use of force by law enforcement officials and that its provisions will provide a legal framework for the rights to free-

dom of peaceful assembly and association.

However, the measures taken to improve crowd control operations have proved insufficient, and force continues to be used to deal with peaceful demonstration, as was shown just three days after the Special Rapporteur's departure from East Timor.

It was reported that on 14 July 1994, security forces violently broke up what was described by eye-witnesses as a largely peaceful demonstration at the University of East Timor (UNTIM) campus. The demonstration followed an incident which had occurred the day before, when three Indonesian students (some sources alleged that they may have been undercover military intelligence agents) insulted two Roman Catholic nuns. According to the information communicated to the Special Rapporteur by the Government of Indonesia, the situation became uncontrollable when the students started throwing stones at the police. Clashes broke out between the crowd and the policemen. Many students were injured when they tried to jump over a fence in the commotion. The Government admitted that 15 persons were injured, of whom 11 were treated and discharged and 4 were hospitalized. However, the eye-witness account of the rector of UNTIM rejected the Government's version of the incident:

"It is true that the demonstration initially proceeded in an orderly and peaceful fashion, as it had been granted a permit by the local police ... It is not true that the mass rally turned brutal and highly emotional because of issues and incitement by irresponsible elements ... It is our impression that the initiative for the physical clash started with the security forces violently attacking the demonstrators, which they did first with batons, kicks and striking people with their shields, teargas and attacks by two sniffer dogs. The East Timor Chief of Police in his press conference of 14 July 1994 even admitted that the wounded people were bruised all over and that their bodies were lacerated."

76. As noted earlier, the access of victims of human rights violations to the judiciary or to non-governmental organizations has not improved; no appropriate mechanisms to request an investigation or to file a complaint have been instituted. Institutionalized monitoring of the human rights situation in East Timor is not yet allowed. The fear of families of victims still prevents them from making their case known publicly. This was illustrated by the difficulties the Special Rapporteur encountered in trying to persuade victims or witnesses of human rights violations to meet with him in order to testify, and the precautions taken before, during and after such meetings. The Special Rapporteur clearly sensed terror among many East Timorese he had the opportunity to meet.

III. RECOMMENDATIONS

77. The Special Rapporteur believes that the Santa Cruz killings should not be considered as a thing of the past. They must not be forgotten, and there is still time to correct the shortcomings, noted at all levels, in the way in which violations of the right to life have been dealt with by the Indonesian authorities in East Timor: it is not too late to conduct proper investigations, to identify and bring to justice the perpetrators, to determine the fate and whereabouts of the missing persons, to grant compensation to the victims or their relatives, and to prevent the occurrence of further killings.

78. The Special Rapporteur urges the Indonesian authorities to carry out thorough, prompt and impartial investigations of all suspected cases of extrajudicial, summary or arbitrary executions and enforced or involuntary disappearances. Those investigations should be in accordance with international standards set forth in the various instruments mentioned in this report, and should involve the armed forces, the relatives of the victims, the local clergy, non-governmental organizations, and, particularly, civilian

authorities

The Special Rapporteur calls on the Goverrment of Indonesia to establish a civilian police force as a matter of urgency. This police force should be placed under the authority of the Prosecutor. The Special Rapporteur wishes to recall that the recommendation to establish a civilian police force had already been made by the Special Rapporteur on the question of torture after his visit to Indonesia and East Timor in 1991 (E/CN.4/1992/17)

79. In the case of the Santa Cruz killings and alleged subsequent grave human rights violations, the findings of the military inquiry should be made public and an additional investigation should be conducted by a new commission of inquiry. In this respect, and in addition to what was said earlier, the Special Rapporteur feels that the following aspects should be taken into consideration.

(a) The new commission of inquiry should be composed of individuals of recognized independence, impartiality and expertise. it should include specialists in anthropology, forensic science, ballistics, etc. If this expertise is not available in East Timor or in Indonesia, it should be provided internationally, through the United Nations or non-governmental organizations;

(b) The credibility of such an investigation could be increased by the participation of experts internationally recognized for their objectivity and competence. Such a presence would help to reduce amongst the East Timnorese population the fear and mistrust which were so detrimental to the investigation of NCI;

(c) The commission should have at its disposal all the necessary budgetary and technical resources for effective investiation and shall have the authority to obtain all information necessary to the inquiry;

(d) All the necessary measures should be taken to protect complainants, witnesses and their familiies from violence, threats of violence, arrest or prosecution, or from any other form of intimidation;

(e) The families of the victims shall be informed of and have access to any hearing, as well as any information relevant to the investigation, and shall be entitled to present evidence.

80. The purpose of the investigation should be to determine the following points:

(a) The circumstances of the killings;

(b) The number of persons killed, their identity and the location of their graves;

(c) The number of missing persons, their identity, their fate and exact whereabouts;

(d) The chain of command and the identity of all perpetrators and their superiors, and their individual responsibility in the human rights violations.

81. The Special Rapporteur strongly believes that no confidence-building measures can be effective and no solution to the problems facing East Timor can be found before justice has been done. The first step for the Government should be to recognize its responsibility and declare that killings, and not an "incident", took place in Santa Cruz. Full light should be shed, publicly, on all the tragic events described in this report, in accordance with the standards referred to above. An end should be put to impunity enjoyed by members of the Indonesian armed forces responsible for abuses. To that purpose, the Special Rapporteur recommends the following:

(a) The jurisdiction over such cases should be handed over to the ordinary civilian judiciary;

(b) The independence, fairness and transparency of the judiciary should be improved and guaranteed. Interference of the military at any stage of the proceedings, including the investigation, should be avoided. This should not exclude its cooperation, when it is requested. Corruption should be effectively fought;

(c) Provision should be made to allow victims or their families to initiate judicial proceedings. In particular, investigations into complaints by victims or their families should be compulsory and not left to the discretion of police full participation in the proceedings, and free choice of independent counsel should be guaranteed;

(d) Persons identified by the investigation as being responsible for abuses, whoever they are, should be brought to justice. The proceedings should be public. Human rights violations should be offences under criminal law punishable by appropriate penalties, fully taking into account their seriousness;

(e) Acts constituting enforced disappearances should be considered as a continuing offence as long as the perpetrators continue to conceal the fate and whereabouts of persons who have disappeared and these facts remain unclarified;

(f) Equitable compensation should be granted without delay to the victims or their dependents and families.

82. As regards the access to justice for the victims or their relatives, the Special Rapporteur recommends that the Indonesian authorities apply, in addition to the various international principles referred to in this report, the following points embodied in the Declaration of Basic Principles of Justice for Victims of Crime and Abuse of Power, adopted by the General Assembly in its resolution 40/34 of 29 November 1985:

"4. Victims /8/ should be treated with compassion and respect for their dignity.

They are entitled to access to the mechanisms of justice and to prompt redress, as provided for by national legislation, for the harm that they have suffered.

"5. Judicial and administrative mechanisms should be e*stablished and* strengthened where necessary to enable victims to obtain redress through formal or informal procedures that are expeditious, fair, inexpensive and accessible.

Victims should be informed of their rights in seeking redress through such mechanisms.

"6. The responsiveness of judicial and administrative processes to the needs of the victims should be facilitated by:

"(a) Informing victims of their role and the scope, timing and progress of the proceedings and the disposition of their cases, especially where serious crimes are involved and where they have requested such information;

"(b) Allowing the views and concerns of victims to be presented and considered at appropriate stages of the proceedings where their personal interests are affected, without prejudice to the accused and consistent with the relevant national criminal justice system;

"(c) Providing proper assistance to victims through the legal process;

"(d) Taking measures to minimize inconvenience to victims, protect their privacy, when necessary, and ensure their safety, as well as that of their families and witnesses on their behalf, from intimidation and retaliation;

"(e) Avoiding unnecessary delay in the disposition of cases and the execution of orders or decrees granting awards to victims".

83. As mentioned earlier, the involvement of the relatives of missing or killed persons into any sort of investigation is essential. The Special Rapporteur could notice himself that in the atmosphere of fear and suspicion currently prevailing in East Timor. the conditions conducive to such participation are not present.

The Special Rapporteur therefore believes that a drastic reduction of the military presence in East Timor is a prerequisite for confidence-building measures allowing the families to feel safe enough to report about their missing or killed relatives. This reduction should not only affect combat units, but all troops present in the territory, including territorial battalions and military intelligence. In that regard, the Special Rapporteur welcomes the dissolution of the Special Military Command in East Timor in 1993, as well as the reductions of troops, especially combat battalions, already carried out.

84. The Special Rapporteur believes that the involvement of non-governmental organizations

in all questions relating to human rights in East Timor - e.g. investigation, monitoring, legal assistance, information and training should be allowed and encouraged by the Indonesian authorities:

(a) Independent NGOs should be created in East Timor and allowed to operate freely throughout the territory. At this stage, the Special Rapporteur feels that the involvement of the Catholic clergy (which at the moment is the only institution whose involvement with human rights questions is tolerated, by the Indonesian authorities) in such organizations would be essential;

(b) Indonesian and international human rights NGOs should be granted full access to East Timor.

85. The Special Rapporteur believes that the National Human Rights Commission is not the most appropriate mechanism to deal with human rights violations in East Timor. Its mandate, the means of action at its disposal and its methods of work are insufficient. Furthermore, it is not trusted by the population of East Timor. In any event, it has not dealt with questions relating to East Timor. Consequently, the Special Rapporteur recommends that a commission for human rights in East Timor he created to monitor the situation of human rights, receive and independently investigate complaints, make recommendations to the competent authorities, and disseminate information about human rights. Its characteristics should be in accordance with the Principles relating to the status of national institutions (Commission on Human Rights resolution 1992/54, annex, adopted without a vote on 3 March 1992).

The Special Rapporteur recommends that such a commission should be composed of individuals of recognized impartiality and independence representing the civil society of East Timor, including NGOs.

86. As provided for in article 3 of the Declaration on the Protection of All Persons from Enforced Disappearances the Special Rapporteur recommends that the Indonesian authorities "take effective legislative, administrative, judicial or other measures to prevent and terminate acts of enforced disappearance".

Following article 4. paragraph 2, of the Declaration. the Special Rapporteur suggests that "mitigating circumstances may be established in national legislation for persons who, having participated in enforced isappearances, are instrumental in bringing the victims forward alive or in providing voluntarily information which could contribute to clarifying cases of enforced disappearance"

87. Measures should be taken to ensure that peaceful demonstrations of political dissent are dealt

with in conformity with international standards In particular, the use of force by law enforcement officials should be restricted accordingly.

Furthermore, members of the security forces should be better trained in proper crowd control methods, and the appropriate non-lethal equipment for such operations should be made available to them. Training should also place more emphasis on human rights questions and should stress that a soldier receiving an order contrary to human rights has the right and duty not to obey it.

88. The Special Rapporteur recommends that the Indonesian Government invite the Working Group on Enforced or Involuntary Disappearances to carry out a mission. He expresses the hope that his recommendations will be implemented, in conjunction with those formulated by the Special Rapporteur on the question of torture after his visit to Indonesia and East Timor in November 1991. In particular, he encourages the Government to accede to major human rights Rights and the Convention against Torture and Other Cruel, Inhuman or Degrading Treatment or Punishment.

Notes

1/ For activities undertaken in 1992 and 1993: on extrajudicial, summary or arbitrary executions, E/CN.4/1993/46, paras. 348-353, E/CN.4/1994/7. paras.343-356; for torture, E/CN.4/1993/26. paras. 270-274, E/CN.4/1994/31, paras. 325-343; on arbitrary detention, E/CN.4/1994/27, annex II, decision No. 36/1993; on enforced or involuntary disappearances. E/CN.4/1993/25, para. 278-290. E/CN.4/1994:26, paras. 260, 261 and 269.

2/ The Chief of the East Timor Police estimated that the shooting lasted for 10 to 15 minutes.

3/ See: E/CN.4/1994/26, para. 265 and Asia Watch, "Remembering History in East Timor". vol. 5, No. 8, April 1993, pp. 21-22.

4/ The Special Rapporteur will refer to the events of the 12 November as "killings", a word that, in his opinion, is more appropriate than the term "incident", used by many. including the Indonesian authorities.

Indeed, in view of the number of victims, the Special Rapporteur deems it appropriate to speak of a "massacre".

5/ The presidential decree spells out that the NHRC shall "monitor and investigate the implementation of human rights and present views, considerations and suggestions to State institutions on the implementation of human rights'.

6/ The Special Rapporteur was informed that the NHCR has a very limited budget, office facilities and staff and has no formal authority.

7/ The Pancasila is the state philosophy, which consists of the following five principles: (i) belief in one Supreme God; (ii) just and civilized humanity; (iii) the unity of Indonesia; (iv) democracy led by the inner wisdom of unanimity arising out of the deliberation among representatives;

(v) social justice for the whole of the Indonesian people.

8/ In the terms of the Declaration, "the term 'victim' also includes, where appropriate, the immediate family or dependents of the direct victim..." (para. 3)

Document 9

UN Commission on Human Rights: Resolution on East Timor, 49th Session, March 1993

The Commission on Human Rights, guided by the Universal Declaration of Human Rights, the International Covenants on Human Rights and the universally accepted rules of international law,

Bearing in mind the statement on the situation of human rights in East Timor as agreed by consensus by the Commission on Human Rights at its forty-eighth session (see E/CN-4/1992/84 para-457) following the violent incident of 12 November 1991 in Dili,

Recalling the resolution 1992/20 of 27 August 1992 of the Sub-Commission on Prevention of Discrimination and Protection of Minorities,

Gravely concerned at the continuing allegations of serious human violations and noting with concern in this context the reports of the Special Rapporteur on the question of torture (E/CN.4/1993/26), of the Special Rapporteur on extrajudicial, summary or arbitrary executions (E/CN.4/.1993/26) and of the Working Group on enforced or involuntary disappearances (E/CN/1993/25);

Bearing in mind the Body of Principles for the Protection of All Persons under Any Form of Detention or Imprisonment approved by the General Assembly in its Resolution 43/173 of 9 December 1988 and the Principles on the Effective Prevention and Investigation of Extra Legal and Arbitrary and Summary executions, endorsed by the General Assembly in its resolution 44/162 of 15 December 1989,

Taking note of the information that the Government of Indonesia has provided to the Commission on its actions its actions it has taken during the past year,

Welcoming the recent access to East Timor to human rights organisations as to some other relevant human rights observers, but remaining disappointed that such access is frequently denied,

Having examined the report of the Secretary-General on the situation in East Timor (E/CN.4/1993/49),

1. **Expresses** its deep concern at the reports of continuing rights violations in the territory of East Timor;

2. **Recalls** that the Commission has commended the decision of the Government of Indonesia to set up an inquiry Commission but regrets that the Indonesian investigation into the actions of the members of its security personnel on 12 November 1991, from which resulted in loss of life, injuries and disappearances, failed

to clearly identify those responsible for those actions,

3. **Expresses** its concern at the lack of clear information about the number of people killed on 12 November 1991 and at the persons still unaccounted for and urges the Government of Indonesia to account fully for those still missing since 12 November 1991;

4. **Regrets** the disparity in the severity of sentences on those civilians not indicted for violent activities who - should have been released without delay - on the one hand and to the military involved in the violent incident, on the other,

5. **Calls** upon the Government of Indonesia to honour fully its commitments undertaken in the statement on the situation of human rights in East Timor, agreed by consensus by the Commission on Human Rights at its 48th session;

6. **Calls** upon the Government of Indonesia to ensure that all the East Timorese in custody, including main public figures, be treated humanely and with their rights fully respected that all trials be fair, just, and recognise the right to proper legal representation, in accordance with international humanitarian law, and, those not involved in violent activities will be released without delay;

7. **Welcomes** the greater access recently granted by the Indonesian authorities to human rights organizations and additional human rights organizations and calls upon the Indonesian government to expand this further,

8. **Encourages** once again the Indonesian authorities to take the necessary steps to implement the recommendation presented by the Special Rapporteur on torture in its report (Doc. E/C. 4/1992/ 17/Add.1) following his visit to Indonesia and East Timor and to keep the Special Rapporteur informed of the progress made towards their implementation;

9. **Urges** the Government of Indonesia to invite the Special Rapporteur on Torture, the Special Rapporteur on extrajudicial, summary or arbitrary executions, the Working Group on Arbitrary Detention and the Working Group on Enforced or Involuntary Disappearances to visit East Timor and to facilitate the discharge of their mandates;

10. **Welcomes** the agreement given by the Government of Indonesia to the proposal of the Secretary General for a new visit to Indonesia and East Timor by his personal envoy in the coming months, and, invites the Secretary-General to consider transmitting the full report of Mr. Wako's previous and next visit to the Commission on Human Rights;

11. **Also** welcomes the resumption of talks about the question of East Timor and encourages the Secretary-General to con-

tinue his good offices for achieving a just, comprehensive and internationally acceptable settlement of the question of East Timor;

12. **Decides** to consider the situation in East Timor at its fiftieth session on the basis of the reports of the Special rapporteurs and Working Group's and that of the Secretary-General, which would include an analytical compilation of information received from, inter alia, Governments, intergovernmental and non-governmental organisations.

Document 10

UN Commission on Human Rights: 53rd session, Resolution 1997/63

E/CN.4/1997/L.96, 10 April 1997 (adopted 16 April 1997)

Situation of human rights in East Timor

The Commission on Human Rights,

Reaffirming that all Member States have an obligation to promote and protect human rights and fundamental freedoms as stated in the Charter of the United Nations and as elaborated in the Universal Declaration of Human Rights, the International Covenants on Human Rights and other applicable instruments,

Mindful that Indonesia is a party to the Convention on the Rights of the Child, the Convention on the Elimination of All Forms of Discrimination against Women and to the Geneva Conventions of 1949 on the protection of victims of war,

Recalling its resolution 1993/97 of 11 March 1993, and bearing in mind statements by the Chairman of the Commission on the situation of human rights on East Timor at its forty-eighth, fiftieth, fifty-first and fifty-second sessions,

1. Welcomes

(a) The report of the Secretary-General (E/CN.4/1997/51) and his recent nomination of a special representative;

(b) The continuing efforts of the Indonesian National Commission on Human Rights to investigate human rights violations, and its decision to establish an office in Dili, East Timor;

(c) The commitments by the Government of Indonesia to continue the dialogue under the auspices of the Secretary-General for achieving a just, comprehensive and internationally acceptable solution to the question of East Timor;

2. Expresses its deep concern

(a) At the continuing reports of violations of human rights in East Timor, including reports of extrajudicial killings, disappearances, torture and arbitrary detention as reported in the reports of the Special Rapporteur on torture (E/CN.4/1997/7), the Special Rapporteur on extrajudicial, summary or arbitrary executions (E/CN.4/1997/60), the Working Group on Arbitrary Detention (E/CN.4/1997/4 and Add.1) and the Working Group on Enforced or Involuntary Disappearances (E/CN.4/1997/34);

(b) At the lack of progress made by the Indonesian authorities towards complying with their commitments undertaken in statements agreed by consensus at previous sessions of the Commission;

(c) That the Government of

Indonesia has not yet invited thematic rapporteurs and working groups of the Commission to East Timor, in spite of commitments undertaken to do so in 1997;

(d) At the policy of systematic migration of persons to East Timor;

3. Calls upon the Government of Indonesia

(a) To take the necessary measures in order to ensure full respect for the human rights and fundamental freedoms of the people of East Timor;

(b) To ensure the early release of East Timorese detained or convicted for political reasons and to clarify further the circumstances surrounding the violent incident that took place in Dili in November 1991;

(c) To ensure that all East Timorese in custody are treated humanely and in accordance with international standards, and that all trials in East Timor are conducted in accordance with international standards;

(d) To cooperate fully with the Commission and its thematic rapporteurs and working groups and to invite these rapporteurs and working groups to visit East Timor, in particular the Special Rapporteur on torture, in line with the commitment undertaken to invite a thematic rapporteur in 1997;

(e) To undertake all necessary action in order to upgrade the memorandum of intent of 26 October 1994 on technical cooperation into the envisaged memorandum of understanding, and requests in this regard the United Nations High Commissioner for Human Rights to report on the follow-up to the memorandum of intent;

(f) To bring about the envisaged assignment of a programme officer of the Office of the United Nations High Commissioner for Human Rights at the Jakarta office of the United Nations Development Programme, as follow-up to the commitment undertaken, and to provide this officer with unhindered access to East Timor;

(g) To provide access to East Timor for human rights organizations;

4. Decides

(a) To consider the situation in East Timor at its fifty-fourth session under the agenda item entitled "Question of the violation of human rights and fundamental freedoms in any part of the world" on the basis of the reports of special rapporteurs and working groups and that of the Secretary-General;

(b) To encourage the Secretary-General to continue his good offices mission for achieving a just, comprehensive and internationally acceptable solution to the question of East Timor and in this framework to encourage the all-inclusive intra-East Timorese dialogue to continue under the auspices of the United Nations.

Document 11

UNITED NATIONS
Economic and Social Council
Distr.
GENERAL
E/CN.4/1997/51
21 February 1997
Original: ENGLISH

COMMISSION ON HUMAN
RIGHTS
Fifty third session
Item 10 of the provisional
agenda

QUESTION OF THE VIOLA-
TION OF HUMAN RIGHTS
AND FUNDAMENTAL
FREEDOMS IN ANY PART
OF THE WORLD, WITH
PARTICULAR REFERENCE
TO COLONIAL AND OTHER
DEPENDENT COUNTRIES
AND TERRITORIES

Situation in East Timor
Report of the Secretary-General

CONTENTS
Paragraphs
Introduction.................
I. Update on the good offices activities of the Secretary-General concerning the question of East Timor.................
II. Actions taken by the thematic rapporteurs and working groups of the Commission on Human Rights concerning East Timor.........
Annexes [not included here]
I. Information provided by the Government of Indonesia
II. Information provided by the Government of Portugal
III. Material provided by non governmental sources

Introduction

1. At its fifty-second session, the Chairman of the Commission on Human Rights made a statement on 23 April 1996, agreed by consensus, on the situation of human rights in East Timor (E/1996/23-E/CN.4/1996/177, para.370). In that statement, the Commission, inter alia, welcomed the intention of the Government of Indonesia to continue to cooperate with the Commission on Human Rights and its mechanisms as well as its intention to invite a thematic rapporteur in 1997. It encouraged the Secretary-General to continue his good offices in order to achieve a just, comprehensive and internationally acceptable solution to the question of East Timor, and requested the Secretary-General to keep it informed on the situation of human rights in East Timor, which it would consider at its fifty-third session.

2. The present report has been prepared in response to the request contained in the above-mentioned statement.

3. Section I of the report contains an update on the good offices activities of the Secretary-

General concerning the question of East Timor; section II contains a summarized description of action taken by various thematic special rapporteurs and working groups of the Commission. Annex I of the report contains information provided by the Government of Indonesia; annex II contains information provided by the Government of Portugal; annex III contains a summary of reports and other pertinent material provided by non-governmental sources.

4. The attention of the Commission on Human Rights is also drawn to the progress report of the Secretary-General on the question of East Timor (A/51/361) of 16 September 1996 in which he refers to the talks held between the Governments of Indonesia and Portugal in the framework of his continuing good offices.

I. UPDATE ON THE GOOD OFFICES ACTIVITIES OF THE SECRETARY-GENERAL CONCERNING THE QUESTION OF EAST TIMOR

5. In the past year, the Secretary-General has continued his good offices aimed at finding a just, comprehesive and internationally acceptable solution to the question of East Timor. He held an eighth round of discussions with Foreign Ministers Ali Alatas of Indonesia and Jaime Gama of Portugal in Geneva on 27 June 1996. This had been preceded by preparatory meetings in New York between the Permanent Representatives of the two Governments, led by the Secretary-General's Special Adviser, Mr. Ismat Kittani, which were also continued in Geneva in the days preceding the ministerial meeting.

6. The Foreign Ministers discussed in greater detail the substantive issues related to an eventual framework for a solution to the question of East Timor.

At the conclusion of the meeting, the Foreign Ministers and the Secretary-General agreed that the discussions should continue at the level of the Permanent Representatives in New York through his Special Adviser and to hold a ninth round of talks on 21 December 1996 in New York. While the contacts with the two sides continued in subsequent months, various matters not directly related to the issue obstructed the preparatory meetings required for the ministerial talks. Consequently, at the suggestion of the Secretary-General, the ninth round of ministerial talks was postponed to a later date.

7. The new Secretary-General, Mr. Kofi Annan, has been in touch with the two Governments and has expressed his desire to give a new impetus to his good offices. On 12 February, he announced the appointment of Mr. Jamsheed Marker (Pakistan) as his Personal Representative for

East Timor. The Secretary-General will remain personally engaged in the efforts to find a solution to the problem while the Personal Representative will represent him in all aspects of his good offices function, including the talks between the two Governments and the consultations that the Secretary-General conducts with a cross-section of East Timorese society. Mr. Marker has begun consultations with the two Governments and intends shortly to follow up the Secretary-Genera'ls desire to give new momentum to these efforts.

8. With the agreement of the two Governments, the Secretary-General facilitated a second meeting of the All-inclusive Intra-East Timorese Dialogue (AIETD) from 19 to 22 March 1996 at Burg Schlaining, Austria. The meeting, which was held under the same terms of reference as the first one, held in June 1995, adopted the "Burg Sclaining Declaration–1996 II, in which the participants, inter alia, expressed their desire to continue the Dialogue and reaffirmed "the need to implement the necessary measures in the field of human rights … including the protection of women … ". The Foreign Ministers of Indonesia and Portugal considered the Declaration at their eighth round of talks in June 1996 and agreed to have further consultations on the proposals of the AIETD relating to the estab-lishment of an East Timorese cultural centre in Dili and to the development of East Timor's human resources. They also "took note positively" of the Secretary-General's intention to facilitate another meeting of the AIETD, under the same terms of reference as the two first meetings.

II. ACTIONS TAKEN BY THEMATIC SPECIAL RAPPORTEURS AND WORKING GROUPS OF THE COMMISSION ON HUMAN RIGHTS CONCERNING EAST TIMOR

Special Rapporteur on the question of torture

9. Information regarding the action taken by the Special Rapporteur on torture with regard to East Timor is described in his report to the Commission (see E/CN.4/1997/7, paras. 91-111 and E/CN.4/1997/7/Add.1, paras. 2 09-241)

10. During 1996 the Special Rapporteur transmitted to the Government of Indonesia 12 cases of East Timorese reported to have been tortured and sent three urgent appeals on behalf of individuals or groups regarding whom fears were expressed that they might be subjected to torture. The Government replied to all these cases stating basically that the allegations or fears were unfounded.

11. The Special Rapporteur

also included in his report information about his two-day visit to Lisbon, at the invitation by the Portuguese Government, in order to meet a number of East Timorese residing in Portugal who had allegedly been tortured by Indonesian security forces prior to leaving their country. The Special Rapporteur indicated that he had decided to accept the invitation partly due to the fact that the Government of Indonesia had replied negatively (at least until spring 1997) to his request for a visit to Indonesia and East Timor, and therefore the visit to Portugal was an opportunity for him to obtain first-hand information that would help him to assess the situation regrding the use of torture against East Timorese. The report also included summaries of the general allegations received from nongovernmental organizations, the oral accounts of torture he received from the alleged victims and the Government's replies to them, as well as its comments on the invitation by the Government of Portugal to the Special Rapporteur.

Working Group on Arbitrary Detention

12. The Working Group adopted decision No. 36/1996 regarding a number of East Timorese in detention. The text of the decision, which declares the detention of one person to be arbitrary, is included in the report of the Working Group (E/CN.4/1997/4/Add.1).

Working Group on Enforced or Involuntary Disappearances

13. Information regarding the action taken by the Working Group with regard to East Timor is included in its report to the Commission (E/CN.4/1997/34, paras. 190-195). According to the Working Group, between November 1995 and November 1996 it transmitted nine newly reported cases of disappearance to the Indonesian Government. Despite the government responses the cases remained unclarified. The Group also pointed out that it had in its files a total of 378 cases that had not yet been clarified.

Special Rapporteur on extrajudicial, summary or arbitrary executions.

14. Information regarding the action taken by the Special Rapporteur with regard to East Timor is described in his report to the Commission (E/CN.4/1997/60/Add.1, paras. 231-247). The Special Rapporteur again indicated that he never received any reaction from the Government to the report he had prepared following his visit to East Timor in 1994.

Document 12

**Commission on Human Rights
53rd session, Agenda item 10**

**Statement by José Ramos-Horta,
1996 Nobel Peace Prize co-
Laureate, on behalf of
International Service for Human
Rights, Pax Christi International
and the Movement Against
Racism and for Friendship Among
Peoples, Geneva, 7 April 1997**

Mr. President: I thank you for giving me the floor.

As I speak before you today, I pay tribute to the memory of thousands of people who died in prison, torture chambers and streets in the hands of dictators. Their sacrifice has contributed immensely to the progress in the international awareness about human rights and in the UN protection mechanisms.

The Nobel Peace Prize attributed to my compatriot and good friend, Bishop Carlos Filipe Ximenes Belo, and myself, was a tribute to all those individuals and organisations struggling for the human rights and self-determination of peoples all over the world.

The presence every year in Geneva of hundreds of human rights defenders and victims is an evidence of the extremely serious human rights situations in many parts of the world, but also of the illusions and hope of many that there are some international legal remedies available to them.

Hence a major responsibility entrusted to the states to live up to their own obligations to uphold the principles enshrined in the numerous international human rights instruments. If the international community fails to hear the voices and grievances of the poor and the persecuted, there is a real danger that the entire UN and state-based human rights systems might become totally irrelevant. The consequences would be disastrous.

I must also pay tribute to those in government who over the years have done their best for the cause of human rights and resisted the easy temptation of pragmatism and realpolitik.

I do believe that NGOs and governments can work together. Indeed, only a strategic partnership between the NGOs and democratic governments of the North and South will advance the agenda for human rights and democracy.

The roots of the human rights violations in East Timor: the denial of the right to self-determination

The human rights situation in East Timor is intimately linked to the denial of the right of the people of East Timor self-determination. Therefore, allow me, Mr. President, to elaborate on this fundamental human right.

The UN General Assembly

and Security Council have adopted a total of 10 resolutions on the question of East Timor all reaffirming the right to self-determination. In its ruling of 30 June 1995 on the Case Concerning East Timor, Portugal Vs Australia, the International Court of Justice stated that this right has an *erga omnes* character and that the East Timorese were entitled to it.

The current boundary of the Republic of Indonesia is a product of the Dutch East Indies administration. West New Guinea was absorbed by the Republic not because of any valid historical, cultural, ethnic kinship or geographic continuity.

The only link that justified its forcible annexation was West New Guinea's brief colonisation by the Dutch.

A strict respect for the colonial boundaries, as unfair as most might be, has provided some peace and stability and kept most of Africa, Latin America and Asia from disintegrating.

There is genuine fear and suspicion among many states that self-determination leads to the break-up of the nation states. However, this is unfounded. While the de-colonisation process of the non-self-governing territories almost always led to independence, this is not the case in most claims today.

I understand the legitimate concerns of countries in preserving their national unity and territorial integrity. Many developing countries, Indonesia being a prime example, experienced a traumatic nation-building process with numerous attempts from within and without to undermine the unity of the state.

I do not hold the view that an independent state has to be homogenous, ethnically, culturally or religiously. Examples abound of multi-ethnic states that live in peace, based on shared concerns and destiny, on a degree of genuine political and administrative autonomy for each component, and of deep respect for each others heritage and aspirations.

A pattern of gross and systematic violation of human rights

More than two decades after the invasion, the conflict in East Timor remains unresolved.

The massacre of 271 Timorese civilians in Dili on 12 November 1991 was not an isolated incident. It followed a well documented pattern of gross and systematic human rights abuses in many parts of East Timor perpetrated by the members of the Indonesian armed forces.

The highest ranking officers in the Indonesian army had full knowledge of, and took active part in these atrocities. These violations are continuing today. Bishop Carlos Filipe Ximenes Belo, head of the Diocese of Dili, 1996 Nobel Peace Prize co-Laureate, stated in a recent message addressed to this Commission dated 21 March 1997. I quote:

... prisoners are tortured, slapped around, kicked and punched. They are plunged into water tanks, burnt with cigarettes. The families of suspected youths know no peace at night: their houses are searched in the middle of the night, are showered with stones. Individuals are humiliated.

The arrogance and brutality of the Indonesian army have been once again demonstrated when on 23 March 1997 a peaceful assembly was fired on by the army. During a visit to East Timor by the Secretary-General's Personal resentative, Ambassador Jamsheed Marker of Pakistan, a group of 250 East Timorese students went to hotel Makota in Dili to deliver a petition to Mr. Marker.

While most of the students stayed outside, a small delegation entered the hotel at about 7AM requesting to see Ambassador Marker. They were met by an aide to Mr. Marker who received the petition. Suddenly, Indonesian troops and police opened fire on the students inside the hotel. Bayonet and batons were also used against them.

We now have evidence that four students were killed and at least 20 were seriously injured.

In Jakarta a group of 30 East Timorese students entered the Austrian Embassy on March 25.

They demanded to see the UN Special Envoy. They were all arrested, questioned and subsequently released. However, two were murdered soon after their release the very same day.

I have with me photographic evidence of the Indonesian army's recent brutality. This happened right under the nose of the Special Representative of the Secretary-General. You can then imagine what is the daily life of the East Timorese under military occupation in one of the most isolated regions of the world.

I shall not elaborate any further on this and on the so many other cases of senseless killing in East Timor. The Special Rapporteur on Extra-judicial, summary or arbitrary executions, Mr. Bacre Waly Ndiaye, of Senegal, a much more authoritative person than I, has detailed at length the circumstances surrounding the 12 November 1991 massacre in Dili, as well as a pattern of widespread abuses.

His report was preceded by an earlier one, that of the Special Rapporteur on Torture, Prof. Peter Kooijman, of the Netherlands, who happened to be in Dili on 12 November 1991.

The US State Department 1996 report devotes a large section on the human rights situation in East Timor and I commend it for the honest effort in presenting the tragic reality in the territory as it is.

Mr. President:

Time and again the Indonesian government has levelled attacks against the FRETILIN movement and accused it of crimes that occurred in August 1975 during a brief but violent civil war in which this organization was involved with another East Timorese group, the União Democratica Timorese (UDT).

On more than one occasion, the FRETILIN leadership has accepted responsibilities for the violence and deaths of innocent people which occurred during the period August-December 1975. A crime is a crime and there is no acceptable intellectual or political justification for it.

The FRETILIN leadership has repeatedly called for an international investigation into the events that took place between August and December 1975 to ascertain the responsibilities of all parties during that period, and into the 22 years of Indonesian occupation after December 1975.

I urge the Indonesian government to show its good faith by accepting this challenge.

The East Timorese resistance leadership has stated its solemn commitment to uphold international human rights standards when the country is free.

In an independent East Timor, all international human rights treaties will be submitted to the Parliament for ratification. We believe that human rights transcend boundaries and prevail over state sovereignty.

We will seek the co-operation of UN human rights agencies as well as NGOs to assist us in our efforts to promote respect for human rights and the rule of law in our country. East Timorese now serving in the Indonesian administration in East Timor, the security forces and police will be invited to stay on as their full and active involvement in running the country will be necessary to insure a smooth transition. On day one of independence, we will proclaim a general amnesty and national reconciliation.

Our society will not be based on hatred and revenge.

Because of its credibility and standing over the past twenty years, the Catholic Church will be expected to play a major role in the healing process of our society.

Our people are fortunate to have outstanding leaders, Xanana Gusmão as the political leader, and Bishops Carlos Filipe Ximenes Belo and Basilio de Nascimento, as the spiritual leaders, whose combined moral authority and vision will guarantee that the people of East Timor will heal the wounds of the war and embrace each other and their neighbours.

Human rights and Asian values

The movement for democracy, human rights and rule of law is irreversible. Even in our tortured region, Asia, unprecedented events are taking place.

The overthrow of the dictatorship in South Korea is of enormous significance for democracy and the rule of law in the entire Asia region. The brave people of Korea who endured decades of dictatorship won the struggle for democracy not with guns but peacefully confronting the troops in the streets of Seoul and Kwangju.

For the first time in the history of Asia, former heads of states and other leaders are being prosecuted for their crimes whilst in office. The people of South Korea are challenging the impunity of public office and the sacrosanct myth of national security interest which allows leaders to imprison, torture and murder with impunity.

The situation in Burma demands action beyond the annual ritual of the UN General Assembly and CHR resolutions.

While I commend the US, EU and Norway for the moral stance they have taken and the modest punitive sanctions adopted so far, new initiatives must be pursued.

The military junta in Burma which defrauded the Burmese people and the international community should be denied a seat in the UN General Assembly, as the South African apartheid regime was denied a seat in the past.

In the late 70's, the ASEAN countries, supported by the US,

also succeeded in blocking recognition of the government installed in Phnom Penh after the Vietnamese intervention in 1978.

If the international community wishes to move beyond rhetoric and send a clear signal to the SLORC, the denial of its credentials by the GA Credentials Committee is one course of action to be considered.

The peoples of the Chittagong Hilltrack in Bangladesh, of Bougainville, Burma, Thailand, Tibet, the Philippines, South Korea, Assam and Nagaland in India, the democracy movements in China and Indonesia, the Ogoni people in Nigeria are telling the rest of the world that the struggle for democracy and human rights is not an invention of the West or of Western NGOs.

Throughout the sixties and seventies, we heard in this very room the argument that human rights and fundamental freedoms were a Western concept which stood against the collective rights espoused by the communist bloc.

The Stalinist regimes of Eastern and Central Europe led by the USSR attempted to derail the UN human rights bodies by injecting ideology into the human rights debate. Ironically with the collapse of the communist bloc this argument has been appropriated by the certain Asian regimes.

Countries in all parts of the world, Argentina, Brazil, Chile, Costa Rica in Latin America, or

South Africa, Mozambique, Cape Verde, Botswana in Africa, or the Philippines, Malaysia, Thailand, South Korea in Asia stand out as living proof that human rights, fundamental freedoms, rule of law and democracy are universal values, they go hand in hand with economic development.

Tens of thousands of Argentineans, Brazilians, Chileans, Uruguayans, Paraguayans, Guatemalans, South Africans and Filippinos were tortured, killed or exiled. Their sacrifice has not been in vain.

Although there are still some extremely serious human rights situations in Latin America today that continent is a shining example of pluralism, democracy and economic progress.

No other country has endured more pain and humiliation than South Africa. Yet South Africa is today a model of tolerance, reconciliation and democracy for the rest of world. South African blacks, whites, Asians and mixed race are telling the rest of the world that human rights are universal, colour blind, and know no geographic boundaries.

Human rights violations must be forcefully denounced no matter where and how they occur, there must be caution in addressing the often complex political situations in certain regions and countries.

I believe that a grave injustice has been committed against the people of Kashmir in India and the Tamils in Sri Lanka, and that the international community must seriously address these conflicts. However, the responsibility for these problems cannot be assigned only to the Indian and Sri Lanka governments, respectively.

There are other parties that must share the blame for the human rights violations taking place there and they must make a commitment in co-operating towards bringing about a peaceful resolution of these two conflicts.

The massacre of the Armenian people by the Ottoman empire, the Jewish holocaust, the wanton killing of the gypsies by the Nazis and the genocide of indigenous peoples in so many regions of the world, stand out as the most barbaric and shameful chapters of human history. Unfortunately, humanity has allowed similar crimes to continue till this very day.

The rights of Indigenous peoples

With regards to the violation of human rights and fundamental freedoms of the world's indigenous people a number of concrete actions can immediately be taken by the Commission on Human Rights: support the matters addressed in Item 24, Indigenous issues, acknowledge the link between the human rights problems and historical, ongoing depravation of ancestral rights over their land.

Moreover, the indigenous peoples are calling for their right to full and direct participation within the UN, and in particular processes which directly affect their rights, lives and destinies.

I would like to express my support for the creation of a Permanent Forum for indigenous peoples within the UN. A declaration to protect their rights should be adopted, and this should be done before the Decade of the World's Indigenous People is over. However, this declaration should not contain any definition of the term indigenous peoples, as this matter is an important aspect of the right to self-determination, which should not be prescribed or limited.

Justice Robert Jackson, Chief Prosecutor of the Nuremberg War Crime Tribunals, said:

The wrongs which we seek to condemn and punish have been so calculated, so malignant and so devastating, that civilisation cannot tolerate their being ignored, because it cannot survive their being repeated.

The continuing persecution of the Kurds and the denial of their rights, the slaughter of more than one million peasants and Chinese merchants by the Suharto regime in Indonesia in 1965-66, the mass killings perpetrated by the Pol Pot regime on the Cambodian people, the tragedy in the Great Lakes region, the barbaric violence inflicted on the East Timorese and the peoples of West Papua, Moslems of Aceh, indigenous peoples of Kalimantan, Sulawesi and the Moluccas, the repression of Palestinian rights are an indictment of the entire international community.

These crimes are continuing because those in government allow them to happen. The Jewish holocaust happened because the powers that be at the time chose pragmatism and appeasement over moral leadership and humanity. The defenceless Jews were a mere footnote to the apologists of realpolitik and pragmatism in their pursuit of appeasement towards Hitler.

Mr. President, your country is free today. You have an outstanding individual as Head of State. Vaclav Havel spent years in prison as did tens of thousands of others in Central and Eastern Europe, in the Baltic States, in the Russian gulags.

As did Nelson Mandela. As Daw Aung San Suu Kyi today. As my leader and brother, Xanana Gusmão, who is now serving an unjust prison sentence in Indonesia for the same crime, the crime of wanting freedom.

On this note, I will end with renewed hope that no matter the level of brute force used against us, our dreams will never die.

Document 13

Statement from Xanana Gusmão, head of the National Council of Maubere Resistance, to the U.N. Decolonization Committee in New York, July 27, 1992. Translated from the Portuguese and delivered by José Ramos-Horta, External Spokesman, CNRM.

EAST TIMOR NATIONAL COUNCIL OF MAUBERE RESISTANCE NATIONAL LIBERATION ARMED FORCES OF EAST TIMOR

Mr. Chairman,

Distinguished members of the Special Committee on Decolonization:

I have the honor to address this Committee on behalf of the people of East Timor.

It is with faith that I am addressing this prestigious United Nations body in the current international context. I believe it to be appropriate to note that so many independent States were born in the shadows of the principles that are embodied in this Committee. These are the same principles that are inspiring the birth of new states in the old Continent.

This Committee took upon itself the task of eradicating colonialism by the Year 2,000. With this promising vision the Special Committee on Decolonization asserts itself as the guardian of the hopes and aspirations of the peoples still under a backward system of domination.

In the decades that crowned the struggles for national liberation, this Committee was the forum for the defence of the international rights of the colonial countries and peoples. These historical achievements are our source of faith and hope and this is even more so with the approaching end of colonialism from the face of the Earth.

Mr. Chairman,

Distinguished members of the Special Committee on Decolonization:

With the inclusion of East Timor in 1960 on the UNGA List of Non Self-Governing Territories, this committee undertook total responsibility to see to it that the principles embodied in the Charter are fully applied to this territory.

In the history of the struggle against colonial expansionism, the oppressed peoples were always left with no alternative but to resort to violence to assert their rights in the face of the arrogant use of force by the colonizers. This is what happened to us when we were brutally invaded on 7 December 1975. Till this very day we are resisting the Indonesian criminal military occupation by all means available to us, including armed resistance.

However, we are in the midst of a historical whirlwind, underscored by political changes in various latitudes. Terrorist states have seen their very foundation smoldered by the democratic conscience of their citizens.

Totalitarian regimes are now on the path towards the full respect fo fundamental freedoms. Dictatorships in the Third World, installed by the West, are being overthrown in the face of popular protests. Humanity is indeed on the road towards a New World Order.

We have to continue to build a New World Order that is based on the elimination of all the evils that affect so many regions of this planet.

This Committee, with only eight years ahead before the Year 2,000, has the daunting task of sweeping from the face of the Earth all the manifestations of colonialism.

Regrettably, some Member States use double standards on identical situations, namely, East Timor and Kuwait. In spite of this, I am certain, the Special Committee on Decolonization will not betray the sacred principles that gave birth to it. We are also certain that in dealing with the question of East Timor it will be guided by International Law and all the relevant norms on self-determination and independence.

We are certain that East Timor will not be an exception in the decolonization process. Indonesia, a member of this august body, used it in the past as a forum to denounce Portuguese colonialism. Now again it is using this Committee as a forum to defend its own colonial aggression, annexation and military occupation of East Timor in complete disregard for the relevant Security Council Resolutions 384 (1975) and 389 (1976).

Mr. Chairman,

Distinguished members of the Committee:

It was only yesterday, so to speak, that the world was divided into two major military blocs, led by the U.S. and the U.S.S.R., both sides using at will the veto power to preserve their respective spheres of influence.

We note with consternation that even after the dismantling of the old Soviet empire and the communist bloc, the West continues to make use of its veto power whenever just causes affect their economic interests.

The sanctions against Iraq seemed to suggest that gone is the taboo of state sovereignty and domestic jurisdiction; the measures adopted against Libya seem to suggest that the universal concept of justice should breach national boundaries when it comes to the application of universal princi- ples; the Security Council resolu- tions on Yugoslavia seem to sug- gest that it now belongs to the past the notion that only the powerful and rich could determine the fate of peoples and that the universal principles of self-determination should prevail in tme, in all lati- tudes and in all circumstances.

More than 200,000 dead and a continuing practice of persecu- tion, imprisonment and massacres are the balance of more than 16 years of our resistance to Indone- sia's military occupation of our country.

The 12 November 1991 mas- sacre of East Timorese civilians jolted the international con- science. Some governments, even though accomplices in the physi- cal, ethnic and cultural genocide of our people, were not able not able to hide their horror in the face of the Santa Cruz massacre. However, a few months have elapsed, and their conscience slipped back to business as usual.

Much has been said about the 12 November 1991 massacre and the images of the massacre re- vealed the nature of the annexa- tion of East Timor. 12 November underscored the historical fact that people's nationalism cannot be liquidated by repression, nor

can it be alienated by so-called economic development. Namibia emerged as an independent state 40 years later. Small and large independent states whose right to self-determination and independ- ence were denied blossomed 40 years later.

The referenda in the Baltic States were a model in conflict resolution. The world is shocked by the armed conflicts in Yugo- slavia and Armenia. However, the international community is only harvesting the fruits of historical mistakes perpetrated by oppres- sive regimes that assaulted human conscience and regarded their fel- low beings as mere pawns of the ambitions of the economic oligar- chy to which they belonged.

A referendum process is now in preparation in Western Sahara. We are perplexed by the news that Indonesia reportedly offered a contingent to participate in the UN multinational force in West- ern Sahara.

Mr. Chairman,

Distinguished members of the Committee:

Indonesia claims that the peo- ple of East Timor have already chosen integration by "free will". If this is the case, then why so many restrictions in East Timor? If this is so, why does it, fear a ratification of the act under inter- national supervision? if this is so, why did it create so many obstacles that aborted the projected Portuguese Parliamentary Mission to East Timor? Why did Indonesia close the territory following the 12 November massacre? Why are foreign visitors subjected to pro-Indonesia criteria? Why does East Timor remains closed to international humanitarian organizations?

Why all this if the people of East Timor chose by its free will integration with Indonesia? Why all this if, according to the Indonesian generals, only a few "marginal" continue to think about independence?

The new democracies, conscious that they are part of the community of nations, have shown political good will by inviting international supervision of their inaugural electoral processes. Why does the international community allow East Timor to remain a large prison? Is it because the people of East Timor wanted their island to be a prison?

Mr. Chairman,

Distinguished Members of the Special Committee on Decolonization:

I believe that in regard to East Timor, there are three fundamental resolutions that should be taken into consideration:

a. Security Council Res. 384 of 22 December 1975 and 389 of 26 April 1976 which, inter alia, reaffirm:

"the inalienable right of the people of East Timor to self-determination and independence in accordance with the principles of the United Nations Charter and the Declaration on the Granting of Independence to Colonial Countries and Peoples contained in General Assembly Res. 1514 (XV) of 14 December 1960".

The above-mentioned resolutions called 'on all States to respect the territorial integrity of East Timor as well as the inalienable right of its people to Self-determination in accordance with GA Res. 1514 (XV); and the government of Indonesia to withdraw without delay all its forces from the territory".

The Security Council finally called upon "all states and all interested parties to cooperate fully with the United Nations in its efforts to finding a peaceful solution to the prevailing situation and to facilitate the decolonization of the territory".

b. Yearly resolutions between 1975 and 1981 met with the indifference of the international community which in turn served only to encourage inflexibility on the part of Indonesia. In 1982, the General Assembly adopted Res. 37/30 which states and I quote:

"Recognizing the inalienable right of all peoples to self-determination and independence in accordance with the United Nations Charter and the Declaration on the Granting of Independence to Colonial Countries and Peoples, contained in Res. 1514 (XV) of the General Assembly, of 14 December 1960,

"Requests the Secretary-General to initiate consultations with all parties directly concerned with a view to exploring the avenues for achieving a comprehensive settlement of the problem and to report thereon to the General Assembly at its 38th session".

Mr. Chairman,

Any solution to the problem of East Timor must be based on the respect for the expressed will of the people of East Timor. We are conscious of the fact that it is particularly difficult for the government of Indonesia a solution that put in question the fundamental interests of the Indonesian state, but we cannot abdicate from our own interests and rights.

Dialogue is the means to solve conflicts. This is the trend in today's world. Indonesia herself continues to play an important role in the resolution of the Cambodian conflict. The whole argument of "internal affair" has been invoked time and again by the powerful. We witnessed it in the Gulf. What is happening in Yugoslavia, now focus of peace-making efforts by the UN and the EC, exposes the arrogance of those who continue to create obstacles to the peaceful resolution of conlicts.

Dialogue without pre-conditions preserves the mutual interests of the parties to the conflict. Both Portugal and the Maubere People are ready for dialogue. However, the government of Indonesia, enjoying the status as benefactor of Western economic and financial largesse, feels strong enough to reject the inclusion of the East Timorese themselves in the peace talks. We continue to invite Indonesia to round-table talks and we reaffirm our political will in endeavoring to find the best way to balance the interests of all parties to the conflict.

Portugal, the Administering power recognized by the UN, stands for a process of dialogue with the inclusion of the East Timorese, without pre-conditions.

Our flexibility regarding the involvement of the East Timorese aims at helping Portugal face the negotiation process seriously. It is the role of Portugal, legal Administering power of East Timor, in the context of its responsibilities, to work with the East Timorese towards finding formulas that might lead towards a comprehensive and lasting solution.

The Special Representative of the National Council of Maubere Resistance, Mr. José Ramos-Horta, conceived and outlined a set of key-ideas with a view to contributing to a solution. I wish to elaborate on this plan. Three elements emerge from this plan:

a. An extremely important element to emphasise, without any doubt, is the fact that the territory remains under UN responsibility until a final solution of the problem;

b. Concerning the Portuguese role in the process, I believe that the role of Portugal has to be seen in the context of its commitment to engage in dialogue with Indonesia. Its role in the whole peace process is vital.

c. In accepting a transition situation and recognizing that a "de facto" situation exists in East Timor (Namibia was under South African domination and yet the UN did not relinquish its responsibilities), we wish to create favorable political conditions so that through democratic means and in a peaceful climate each party may persuade the people about the advantages of its policies. An act of self-determination, as the result and goal of this transition period, would be the true political act of free choice by our people.

I reaffirm our collective political will to abide by the popular verdict if the Mauere people, under international supervision, decide to opt for integration with the Republic of Indonesia.

We do not fight against Indonesia, we are not fighting against the people of Indonesia. We respect the great Indonesian nation, we respect our Indonesian brothers.

In an independent East Timor we will strive to have privileged relations of friendship and cooperation between our two peoples; we will strive to promote the instruments of bilateral and regional cooperation in the framework of ASEAN. We will spare no effort to enhance ASEAN and its role in promoting political and economic cooperation as well as promoting the region as a zone of peace and prosperity.

An independent East Timor will seek membership with the South Pacific Forum. We share the same aspirations with the small island-states of the Pacific and we will strive to foster cooperation for the benefit of our peoples.

An independent East Timor will reject the existence of armed forces as our real contribution towards regional and world peace. We oppose militarization because we are against armed conflicts. We oppose militarization because as part of the Humanity that desires peace we do not fear our powerful neighbors. We oppose militarization because we believe the conscience of mankind opts for dialogue to resolve differences. If dialogue means democratic practice, if, above all, it is a concept of justice, if dialogue means respect for fundamental rights and freedoms of peoples, we are then against the use of force, we are against war, we are against oppression.

We are convinced that if all share the same convictions, Southeast Asia could become a model in the new world we all wish to build.

We hope that the Indonesian leaders understand our message of peace, our gesture of reconciliation and that our resistance is not aimed at the Indonesian state or people. In equal circumstances of rights and obligations we will know how to honor the friendship of the great Indonesian nation may offer us.

We appeal to the Special Committee on Decolonization to spare no effort to see to it that the UN relevant resolutions on East Timor are fully implemented.

Headquarters of the National Council of Maubere Resistance, in East Timor, 20 June 1992.

For the CNRM,
Kayrala Xanana Gusmão
Commandante das FALINTIL

Document 14

United Nations General Assembly A/AC.109/2026 22 June 1995: Original: English (full text)

SPECIAL COMMITTEE ON THE SITUATION WITH RE-GARD TO THE IMPLEMENTA-TION OF THE DECLARATION ON THE GRANTING OF INDE-PENDENCE TO COLONIAL COUNTRIES AND PEOPLES

EAST TIMOR

Working paper prepared by the Secretariat

I. GENERAL

1. The Territory of East Timor comprises the eastern part of the island of Timor, which is located at the top of the chain of islands forming the Republic of Indonesia; the enclave of Oecusse Ambeno; the island of Atauro, off the northern coast of Timor; and the island of Jaco, off its extreme eastern tip. It lies between latitudes 8 17'S and 10 22'S and longitudes 123 25'E and 127 19'E. The 1980 census recorded the total population of the Territory at 555,350. According to the latest estimates, as of 1993, the population of the Territory was

783,000 (ST/ESA/STAT/SER.A/ 193).

II. POLITICAL DEVELOP-MENTS

A. Background

2. According to Indonesian Law 7/76 of 17 July 1976, East Timor is a province or a "first-level region" of Indonesia with a Government consisting of a "Regional Secretariat" and a "Regional House of Representatives". East Timor is represented in the National House of Representatives and in the People's Consultative Assembly of Indonesia.

3. In its resolution 32/34 of 28 November 1977, the General Assembly rejected the claim that East Timor had been integrated into Indonesia, inasmuch as the people of the Territory had not been able to exercise freely their right to self-determination and independence.

B. Recent developments

4. According to press reports, on 14 July 1994, a group of East Timorese students held a march in Dili to protest the alleged "Islamization" of the Territory, The Indonesian police dispersed the demonstrators, injuring some 20 persons. Published reports also indicate that two participants were arrested and tortured by the

military. Monsignor Belo, the Catholic Bishop of East Timor, stated in connection with the incident that the problem of East Timor would be resolved only after the Indonesian military had withdrawn from the Territory. He also expressed concerns over the distribution in East Timor of pamphlets containing calls for the "Islamization" of the population and warned against possible religious clashes. The Foreign minister of Indonesia, in. connection with the events of 14 July, reportedly refuted allegations of religious intolerance and police brutality. (1) However, the Permanent Mission of Indonesia to the United Nations described the above incident as follows:

"On 14 July 1994, a few East Timorese students held a protest against rude behaviour of two low-ranking soldiers who allegedly indulged in insulting behaviour against the Santo Yoseph Remexio church. In connection with this incident, the local military commander, Col. Johnny J. Lumintang, apologized to the Catholics in East Timor. The Dili District Court tried the two accused individuals and they were sentenced to prison and dismissed from the armed forces."

5. Press reports indicate that at the end of July 1994, six Indonesian soldiers were killed during clashes with East Timorese guer-rillas near Laleia, approximately 70 kilometres from Dili. (2)

6. According to press reports, on 1 August 1994, the Indonesian military barred protests and demonstrations in East Timor in connection with a visit to the Territory by a group of Japanese lawmakers and journalists. (3) The Permanent Mission of Indonesia to the United Nations noted in that connection that in addition to a group of Japanese lawmakers and journalists, the following personalities have visited East Timor during 1994:

Five members of the Japanese Diet, consisting of two MPs from the Liberal Democratic Party, two MPs from the Social Democratic Party and one from the New Party, from 10 to 13 August 1994. They were accompanied by two journalists from the NHK and two journalists from Asahi TV; Mr. Gerhart Baum, a Member of Parliament of the Federal Republic of Germany and Former Minister for Home Affairs, accompanied by Mr. Wolfgang Sachsenroder, Head of the Regional Office of the Friedrich Naumann Foundation for South-East Asia and East Asia, on 12 and 13 August 1994; Six staff members of the United States Congress from 21 to 28 August 1994; Six members of the Anglo-Indonesian Parliamentary Group, consisting of three MPs from the Conservative Party and three MPs from the Ulster Unionists from 18 to 20 September

1994; A delegation of four members of the Australian Parliament, consisting of two Liberal Party MPs, one Labor Party MP and one secretary, from 25 September to 1 October 1994; Five Members of the New Zealand Parliament, consisting of two MPs from the National Party, two MPs from the Labour Party and one MP from the First New Zealand Party, from 29 October to 1 November 1994; Approximately 40 foreign journalists attending the APEC meeting in November 1994, including one Portuguese journalist; Special envoys of the United Nations Secretary-General, Mr. Francesc Vendrell and Mr. Tamrat Samuel, from 30 November to 3 December 1994.

7. On 25 August, Bishop Belo inaugurated in East Timor a Commission on Peace and Justice. It was expected that the commission would have offices in 13 towns, 63 districts and 442 villages throughout the Territory. The Commission, according to Bishop Belo, "aims at learning about and analysing problems related to justice and peace ... to help people fully understand their role and function in the fields of justice, peace and human rights". (4)

8. In August 1994, the Indonesian Government reportedly announced its intention to relocate some 1,000 Catholic families from Java and Bali to East Timor. That decision reportedly was taken within the framework of the Indonesian "transmigration programme". (5)

9. According to press reports, on 11 September 1994, the Indonesian military arrested two members of the Frente Revolucionaria de Timor Leste Independente (FRETILIN). (6) Colonel Syahnakry, the Indonesian military commander in East Timor, confirmed the arrests and stated that in East Timor "there were only some 228 members of FRETILIN with 107 rifles and a small quantity of ammunition". He also reiterated the validity of the clemency decree proclaimed by the President of Indonesia for FRETILIN fighters who surrender.

10. It was further reported that in October 1994, the East Timorese resistance fighters had announced that they would be prepared to announce a unilateral cease-fire and "suspend all military activities, except as demands of legitimate defence", if the Indonesian authorities agreed to free imprisoned East Timorese leader José Alexandre "Xanana" Gusmão and to hold immediate negotiations "at the highest level" with the resistance fighters. (7) The same sources indicated that on 11 October, the Indonesian military had rejected the unilateral cease-fire declared by the resistance fighters. The Indonesian military spokesman in East Timor, Major Simbolou, (sic) re-

portedly stated the following: "It's good that they have called for a cease-fire but that's not enough. They must now surrender themselves and their weapons. We are prepared to grant them amnesty if they surrender. But there will be no negotiations or dialogue with them."

11. According to press reports, Bishop Belo announced on 27 October that he was working with "all parties", including the Indonesian Government, todefine a "special status" for East Timor for a transitional period towardsan act of self-determination. (8) According to the Permanent Mission of Indonesia to the United Nations minister/State Secretary Moerdiono said that the Government of Indonesia would not give special autonomy to East Timor, which would make its status different from 26 Indonesian provinces.

12. The United States information Service reported that on 12 November 1994 "there was a small demonstration in front of the United States Embassy in Jakarta. The demonstrators were seeking to express their views on the situation in East Timor. Several entered the Embassy compound and remained there". The demonstration took place one day before the arrival in Jakarta of President Bill Clinton for the meeting of the Asia-Pacific Economic Cooperation (APEC) forum. The demonstration had been preceded by a letter dated 7 November 1994 from Mr. Gusmão addressed to President Clinton, in which he expressed his gratitude to the United States for its past attention to East Timor and appealed for the support of President Clinton in raising with President Suharto on the occasion of the APEC summit the need for Jakarta to display greater political goodwill in addressing the problems. (9) Some 29 East Timorese protestors who entered staged a 12-day sit-in there and demanded the immediate release of Mr. Gusmão. On 23 November, the protesters were allowed by the Government of Indonesia to leave the country for any country of their choice, On the same date, they left Indonesia for exile in Portugal. (10)

13. Press reports stated that a number of pro-independence demonstrations were held in East Timor during the period 12-24 November 1994. (11) The same sources indicated that the Indonesian security forces used truncheons and tear gas to disperse the protestors; they also resumed night-time detentions of youths suspected of having pro-independence sympathies. Approximately 135 East Timorese were reportedly arrested for participating in those demonstrations. Many of them reportedly were taken from their homes and beaten by the Indonesian security forces. The police acknowledged

80 arrests. (12) In November 1994, the Indonesian authorities announced that 30 East Timorese would be prosecuted for alleged involvement in pro-independent protests in East Timor between 10 and 24 November. (13)

14. It was later reported (14) that on 26 November, a pro-Indonesian demonstration had been held in Dili. The demonstration was reportedly disrupted by a group of pro-independence East Timorese.

15. On 14 January 1995, as reported by the press, the Indonesian security task force (Tintim Saka) killed six East Timorese near the village of Gauana. The Indonesian authorities stated that the six victims were FRETILIN guerrillas. (15) In February, the United States, Australia and Canada expressed their concern to the Indonesian authorities over the alleged killing of the six FRETILIN members. They stated that they had enough evidence to contradict official Indonesian accounts that the incident had been a clash between troops and anti-Indonesian guerrillas. (16) Also in February, the Indonesian military established a special investigation team to examine the incident. (17) Following the investigation, the Indonesian Government acknowledged that the military had committed "irregularities" in the killing of the six East Timorese and "had acted beyond established procedures". A spe-

cial inquiry was initiated following the above acknowledgement. (18) On 24 February, it was announced that the Indonesian military had established a 36-member committee to investigate the killings. (19) On the same date it was also announced that the Indonesian military at Liquica had arrested 10 East Timorese for questioning on charges of conspiring against the Government. (20) On 27 February, the Indonesian military admitted that the six people killed by the soldiers were "victims of mistaken identity". (21) On 5 April, the Indonesian army decided to court-martial two soldiers who had been found guilty in the killing of the six East Timorese on 14 January. (22)

16. According to press reports, (23) on 1 January 1995, an ethnic riot took place at Baucau following an alleged killing of an East Timorese by an Indonesian immigrant. Some 200 youths reportedly burned a market, shops and houses belonging to Indonesian merchants. Police clashed with the rioters and dispersed the crowd. It was further reported that three persons had been killed and three injured during the incident. Police reportedly arrested 20 East Timorese for questioning. In accordance with the press release of the Indonesian Mission to the United Nations of 18 November 1994, the above incident was described as follows:

"On 1 January 1995, an outbreak of violence occurred as a result of a personal quarrel between two traders, one from Sulawesi and one from East Timor, in which the latter was killed. The police officials thereafter contained the violence and restored order. The South Sulawesi man was promptly arrested, tried by the Dili District court and sentenced to 11 years in prison for the murder of the East Timorese trader on 17 January 1995."

17. Press reports (24) in February 1995 indicated that in that month several so-called "Ninja gangs", which were allegedly operating with the connivance of the Indonesian military, had attacked and burned residences of many pro-independence East Timorese. Four East Timorese youths were reported to have been abducted by those gangs. Bishop Belo, speaking on a Lisbon radio station on 10 February 1995, said that the international community should help to guarantee the return of East Timor to tranquillity. On 15 February, the Indonesian military reportedly arrested 12 alleged members of the "Ninja gangs" and stated that the 12 arrested individuals were believed to be members or sympathizers of an urban pro-independence movement known as "Clandestine". (25)

18. On 15 February, Mr. José Antonio Neves, an East Timorese theology student and Secretary of the Student Resistance Organiza-

tion, was sentenced by an Indonesian court to four years imprisonment. Mr. Neves had been arrested in May 1994 at Malang, Central Java, while sending faxes to human rights monitors overseas, citing violations of human rights in East Timor. (26)

19. On 6 March 1995, Indonesian military authorities arrested some 30 pro-independence activists in East Timor. Colonel Kiki Syahnakri, Chief of the East Timor Military Command, said that the arrested East Timorese were "supporters and followers of FRETILIN". (27)

20. According to press reports, (28) on 30 May 1995, a group of 17 East Timorese refugees arrived by boat in Darwin, Australia. The same sources indicated that the refugees were members of the Clandestine Resistance front and had fled from East Timor for political reasons.

III. HUMAN RIGHTS SITUATION

21. A member of the Commission on Human Rights since 1991, Indonesia has repeatedly affirmed its commitment to international human rights principles.

22. According to a United States Department of State report, (29) in East Timor, "troop levels remained unjustifiably high... somewhat greater access was permitted to foreign journalists and others ... although some repre-

sentatives of non-governmental organizations and foreign journalists continued to encounter difficulties or were denied access to East Timor. About 6,000 army troops from outside East Timor reinforced the normal garrison there. There were also about 3,000 police in East Timor".

Disappearances

23. With regard to disappearances, the report of the State Department indicated that the efforts of the Indonesian Government to account for the missing and dead from the 12 November 1991 military shootings of civilians in Dili remained inadequate. No additional cases of those still listed as missing were resolved during 1994. (29)

Torture and other cruel, inhuman or degrading treatment or punishment

24. The report further stated that security forces continued to employ torture and other forms of mistreatment, although the use of torture had declined. Torture continued to be used before releasing suspects to police custody, although its incidence decreased. Political prisoners were usually mixed with the general prison population, although high-profile political prisoners were segregated. (29)

Arbitrary arrest, detention or exile

25. According to the report, in the areas where active guerrilla movements exist, people were routinely detained without warrants, charges or court proceedings. Bail was rarely granted, especially in political cases. Military authorities continued the practice of detaining people without charges for short periods and then releasing them, with the requirement that they report weekly or daily to police. (29)

Arbitrary interference with privacy, family, home or correspondence

26. The report also stated that judicial warrants for earches were required except for cases involving subversion, economic crimes and corruption, although security agencies regularly make forced or surreptitious entries. The "transmigration policy" of the Indonesian Government (also see para. 8 above) was considered by human rights monitors to be a violation of the rights of the indigenous people as well as of the transmigrants. (29)

Freedom of speech and press

27. According to the report, during 1994, the staff of East Timor's only newspaper were subjected to various forms of intimidation, and a vehicle owned by the newspaper was burned following the newspaper's coverage of the

mid-July demonstrations at Dili, which was at variance with the official account. In 1994, the authorities denied permission for non-governmental organizations and the local university to hold a seminar on development and local environment. Special permission from the Indonesian authorities continued to be required for foreign journalists to visit East Timor, although a number of group tours to the Territory were organized by the authorities for the media during 1994. Some journalists were denied access to the Territory. (29)

Freedom of peaceful assembly and association
28. As noted in the report, the Indonesian Government continued to place restrictions and control on the public marches and demonstrations in the Territory. During the period under review, several demonstrations were dispersed by the police, leaving a number of participants killed, injured or arrested (also see paras. 4, 13 and 16 above). (29)

Freedom of religion
29. With regard to the freedom of religion, the report points out that the Constitution provides for religious freedom. Two Indonesian soldiers found guilty of provocative behaviour during a Catholic mass at Dili in July1994 were court-martialled and in October 1994 were expelled from the

army and sentenced to prison. (29)

Freedom of movement within the country, foreign travel, emigration and repatriation
30. According to the report, during 1994, the military continued to carry out security checks, which affected transportation and travel to and within the Territory, and occasionally introduced curfews in connection with military operations. (29)
31. During the period under review, Amnesty International issued two reports, entitled "East Timor–The Liquiza Killings" (February 1995) and "East Timor Continuing Human Rights Violations" (February 1995). In those reports, Amnesty International reiterated its viewpoint that the Indonesian Government had to improve the human rights situation in the Territory. It regretted the fact that it had not been able to visit EastTimor.
32. In February 1995 the Human Rights Watch/Asia issued a report, entitled "Indonesia/East Timor–Deteriorating Human Rights in East Timor", in which it called upon the Indonesian Government to take all necessary measures with a view to complying in full with international human rights standards. The Human Rights Watch/Asia regretted the fact that it had not been able to visit East Timor.
33. The United Nations Special Rapporteur on Extrajudicial,

Summary or Arbitrary Executions, Mr. Bacre Waly Ndiaye, issued a report on his mission to Indonesia and East Timor from 3 to 13 July 1994. The report is contained in document E/CN.4/1995/61/Add.1 dated 1 November 1994.

IV. ECONOMIC, SOCIAL AND EDUCATIONAL CONDITIONS

34. In the absence of information submitted by the administering Power under Article 73e of the Charter of the United Nations and for reasons explained in paragraph 36 below, information on economic, social and educational conditions in the Territory during the period under review was derived from the submission of the Permanent Mission of Indonesia to the United Nations and is set out below:

"According to East Timor Governor Abilio José Osorio Soares poverty and low-quality human resources remain major challenges and after these are dealt with, the goal of creating a prosperous, advanced and self-reliant East Timor could be accomplished. The statistics reflect that foreign and domestic investments now amount to a total of Rp 283.4 billion and these investments have provided employment for 28,923 workers in various sectors. (ANTARA News Agency, 25 and 27 January 1995)

"Primary importance has to be accorded to East Timor's economy to make it more self-supporting." Mr. João Mariano De Sousa Saldhana, a research fellow at the Northern Territory University (NTU) and author of a book entitled *East Timor's Economy, Politics and Development,* cited unemployment as an important social problem facing the region. He also addressed the fact that until now there was an unbalanced amount between the development fund provided by the Central Government and East Timor's own income. (ANTARA News Agency, 3 December 1994)

"The Ministry of Public Works has built bridges of a total length of 2,628 kilometres in the southern part of East Timor. In addition, it has constructed 446 kilometres of national level roads, 765 kilometres of provincial roads and 1,035 kilometres of regency level roads and 26 irrigation systems in the regencies of Liquisa and Viqueque. (ANTARA News Agency, 29 January 1995)

"The Governor of East Timor has emphasized the need to bolster investments in telecommunications to encourage foreign businesses to invest in the province. The local capital investment coordinating Board has informed us that businessmen from both Australia and local East Timorese will cooperate in the development of the Timor Gap prodect with a view to maximizing the gains to be derived from the project. (ANTARA News Agency, 30 January 1995)

"Efforts towards environment conservation in East Timor will be intensified. According to the Head of the Environment Section of East Timor, such efforts are fundamental to maintain the nature and environment in the region. (ANTARA News Agency, 8 October 1994)

"Banks in East Timor have accumulated funds of Rp 58 billion in the first semester of the 1994/1995 fiscal year, an increase of 34.24 per cent. According to the manager of the East Timor bank, the increase was caused by conversion into cash of government funds for the financing of several projects, including health projects, presidential instruction programme for backward regions and increases in salaries for civil servants. At the same time, it was noted that bank credit growth rate increased to Rp 17.92 billion or 40.26 per cent. The presence of banks have improved the economy and lifestyle of people in the province. As can be seen, an increasing amount of people are using the services of banks. It is hoped that this trend continues for it will contribute greatly to the development of the province. (ANTARA

News Agency, 12 December 1994 and 12 February 1995)

"A total of 140 of East Timor's 442 villages received electricity. The rural electrification programme in the region failed to be fully implemented owing to the mountainous geographical conditions. The local branch of the electric company will continue to give priority to this project. (ANTRA News Agency, 6 December 1994)

"Eighteen State cooperatives and businesses are assisting in developing cooperatives and small businesses in East Timor. The East Timor provincial administration will provide the necessary support to encourage investment in the forestry sector. The industrial growth in the province is also encouraging. It has grown by an average of 24.9 per cent per year. Small establishments have contributed to the growth of the industrial sector. (ANTARA News Agency, 28 November 1994)

"East Timor's health services have greatly improved since integration. According to the Head of the Local Population and Environment Office, Ms. Maria de Laourdes, adequate health facilities have been made available to most districts in the region. East Timor now has 67 public health centres and an addition of 2 hospitals to serve the population of 13 districts. (ANTARA News

Agency, 9 September 1994)"

V. CONSIDERATION BY
THE UNITED NATIONS (30)

35. Between 1961 and 1982, the General Assembly annually reviewed the question of East Timor and adopted resolutions on the basis of reports submitted by the Special Committee on the Situation with regard to the Implementation of the Declaration on the Granting of independence to Colonial Countries and Peoples. (31) Since its thirty-eighth session, the General Assembly has deferred consideration of the item. (32)

36. Since 1977, the Government of Portugal, in its capacity as administering Power of East Timor, has annually informed the Secretary-General that, owing to conditions prevailing in the Territory, namely, the presence of armed forces of Indonesia, it has been de facto prevented from transmitting any information concerning East Timor under Article 73e of the Charter. (33) On 5 June, the Permanent Mission of Portugal addressed to the Secretary-General a note verbale on the above subject (A/50/214).

37. At its thirty-seventh session, by resolution 37/30 of 23 November 1982, the General Assembly requested the Secretary-General to initiate consultations with all parties directly concerned, with a view to exploring avenues for achieving a comprehensive settlement of the problem, and to report to the Assembly at its thirty-eighth session. The Assembly requested the Special Committee to keep the situation in the Territory under active consideration and to render all assistance to the Secretary-General to facilitate implementation of the resolution.

38. Since 1983, the Secretary-General has kept the General Assembly regularly apprised of developments related to the exercise of his good offices. (34) His most recent progress report, submitted to the Assembly at its forty-ninth session, is contained in document A/49/391.

39. The Secretary-General held the fifth round of discussions with the Foreign minister of Indonesia and Portugal at Geneva on 9 January 1995. The information regarding the fifth round of discussions is contained in press releases SG/SM/5519 and SG/T/ 1923. On 9 May 1995, the following statement was issued by the Spokesman for the Secretary-General (SG/SM/5626) :

"Notifications are being sent out to 30 East Timorese of various political views from both inside and outside East Timor to atten the all-inclusive Intra-East Timorese dialogue contemplated inthe Geneva communique issued at the conclusion of the fifth round of talks between Indonesia and Portugal on 9 January. The dialogue is now scheduled to take place in Austria from 2 to 5 June.

"The sixth round of ministerial talks between Indonesia and Portugal under the Secretary-General's auspices will now take place at Geneva on 8 July."

40. The most recent round of the all-inclusive intra-East Timorese dialogue was concluded on 5 June 1995 in Austria. The following press release was issued on that day by the United Nations Information

"Concluding an all-inclusive intra-East Timorese dialogue at Schlaining Castle, Austria, today, 30 East Timorese, representing a broad cross-section of political opinion from inside and outside the Territory, adopted the Burg Schlaining Declaration, calling for a continuation of the dialogue. The meeting was initiated by the Secretary-General in the context of his good offices on the question of East Timor.

"The declaration proposed to the Secretary-General the holding of another intra-Timorese dialogue with a view to continuing the debate on issues annexed to the declaration, while noting that despite the frank and open spirit in which the dialogue was conducted, the fundamental, different political options remained unchanged. Such meetings should precede each round of negotiations on the question of East Timor between the Foreign ministers of Portugal and Indonesia.

"Adopted by consensus, the declaration reaffirms the need to implement measures in the field of human rights and other areas with a view to promoting peace, stability, justice and social harmony. It also reaffirms the necessity of the social and cultural development of East Timor to be based on the preservation of the cultural identity of the people, including the teaching of the Tetun and Portuguese languages.

"The declaration also calls for the involvement of all East Timorese without discrimination in the development of the Territory in a climate of mutual understanding, tolerance and harmony.

"The participants affirmed the importance of the ongoing negotiations between the Governments of Portugal and Indonesia under the auspices of the Secretary-General, which aim at finding a just, comprehensive and internationally acceptable solution to the question of East Timor, according to the provisions, letter and spirit of General Assembly resolution 37/30. The declaration notes with appreciation the consultations undertaken by the United Nations with the various shades of Timorese opinion, aiming at their gradual involvement, as well as the availability of the Ministers of Foreign Affairs of Portugal and Indonesia for direct dialogue with Timorese personalities. The declaration also requests the Secretary-General and the two Governments to facilitate the free movement of Timorese families to and from East Timor.

"The declaration pays special tribute to the contribution of the Catholic Church in East Timor and the participation of Dom Carlos Filipe Ximenes Belo, Apostolic Administrator of the Diocese of Dili, in the dialogue, whose concrete proposals for improving the physical and spiritual conditions of life of the East Timor people were agreed upon.

"Facilitated by the United Nations, the intra-East Timorese dialogue served to explore practical ideas that could have a positive impact on the situation in East Timor and assist in creating a conducive atmosphere for a solution of that question. The Government of Austria provided meeting facilities and accommodation for all participants. A number of other Governments also extended financial support to this initiative."

41. During the general debate at the forty-ninth session of the General Assembly, the representatives of Angola, Brazil, Mozambique, Cape Verde, Ireland, Iceland, Portugal and Guinea-Bissau referred to the question of East Timor in their statement.

42. In the general debate in the Fourth Committee, several representatives made references to the question of East Timor under the agenda item entitled "Implementation of the Declaration on the Granting of independence to Colonial Countries and Peoples": Belarus (A/C.4/49/SR.6), Brazil (on behalf of the Rio Group) (A/C.4/49/SR.5) and Germany (on behalf of the European Union) (A/C.4/49/SR.5).

43. In the general debate in the Third Committee, references to East Timor were made by Germany (on behalf of the European Union), Canada, Norway and Sweden.

44. The Special Committee considered the question of East Timor at its 1431st, and 1435th to 1437th meetings, between 11 and 14 July 1994. During those meetings, the Committee heard statements by representatives of Indonesia (A/AC.109/PV.1431, 1435 and 1437); Sao Tome and Principe (on behalf also of Angola, Cape Verde, Guinea Bissau and Mozambique) (A/AC.109/PV.1436); Portugal, as the administering Power (A/AC.109/PV.1437); the Philippines (A/AC.109/PV.1437); Papua New Guinea (A/AC.109/PV.1437); and Fiji (A/AC.109/PV.1437); as well as by 28 petitioners.

45. At its 1437th meeting, on 14 July, the Special Committee decided to continue consideration of the item at its 1995 session subject to any directives which the General Assembly might give in that connection at its forty-ninth session (A/AC.109/PV.1437).

46. The question of East Timor was considered by the UN Subcommission for Prevention of Discrimination and Protection of Minorities at its 17th, 19th and 29th meetings, on 12, 15 and 29 August 1994 espectively (E/CN.4/Sub.2/1994/SR.17, 19 and 29). The documents pertaining to that consideration are listed below:

(a)   Draft report of the Subcommission on Prevention of Discrimination and Protection of Minorities (E/CN.4/Sub.2/I994/L.10/Add.7 (Part 11) of of 22 September 1994), chapter VII;

(b) Situation in East Timor: draft resolution   (E/CN.4/Sub.2/1994/L.20of 18 August 1994);

(c) Situation in East Timor: note by the Secretariat (E/CN.4/Sub.2/1994/14 and Add.1 of 14 July and 5 August 1994).

47. The question of East Timor was subsequently discussed by the Commission on Human Rights during its fifty-first session at its 7th and 55th meetings, on 9 February and 15 March 1995, respectively (E/CN.4/1995/SR.7 and 55). The documents pertaining to that consideration are listed below:

(a)   Draft report of the com- mission on Human Rights, fifty-first session (E/CN.4/1995/L.10/Add.12);

(b) The right of peoples to self-determination and its application to peoples under colonial or alien domination or occupation. Question of the violations of human rights and fundamental freedoms in any part of the world with particular reference to colonial and other dependent countries and territories, written statement submitted by Amnesty International (E/CN.4/1995/NGO/21);

(c) Letter dated 17 October 1994 from the Permanent Representative of the Republic of Indonesia to the United Nations Office at Geneva addressed to the Assistant Secretary-General for Human Rights (E/CN.4/1995/107);

(d) Letter dated 2 November 1994 from the Permanent Representative of the Republic of Indonesia to the United Nations office at Geneva addressed to the Assistant Secretary-General for Human Rights (E/CN.4/1995/108);

(e) Letter dated 29 November 1994 from the Permanent Representative of the Republic of Indonesia to the United Nations office at Geneva addressed to the Assistant Secretary-General for Human Rights (E/CN.4/1995/117);

(f)   Letter dated 1 January 1995 from the Permanent Representative of the Republic of Indonesia to the United Nations Office at Geneva addressed to the Assistant Secretary-General for Human Rights (E/CN.4/1995/118);

(g). Letter dated 3 March 1995 from the Permanent Representative of the United Kingdom of Great. Britain and Northern Ireland to the United Nations Office at Geneva addressed to the Assistant Secretary-General for Human Rights (E/CN.4/1995/173);

(h) Question of the violation of human rights and fundamental freedoms in any part of the world with particular reference to colonial and other dependent countries and territories: extrajudicial summary or arbitrary executions (E/CN.4/1995/61/Add.1);

(i) Situation in East Timor; report of the Secretary-General (E/CN.4/1995/72).

Notes

1. *Diario de Noticias* (Lisbon), 25 and 27 July 1994; The Australian (Sydney), 26 July 1994; *Publico* (Lisbon) 23 July 1994; and *The Straits Times* (Singapore), 20 July 1994.

2. *Diario de Noticias* (Lisbon), 31 July 1994.

3. *The Times* (London), 3 August 1994.

4. *Jakarta Post*, 26 August 1994.

5. Reuters, 4 September 1994.

6. *Indonesian Observer* (Jakarta), 12 September 1994.

7. Reuters, 10 and 11 Octo-

ber 1994.

8 Agence France-Presse, 28 October 1994.

9. Reuters, 10, 11 and 14 November 1994.

10. Reuters, 25 November 1994.

11. *The Guardian* (London), 25 November 1994; and Agence France-Presse, November 1994.

12. *The International Herald Tribune*, 23 November 1994; and *The New York Times*, 22 November 1994.

13. *The Financial Times* (London), 24 November 1994.

14. Reuters, 28 November 1994.

15. *Indonesian Observer* (Jakarta), 14 January 1995.

16. *The International Herald Tribune*, 9 February 1995.

17. *The Australian* (Sydney), 3 February 1995.

18. *The Australian* (Sydney), 13 February 1995; Reuters, 17 February 1995; *The Financial Review* (Sydney), 13 February 1995; and *The Sydney Morning Herald*, 13 February 1995.

19. Agence France-Presse, 24 February 1995.

20. Reuters, 25 February 1995.

21. *The Financial Times* (London), 27 February 1995.

22. *Jakarta Post*, 5 April 1995.

23. *The Guardian* (London), 3 January 1995; Reuters, 5 Janaury 1995; and *Jakarta News*, 5 January 1995.

24. Reuters, 10 and 14 February 1995.

25. *The International Herald Tribune*, 16 February 1995.

26. Reuters, 25 February 1995.

27. Reuters, 6 March 1995.

28. *The Australian*, 30 May 1995; *Northern Territory News*, 30 May 1995.

29. United States Department of State, Country Reports on Human Rights Practice for 1994, Washington, DC, February 1995, pp.592-607.

30. For details, see corresponding sections of the previous working papers prepared by the Secretariat contained in documents A/AC.109L.1328, and A/AC.109/623, 663, 715, 747, 783, 836, 871, 919, 961, 1001, 115, 1154 and 1187.

31. See General Assembly resolutions 1699 (XVI), 1807 (XVII), 1913 (XVIII), 2107 (XX), 2184 (XXI), 2395 (XXIII), 2507 (XXIV), 2707 (XXV), 2795 (XXVI), 2918 (XXVII), 3113 (XXVIII), 3294 (XXIX), 3485 (XXX) and 31/53, relating to the question of Territories under Portuguese administration, including East Timor; see also Assembly resolutions 32/34, 33/39, 34/40, 35/27, 36/50 and 37/30 on the question of East Timor.

32. General Assembly decisions 38/402, 39/402, 40/402, 43/402 and 46/402; see also A/41/PV.3, A/44/PV.3, A/45/PV.3, A/47/PV.3, A/48/130 and A/49/402.

33. See A/35/233, A/37/160, A/37/125, A/39/136, A/40/159, A/41/190, A/42/171, A/43/219, A/44/262, A/45/172, A/46/131, A/47/189, A/48/130 and A/49/184. Owing to a lack of information from the administering Power, the information contained in the present paper has been derived from other sources.

34. A/39/361, A/40/622, A/41/602, A/42/539, A/43/588, A/44/529, A/45/507, A/46/456 and A/48/418.

Document 15

General Assembly
Security Council

A/46/97
S/22285
28 February 1991
ORIGINAL: ENGLISH

GENERAL ASSEMBLY
SECURITY COUNCIL
Forty-sixth session.
Forty-sixth year
165 of the preliminary list (A/46/50)
Question of EAST TIMOR

Letter dated 28 February 1991 from the Permanent Representative of Portugal to the United Nations addressed to the Secretary-General.

Further to my letter of 20 February 1991 (A/46/93-S/22249), and on instructions from my Government, I have the honour to convey to you the text of a note handed to the Minister for Foreign Affairs of Australia by the Ambassador of Portugal at Canberra on 22 February 1991 (see annex).

I should be grateful if you would kindly arrange for the present letter and annex to be cir-culated as an official document of the General Assembly, under 165 of the preliminary list, and of the Security Council.

(Signed) Fernando REINO

Ambassador of Portugal
Permanent Representative to the
United Nations

ANNEX

Letter handed on 22 February 1991 to the Minister for Foreign Affairs of Australia by the Ambassador of Portugal at Canberra

Upon instructions from my Government, I have the honour to kindly request attention to the following:

The Portuguese Government is aware that Australia is on the way of extending the exploration for and the exploitation of the natural resources of the Timor seas's subsoil, as well as the practice of related acts of jurisdiction, close to East Timor's coastline, inside the area known as the "Timor Gap", located between Timor's southern coast and Australia's northern coast. These activities are supposed to be undertaken beyond the median line, every point of which is equidistant from the nearest points of the baselines from which the breadths of the respective seas are measured. Besides, those activities are also expected to be carried out in the very inside of the so-called "Timor Trough" situated close to the Timor coastline.

This extension is based on a bilateral instrument, concluded not with Portugal, the administering Power of the non-self-governing territory of East Timor, recognized as such by the United nations, but with a third country instead any negotiation with Portugal having been precluded.

The Portuguese Government is of the opinion that the negotiation, the signature, the ratification and the implmentation of the Australian-Indonesian "Treaty", signed on 11 December 1989, constitute a very serious violation of some of the most basic rules of international law, namely, those pertaining to the right to self-determination of peoples, to the territorial integrity of non-self-governing territories and to the permanent sovereignty of peoples over their natural resources. Moreover, they plainly disregard the Charter of the United Nations and the authority assigned to its main bodies. This has been consistently made known to the Australian Government.

Besides this, the Portuguese Government considers that, even independently of their title, the the exploration for and the exploitation of the natural resources located in the "Timor Gap's" continental shelf, be it direct or indirect, alone or together with another country, are abusive and illicit without Portugal's consent, taking into account its capacity as the administering Power of East Timor. In fact, they violate also the rights provided to the territory of East Timor under the provisions of article 2 of the Convention on the Continental Shelf done at Geneva on 29 April 1958. The same applies to any act of jurisdiction related to that exploration or exploitation, as well as to the collection of revenues deriving from them. It is also the Portuguese Government's understanding that all the activities described above undertaken beyond the median line of every point of which is equidistant from the nearest points of the baselines from which the breadths of the territorial seas of East Timor and Australia are measured, constitute a violation of those rights.

As a matter of fact Portugal has always affirmed and still affirms that, under the provisions of article 1, complemented by international custom, and of article 6, paragraph 1 of the Convention on the Continental Shelf, done at Geneva, on 29 April 1958, the boundary of the continental shelf appertaining to East Timor, and to Australia is and shall continue to be the median line, every point of which is equidistant from the nearest points of the baselines from which the breadths of respective territorial seas are measured. In accordance with the provisions of aforesaid article 6, paragraph 1, of the Convention on the Continental Shelf done at Geneva, on 29 April 1958, article 1, paragraph 3, of "Decreto-Lei" 49.369, of 11 November 1969, extended to East Timor on 22 November, 1969, and still in force, states that: "unless an agreement has been concluded with a State whose coasts are adjacent to or opposite to those of the Portuguese State, and providing that no special circumstances justify a different boundary line, the boundary of the continental shelf is the median line, every point of which is equidistant from the nearest points of the baselines from which the breadths of the respective territorial seas are measured".

Portugal, in its capacity as admistering Power of the non-self-governing territory of East Timor, is obliged, under the provisions of Article 73 of the Charter of the United Nations, to promote to the utmost, within the system of international peace and security established by the Charter, the well-being of the inhabitants of that territory. It is therefore also incumbent upon it the responsibility of defending and promoting the rights of the East Timorese. Thus Portugal, in addition to what it has already stated before, namely, through the verbal note of protest handed over to the Department of Foreign Affairs on 11 February 1991, hereby notifies the Australian Government that:

The exploration for and the exploitation of the natural resources of the Timor Sea's seabed and subsoil, in the area known as "Timor, Gap", as well as any other connected activities, carried out directly or indirectly, alone or together with any other country, including the practice of related acts of jurisdiction or the collection of any revenue deriving from them, undertaken beyond the abovementioned median line (and, in all cases, when extended to where Australia has announced its intentions to undertake them), without Portugal's consent and not even with any attempt to negotiate the matter with Portugal, constitute, furthermore, a violation of the rights provided to the territory of East Timor under the provisions of article 2 of the Convention on the Continental Shelf of 29 April 1958.

Portugal and Australia are both parties to the Convention on the Continental Shelf, done at Geneva, on 29 April 1958, as well as to the Optional Protocol of Signature concerning the compulsory settlement of disputes arising out of the interpretation or application of any article of any convention on the law of the sea of 29 April 1958, whose article 3 reads as follows:

"The parties may agree, within a period of two months after one party has notified its opinion to the other that a dispute exists, to resort not to the International Court of Justice, but to an arbitral tribunal. After the expiry to the said period, either party to this Protocol may bring the dispute before the Court by an application"

In accordance with and for the purposes of the aforesaid article 3, the Portuguese Government, in the fulfilment of its duties the administering Power of the non-self-governing territory of East Timor, and namely, in the defense of the rights of its people, hereby notifies the Australian Government that:

(a) It considers that the boundary of the continental shelf appertaining to East Timor and to Australia, in the area known as the "Timor Gap", is and shall continue to be the median line, every point of which is equidistant from the nearest points of the baselines from which the breadths of the respective territorial seas are measured;

(b) It considers that the exploration for and the exploitation of the Timor Sea's seabed and subsoil in the area known as "Timor Gap", as well as any other connected activities, carried out by the Government of Australia, directly or indirectly, alone or together with any other country, including the practice of related acts of jurisdiction or the collection of any revenues deriving from them beyond the above mentioned median line (and, in all cases, when extended to where Australia has announced its intention to unertake them), without Portugal's consent and not with any attempt to negotiate the matter with Portugal, constitute a violation of the rights provided to the territory of East Timor under the provisions of article 2 of the Convention on the Continental Shelf of 29 April 1958;

(c) It considers that a dispute exists between Australia and Portugal concerning the question referred to above, questions which concern the interpretation and the application of articles 1, 2, and 6, paragraph 1, of the Convention on the Continental Shelf of 29 April 1958.

As a consequence of the existence of the aforesaid dispute between Australia and Portugal, the Portuguese Government proposes to the Australian Government that negotiations be held aimed at agreeing upon a mutually acceptable form of settlement of the dispute. This would not, of course, be detrimental to the holding of negotiations on the very substance of that dispute, which have been hitherto precluded by the Australian Government.

The Portuguese Government reserves itself the right to bring the entire dispute referred to above before the International Court of Justice, or a part of that dispute, as provided by article 3 of the above mentioned Optional Protocol of 20 April 1958.

This cannot be construed as a renunciation to any rights or to the possibility of resorting to the Court to uphold them.

My Government will forward a copy of this note to the Secretary-General of the United Nations, taking into account the provisions of Chapter XI of the Charter and also the mandate entrusted to him by General Assembly Resolution 37/30 of 23 November 1982.

Document 16

Press Release ICJ/538 3 July 1995

WORLD COURT DECIDES IT CANNOT ADJUDICATE DISPUTE ON EXPLOITATION OF EAST TIMORESE CONTINENTAL SHELF

Vote on Application by Portugal against Australia is 14-2

THE HAGUE, 30 June (International Court of Justice) — By a vote of 14 to 2, the International today held that it could not adjudicate upon the dispute by Portugal on Australia's exploitation of the shelf of the so-called "Timor Gap".

Portugal had instituted proceedings against Australia in February 1991, stating in its application to the Court that by conducting certain activities in the area concerned, Australia had "failed to observe the obligation to respect the duties and powers of Portugal as the administering Power of East Timor and the right of the people of East Timor to self-determination and the related rights".

Portugal maintained that, in concluding a December 1989 treaty with Indonesia which created a "zone of cooperation in an area between the Indonesian province of East Timor and northern Australia" and in taking measures to apply it, Australia had violated the rights of Portugal and the East Timorese.

Australia objected that there was in reality no dispute between itself and Portugal, and that the case presented by Portugal was artificially limited to the question of the lawfulness of Australia's conduct. The true respondent, Australia maintained, was Indonesia and that Australia was being sued in place of Indonesia.

It also pointed out that while Australia and Portugal had accepted the compulsory jurisdiction of the Court, Indonesia had not. So, for the Court to rule on Australia's conduct, it would first have to rule on the lawfulness of Indonesia's entry into and continuing presence in East Timor, or the validity of the 1989 treaty between Australia and Indonesia. Since the Court did not have jurisdiction over Indonesia's conduct, it could not adjudicate on the matter.

On the first point, the Court found that by virtue of the fact that Portugal had filed a legal complaint against Australia and that Australia had responded with a denial, there was in fact a legal dispute.

However, the Court supported

Australia's second point that Australia's conduct could not be ruled upon without first deciding on the lawfulness of Indonesia's concluding the 1989 treaty; the very subject matter of the Court's decision would necessarily be a determination whether, considering the circumstances in which Indonesia entered and remained in East Timor, it could or could not have acquired the power to enter into treaties on behalf of East Timor on the resources of its continental shelf.

Given the fundamental principle in the Court's Statute that it can only exercise jurisdiction over a State with its consent, the Court found that it could not make a determination of Indonesia's rights and the lawfulness of its conduct in the absence of that State's consent. The Court concluded that it could not rule on Portugal's claims on the merits, "whatever the importance of the questions raised by those claims and of the rules of international law which they bring into play".

In its Judgement, the Court observed, however, that Portugal's assertion that the right of people's to self-determination, as it evolved from the Charter and United Nations practice, had an *erga omnes* [a right that can be asserted against any Power] character, was irreproachable. The principle of self-determination of peoples was one of the essential principles of contemporary international law, it stated. And for the two parties to the dispute, "East Timor remains a Non-Self-Governing Territory and its people has the right to self-determination.

Judges who voted in favour of today's decision were Bediaoui, Schwebel, Oda, Jennings, Guillaume, Shahabuddeen, Aguilar-Mawdsley, Ranjeva, Herczegh, Shi, Fleischhauer, Koroma, Vereshchetin, and Stephen. Judge Weeramantry and Judge ad hoc Skubiszewski voted against and appended dissenting opinions to the Judgment. Separated opinions were also appended by Judges Oda, Shahabuddeen, Ranjeva and Vereschetin.

Document 17

Statement by the Secretary-General's Spokesman on East Timor, 17 September 1993

The Secretary-General held meetings in New York on 17 September 1993 with the Foreign Ministers of Indonesia and Portugal, as had been agreed at the last round of talks hold on 21 April 1993 in Rome. In the context of the ongoing efforts, under his auspices, 'to seek a just, comprehensive and internationally acceptable settlement to the question of East Timor. The Secretary-General met separately with each of the two Ministers and subsequently chaired a Joint meeting.

As they agreed in Rome, the Ministers considered possible confidence-building measures as a means of fostering an atmosphere propitious to addressing the substance of the question on which they reiterated their respective positions of principle. In this connection, the Secretary-General wishes to record the following points, which emerged during their meeting:

1. The Ministers concurred on the importance of the promotion of respect for human rights in all their indivisible aspects (civil, political, economic, social and cultural) and fundamental freedoms in East Timor.

2. They also concurred on the need to create a favourable. and non-confrontational atmosphere in order to allow effective progress towards a comprehensive settlement of the question.

3. Both Ministers reaffimed the importance of the implementation of the recommendations contained in the consensus statement of the Chairman of the Human Rights Commission of 4 March 1992, and the need for further facilitating access to East Timor by United Nations and humanitarian and human rights organizations.

Document 18

General Assembly Document: A/49/391:16 September 1994 Forty-ninth session: Item 87 of the provisional agenda

QUESTION OF EAST TIMOR: Progress report of the Secretary-General

1. The purpose of the present report is to inform the General Assembly, as I have done in past years, of the continuing exercise of my good offices aimed at finding a just, comprehensive and internationally acceptable solution to the question of East Timor. The dialogue between Indonesia and Portugal has been under way since 1983. After an interruption in 1991, it was reactivated towards the end of 1992. Since then, I have held four rounds of discussions with the Foreign Ministers of Indonesia and Portugal. Through my aides, I have also kept in touch with East Timorese groups and personalities representing various shades of political opinion.

2. As indicated in my report last year (A/48/418), the positions of the two Governments on the issue of the Territory's status remain far apart. Nevertheless, an improved atmosphere has recently been achieved in the dialogue. The two sides have shown a manifest interest in avoiding a confrontational approach and have carried out a number of mutually agreed confidence-building measures, primarily of a humanitarian nature. I have urged both parties to build on these steps and to consider a number of concrete ideas that could further advance the talks while improving conditions and fostering confidence inside East Timor. At the last round of talks, held at Geneva on 6 May 1994, agreement was reached on a number of steps to be undertaken by both sides (see press release SG/SM/5283). These points of agreement were arrived at following a series of thorough consultations before the Geneva meeting. The consultations included discussions with the Permanent Representatives of the two sides in New York, and exploratory discussions on a wide range of ideas, in January 1994, in Portugal, Indonesia, East Timor and Australia with senior government officials, East Timorese political and religious leaders and others representing differing trends of Timorese opinion.

3. I will highlight three of the points that were agreed upon at the last round of talks. Firstly, the two Ministers agreed that access to East Timor for the United Nations and human rights and humanitarian organizations, as well as visits to East Timor by

East Timorese living abroad and visits of East Timorese to Portugal, should be continued and expanded. Secondly, I underlined to the two Ministers that a dialogue among East Timorese representatives of all shades of opinion could make important contributions to the ongoing bilateral dialogue under my auspices. The two Ministers have agreed that I should explore ways of convening such an all-inclusive intra-Timorese dialogue. Thirdly, the two Ministers expressed their willingness to meet separately with East Timorese representatives holding opposing views on the political status of East Timor, i.e., the Foreign Minister of Portugal would meet with those who support integration with Indonesia, and the Foreign Minister of Indonesia with those opposed to integration. I intend to facilitate these meetings in the near future.

4. Human rights issues have figured prominently in the dialogue between Indonesia and Portugal under my auspices, among them the full accounting for those who died or are still missing as a result of the violent and tragic incident which took place at Dili on 12 November 1991. I have continued to discuss with the Indonesian Government the situation of East Timorese in custody, including the leader of the armed independence movement, Jose "Xanana" Gusmão, who is serving a 20-year prison term after his capture in November 1992, and the need for taking measures aimed at their early release. In addition, the appropriate human rights organs of the United Nations have continued to deal with the situation in East Timor. In March 1994, the Commission on Human Rights adopted a consensus statement on the subject (see E/1994/24-E/CN.4/1994/132, para. 482). The Subcommission on Prevention of Discrimination and Protection of Minorities also discussed the issue at its forty-sixth session in August 1994. In July 1994, the Commission's Special Rapporteur on extrajudicial, summary or arbitrary executions visited East Timor at the invitation of the Indonesian Government.

5. In the coming months, I intend to assist the two Governments in identifying a series of issues for consideration by them in advance of the next round of talks, including possible avenues towards achieving a just, comprehensive and internationally acceptable solution. I will shortly undertake a series of consultations with various East Timorese groups and personalities with a view to convening an all-inclusive intra-Timorese dialogue.

6. The next round of talks between the two Foreign Ministers will be held at Geneva in the first half of January 1995.

Document 19

UN Press Statement of 9 January 1995

The Secretary-General held a fifth round of meetings in Geneva on 9 January 1995 with the Foreign Minister of Portugal, Mr. J. Durao Barroso and the Foreign Minister of Indonesia, Mr. Ali Alatas. The discussions focused on the Secretary-General's initiative to facilitate the convening of an all-inclusive intra-East Timorese dialogue, on a set of issues to be addressed in future talks and on confidence-building measures. In this regard, the Secretary-General wishes to record the following points of agreement arrived at during the Meeting.

1. The Meeting took note of:

– the dispatch by the Secretary-General of a mission to Jakarta, Dili and Lisbon at the end of 1994 to conduct consultations prior to the present round of talks;
– the presence of a representative sent by the Secretary-General at a meeting of East Timorese from inside and outside East Timor held in Chepstow, Unied Kingdom, at the end of September 1994, to initiate the first in a series of consultations with East Timorese groups and personalities of different political opinions, which was followed by similar consultations elsewhere with other East Timorese;
– the meetings held in October 1994 between the Foreign Ministers of Portugal and Indonesia with leading East Timorese supporters and opponents of integration in conformity with paragraph 9 of the 6 May communique;
– and the visit to East Timor in July 1994 by the Special Rapporteur on Extrajudicial, Summary or Arbitrary Executions of the Commission on Human Rights at the invitation of the Indonesian Government.

2. The two Ministers noted positively the Secretary-General's intention, following his consultations with a broad cross-section of East Timorese representing various trends of opinion, to facilitate and offer the necessary arrangements for the convening of an all-inclusive intra-East Timorese dialogue.

3. The objective of the dialogue will be to provide a forum for continuing the free and informal exchange of views to explore ideas of a practical nature that might have a positive impact on the situation in East Timor and assist in the establishment of an atmosphere conducive to the achievement of a solution to the question of East Timor. The dialogue will not address the political status of East Timor and will in no way constitute a parallel negotiating track or be a substitute

for the Ministerial talks under the auspices of the Secretary-General.

4. In order to create and maintain a propitious climate for a fruitful intra-East Timorese dialogue, the Secretary-General appeals to East Timorese of all shades of opinion to exercise restraint and refrain from actions that could have a detrimental impact, prior to and in the course of the dialogue.

5. The Secretary-General expressed the need for the two governments to cooperate with him in his initiative and to encourage all East Timorese to respond constructively to the initiative and appeal.

6. The two Ministers agreed to consider at the next round of talks substantive issues identified by the Secretary-General regarding possible avenues towards achieving a just, comprehensive and internationally acceptable solution to the question of East Timor.

7. The Ministers recalled the statement issued on 6 May 1994 at the conclusion of the fourth round of talks in which they concurred,– inter alia–, on the need to improve the human rights situation in East Timor, and the relevant Chairman's Statements adopted by consensus by the Human Rights Commission on that question, in particular with regard to access to East Timor, the early release of the East Timorese imprisoned and to the full accounting of the persons dead or missing as a result of the violent incident in Dili of 12 November 1991. In that connection the Meeting took note of the Indonesian Government's intention, in the terms conveyed at the Meeting, to take further steps for the implementation of the undertakings contained therein.

8. They also recalled the statement of 6 May 1994 on the need for continued restraint by both parties in the interest of maintaining a favourable atmosphere for further progress towards a comprehensive solution of the question of East Timor.

Following today's discussion the parties agreed to continue their efforts, with the assistance of the Secretary-General, to find a just, comprehensive and internationally acceptable settlement to the question of East Timor. The sixth round of talks between the Foreign Ministers under the auspices of the Secretary-General will be held on 19 May 1995 in New York. Prior to the Ministerial Meeting, preparatory talks will be held through the Representative of the Secretary-General.

Document 20

General Assembly Document: A/50/436 September 1995 Fiftieth session: Item 94 of the provisional agenda* (A/50/150)

QUESTION OF EAST TIMOR Progress report of the Secretary-General

1. Since the resumption of talks between Indonesia and Portugal on the question of East Timor in 1992, I have held, in the context of my good offices, six rounds of discussions with the Foreign Ministers of the two countries aimed at finding a just, comprehensive and internationally acceptable solution to the question of East Timor. I have reported to the Assembly annually on the progress of these efforts. The last two rounds of talks were held since I submitted my last progress report (A/49/391), and I will highlight here the salient points that emerged from those discussions (see press releases SG/SM/5519 and SG/T/1974).

2. The fifth round of talks with the Foreign Ministers of the two Governments was held at Geneva on 9 January 1995. At that round, the Ministers, inter alia, noted positively my intention to facilitate and offer the necessary arrangements for the convening of an all-inclusive intra-East Timorese dialogue. The objective of the dialogue was to provide a forum for continuing the free and informal exchange of views to explore ideas of a practical nature that might have a positive impact on the situation in East Timor and assist in the establishment of an atmosphere conducive to the achievement of a solution to the question of East Timor. It was understood that the East Timorese dialogue would not address the political status of East Timor and would not constitute a parallel negotiating track or be a substitute for the ministerial talks. In the interest of creating and maintaining a propitious climate for a fruitful dialogue, I issued an appeal to all East Timorese to exercise restraint and refrain from actions that could have a detrimental impact, prior to and during the course of the dialogue. I also expressed the need for the two Governments to cooperate with me in my initiative and to encourage all East Timorese to respond constructively to my initiative and appeal.

The Ministers further agreed to consider at the subsequent round of talks substantive issues identified by me regarding possible avenues towards a solution to the question of East Timor.

4. On human rights, the Ministers recalled the statement issued following the previous round of talks, in May 1994, in

which they had concurred, inter alia, on the need to improve the human rights situation in East Timor, and the relevant Chairman's statements adopted by consensus by the Commission on Human Rights, in particular, with regard to access to East Timor, the early release of the East Timorese imprisoned and the full accounting for the persons dead or missing as a result of the violent incident at Dili on 12 November 1991. The meeting took note of the intention of the Government of Indonesia, in the terms conveyed at the meeting, to take further steps for the implementation of the undertakings contained therein.

5. The first meeting of the All-Inclusive Intra-East-Timorese Dialogue was held at Burg Schlaining, Austria, from 2 to 5 June 1995 and brought together 30 East Timorese of various shades of political opinion residing inside and outside East Timor. Two representatives of the United Nations attended the meeting without taking part in the discussions. The gathering, the first of its kind, was held in a positive and constructive atmosphere and adopted, by consensus, the Burg Schlaining Declaration, which inter alia, proposed to me that further meetings be held within the same framework; reaffirmed the need to implement the necessary measures in the field of human rights and other areas with a view to promoting peace, stabil-

ity, justice and social harmony; reaffirmed the necessity for the social and cultural development of East Timor on the basis of the preservation of the cultural identity of the people, including tradition, religion, history and language, as well as the teaching of Tetun and Portuguese; and expressed the need to create the basis for the involvement of all East Timorese, without discrimination of any sort, in the development of East Timor in every sphere of human life in a climate of mutual understanding, tolerance and harmony.

6. The participants paid tribute to Rev. Dom Carlos Filipe Ximenes Belo, the Apostolic Administrator of Dili, for his contribution to the debate, such as the proposals that were agreed upon with a view to improving the physical and spiritual conditions of the lives of the people of East Timor. They also expressed appreciation for the consultations undertaken by the United Nations with East Timorese of various shades of opinion, aiming at the gradual involvement, as well as the availability of the Foreign Ministers of Portugal and Indonesia for direct dialogue with East Timorese personalities. I am encouraged by the result of this first meeting, and it is my intention, with the consent of the two Governments, to facilitate a further intra-East Timorese-meeting following the seventh round of min-

isterial talks on 16 January 1996.

7. I convened the sixth round of talks between the two Foreign Ministers, also at Geneva, on 8 July 1995, a few weeks later than the time originally envisaged, in order to allow for the meeting of the All-Inclusive Intra-East Timorese Dialogue to take place.

8. At that round, the Ministers discussed developments since the previous round in January, including the implementation of the chairman's statement on the situation of human rights in East Timor, agreed upon by consensus by the Commission on Human Rights at its fifty-first session, the importance of which was stressed.

9. The Ministers welcomed the convening of the All-Inclusive Intra-East Timorese Dialogue, which constituted a positive effort to help create an atmosphere conducive to the achievement of a solution to the question of East Timor. They also welcomed my view on the need for convening a further meeting or meetings of that Dialogue and my intention to pursue the matter with the two parties.

10. Also at the sixth round, the two sides, without prejudice to their respective positions of principle regarding the political status of East Timor, began discussions on the substantive issues identified by me regarding possible avenues for a just, comprehensive and internationally acceptable solution. In that context, they discussed issues related to an eventual framework for the achievement of such a solution and other related issues, including the preservation and promotion of the cultural identity of the East Timorese people and bilateral relations between them. They agreed to continue to discuss these issues.

11. I will hold a seventh round of talks with the two Ministers on 16 January 1996 in London.

Document 21

Communique of UN Talks on East Timor Issued at the Conclusion of the Seventh Round of Talks on the Question of East Timor (SG/SM/5875 16 January 1996).

1. The Secretary-General held the seventh round of talks on the question of East Timor in London on Tuesday 16 January 1996, with the Foreign Minister of Portugal, Mr. Jaime Gama, and the Foreign Minister of Indonesia, Mr. Ali Alatas.

2. The Ministers discussed developments since the sixth round of talks in July 1995 and, in this connection, welcomed the visit of the United Nations High Commissioner for Human Rights, Mr. José Ayala-Lasso, to Jakarta and East Timor in December 1995 in the context of the implementation of the Chairman's Statement adopted by consensus in 1995 by the Human Rights Commission, the importance of which was recognised.

3. The Ministers, without prejudice to their respective positions of principle regarding the political status of East Timor, continued their discussions on those substantive issues which have been identified related to an eventual framework for the achievement of a just, comprehensive and internationally acceptable solution to the question of East Timor, as well as other related issues, inter alia, the preservation and promotion of the cultural identity of the East Timorese people and bilateral relations between Indonesia and Portugal.

4. The Ministers took note positively of the Secretary-General's intention to facilitate and offer the necessary arrangements for another meeting of All-Inclusive Intra-Timorese Dialogue in accordance with the same terms of reference agreed at the fifth round of talks, which will take place in Austria in March 1996.

5. Following today's discussion, the parties agreed to continue their efforts, with the assistance of the Secretary-General, to find a just, comprehensive and internationally acceptable settlement to the question of East Timor. The eighth round of talks between the Foreign Ministers under the auspices of the Secretary-General will be held in Geneva on 29 June 1996. In the interval, talks will continue at the Permanent Representative level with the participation of the Secretary-General's Representative.

London, 16 January 1996

Document 22

Communique Issued at the Conclusion of the Eighth Round of Talks on the Question of East Timor, 27 June 1996

1. The Secretary-General held the eighth round of talks on the question of East Timor in Geneva on Thursday, 27 June 1996 with the Foreign Minister of Indonesia, Mr. Ali Alatas, and the Foreign Minister of Portugal, Mr. Jaime Gama.

2. The Ministers discussed developments since the last round of talks in January 1996, including the implementation of the Chairman's Statement adopted by consensus in 1996 by the fifty-second session of the Commission on Human Rights, the importance of which was recognized.

3. The Ministers, without prejudice to their respective positions of principle regarding the status of East Timor, discussed in greater detail those substantive issues which have been identified related to an eventual framework for the achievement of a just, comprehensive and internationally acceptable solution to the question of East Timor.

4. The Ministers welcomed the convening of the All-inclusive Intra-East Timorese Dialogue (AETD), held at Burg Schlaining, Austria, from 19 to 22 March 1996 with the facilitation of the Secretary-General.

They expressed their gratitude to the Government of Austria for hosting the meeting and to other governments for their support.

5. The Ministers took note positively of the Secretary-General's intention to facilitate and offer the necessary arrangements for another meeting of the All-inclusive Intra-East Timorese dialogue in accordance with the same terms of reference agreed at the fifth round of talks.

6. The Ministers considered the proposals of the AETD and agreed to proceed with consultations on those relating to the establishment of an East Timorese cultural centre in Dili and to the development of human resources in East Timor.

7. Following today's discussions, the parties agreed to continue their efforts, with the assistance of the Secretary-General, to find a just, comprehensive and internationally acceptable settlement to the question of East Timor. The ninth round of talks will be held on 21 December 1996 in New York. In the interval, talks will continue at the Permanent Representative level with the participation of the Secretary-General's Representative.

Geneva, 27 June 1996

Document 23

DECLARAÇÃO DE BURG SCHLAINING, AUSTRIA, 1995

Os timorenses reunidos no dialogo abragente intra-timorense de 3 a 5 de Junho de 1995, em Schlaining, Austria, no quadro da iniciativa do Secretário Geral das Nações Unidas:

Agradecendo e saudando o Secretário Geral da ONU e os seus colaboradores nesta iniciativa; *Registando* com apreço a hospitalidade generosa do Governo austriaco no acolhimento dos participantes; *Agradecendo* a contribuição voluntaria de varios paises para a realização deste encontro; *Reconhecendo* o inestimavel contributo da Igreja católica timorense no passado e no presente de Timor Loro Sa'e; *Tend*o presente o contribute de Sua Excelência Rev. D. Carlos Filipe Ximenes Belo, no decorrer do dialogo intra-timorense; *Ressaltando* que, não obstante o espiritio franco e aberto em que decorreu este Encontro Intra-Timorense se mantem as diferentes opções políticas de fundo;

DECIDEM:

1. Sauder a presenca de Sua Excelência Reverendíssima Bispo D.Carlos Filipe Ximenes Belo, Administrador Apostólico da Diocese de Dili, que com o seu inestimável contributo ao longo dos debates se obtiveram propostas de medidas concretes para a melhoria das condiçoes fisicas e espirituais da vida do povo de Timor Loro Sa'e:

2. *Propor* ao Secretário Geral a realização de de um novos diálogos intra-timorense a ocorrer no quadro em que este foi organizado a fim de continuer a debata os assuntos, a preceder a cada ronda de conversações entre os Chefes das Diplomacias de Portugal e da Indonésia;

3. *Reafirmar* a necessidade de imiplenentação de medidas necessárias na área dos Direitos Humanos e nos mais diversos domínios com vista a promoçáo da paz, estabilidade, justiça e harmonia social.

4. *Reafirmar* a necessidade do desenvolvimento sócio cultural do Timor Loro Sa'e com base na preservação da identidade cultural do seu povo como a tradição, religião, história e língua, incluindo o ensino do tétum e português;

5. *Erpressar* a necessidade de, num clima de mútua compreensão, toterância e concórdia, lançar as bases para a participação de todos os

timorenses, sem discriminações de qualquer ordem no desenvolvimento do Timor Loro Sa'e em todos os niveis da vida humana;

6. Affirmar a importancia das conversações em curso entre os Governos Indonésio e português sob os auspicios do Secretário Geral da ONU a fim de se encontrar uma solução justa e global e internacionalement aceitável para a questão de Timor Leste nos termos da letra e do espírito da Resolução 37/30 da Assembleia Geral da ONU;

7. Registrar com apreço as consultas realizadas pelas Nações Unidas com as diferente sensibilidades timorenses, visando o seu envolvimento crescents, ressaitando a disponsibilidade dos Ministros de Negócios Estrangeiros de Portugal e da Indonesia para diálogo directo com personalidades timorenses;

8. Solicitar os bons oficios do Secretario Geral da ONU e do Govemo de Portugal e da Indonésia no sentido de facilitar a livre circulação de famílias timorenses de e para Timor Loro Sa'e.

Burg Schlaining, 5 de Junho de 1995,

Document 24

BURG SCHLAINING DECLARATION, 1996

Guided by the terms of reference of the meeting as contained in paragraph 3 of the communique issued at the conclusion of the fifth round of Ministerial talks in Geneva on 9 January 1995, the All Inclusive Intra-East Timorese Dialogue on March 19–22, 1996, herewith 1996 AIETD in Burg Schlaining, Austria,

Expressing their gratitude to the Secretary-General and his staff for facilitating the All Inclusive Intra-East Timorese Dialogue in Burg Schlaining,

Expressing their appreciation and thanking the generous hospitality of the Austrian Federal Government in welcoming the participants for the second time,

Taking into consideration the Note to the Burg Schlaining Declaration of June 5, 1995 as contained in the Note of 6 June 1995 submitted by the participants from inside East Timor.

Recognizing the efforts of various East Timorese personalities who made possible the realization of 1995 AIETD.

Deeply concious (sic) of the invaluable role of the Catholic Church in East Timor and commending its positive cooperation with other religions,

Taking note of all contributions by the participants of this meeting,

Bearing in mind the positive atmosphere that prevailed during the course of the 1996 AIETD.

THE PARTICIPANTS

1. Emphasize the importance of the presence of Mgr. José Antonio da Costa, Vicar-General of the Diocese of Dili, as personal representative of Bishop Carlos Filipe Ximenes Belo, SDB, Apostolic Administrator of Dili;

2. Again affirm the importance of ongoing negotiations between the governments of Indonesia and Portugal under the auspices of the UN Secretary-General with a view to finding a just, comprehensive, and internationally acceptable solution to the question of East Timor;

3. Express their interest and readiness in continuing the AIETD, should it be requested by the UN Secretary-General in the same framework in which this one was undertaken with a view to continuing the debate on the concrete and practical issues conducive to the confidence building measures aiming at helping the resolution of the question of East Timor;

4. Express their interest to the Governments of Indonesia and Portugal in the establishment of an East Timorese Cultural Center in Dili with the aim of undertak-

ing research on the culture, such as language (including Tetum and Portuguese), customs and traditions of the East Timorese;

5. Welcome assistance from Portugal to help East Timor's human resources development by concrete measures, such as financial and technical support for East Timor University and practical training for youth in all areas of relevance to the needs of East Timorese people;

6. Encouraged by the substantial role of the East Timorese in the administration and development of East Timor, propose to the Indonesian government the provision of further opportunities for East Timorese to have a greater role in the administration of the territory as well as economic policy, trade and investment activities. The promotion of local small industries, such as handicraft and textile should deserve special attention;

7. Reaffirm the need to implement the necessary measures in the field of human rights in various areas, including the protection of women with a view to promoting peace, stability, justice and social harmony.

Burg Schlaining, March 22, 1996

Document 25

European Parliament Resolution on Indonesia

The following resolution on the situation in East Timor and the violation of human rights in Indonesia was adopted by the European Parliament in its Plenary Session in Strasbourg 20 June 1996.

EUROPEAN PARLIAMENT

19 June 1996

JOINT MOTION FOR A RESOLUTION (Rule 47)

THE EUROPEAN PARLIAMENT,

A. having regard to the illegal occupation of East Timor by Indonesia,

B. whereas Indonesian military repression against the population of East Timor is continuing and has been stepped up over recent days, particularly against young people,

C. deeply concerned at the incidents which occured in Baucau between 9 and 11 June in the wake of the profanation of a Catholic religious image, involving protests by several hundred young Timorese which where repressed by the Indonesian security forces, with at least two of the young killed, large numbers wounded

and several dozen being arrested,

D. whereas the Indonesian government continues to ignore all calls from the international community urging it to respect human rights and the right of self-determination of the people of East Timor,

E. having regard to the developments following the approach made by the Portuguese Prime Minister to the President of Indonesia during the Euro-Asian summit in Bangkok,

F. having regard to the forthcoming meeting between the Indonesian and Portuguese Foreign Ministers to be organized by the UN Secretary-General,

G. having regard to the fatal shooting of 25 year old Imanuel Suares from East Timor on 7 June by the police in Jakarta,

H. whereas hundreds of political prisoners are still being detained in Indonesia and in East Timor,

I. whereas the tension in Indonesia has been increasing, as demonstrated by the incidents which have occured in Irian Jaya (Western Papua), where young people clashed with soldiers, and by the army's brutal invasion of the university campus in Ujung Pandang in order to stop a student demonstration (protesting against a 150% increase in bus fares) which resulted in the death of six young people,

J. whereas the Indonesian authorities accused the former member of parliament Mr Sri-Bintang Pamungkas of being the instigator of demonstrations in Germany,

K. whereas this accusation was subsequently replaced by another alleging that Mr Sri-Bintang Pamungkas had insulted the President of the Republic of Indonesia during a lecture he gave at the Technical University of Berlin on 9 April 1995, which led to his being sentenced to 34 months' imprisonment on 8 May 1996,

L. having regard to its previous resolutions on the situation in East Timor and the violation of human rights in Indonesia,

1. Condemns once more the Indonesian military repression of the people of East Timor and expresses its solidarity with the victims and their families;

2. Deplores the provocative acts perpetrated by the Indonesians against freedom of religion;

3. Reaffirms its solidarity with the people of East Timor in their fight for self-determination, and its condemnation of the illegal occupation of East Timor;

4. Calls for the immediate release of all political prisoners, including Mr Xanana Gusmão;

5. Reaffirms its support for the UN-sponsored negotiations now under way aimed at resolving the problems of the basis of respect for human rights and the right to self-determination;

6. Calls on the Indonesian government to respond to the initiative of the Portuguese government;

7. Reiterates its demand to the Member States of the European Union to halt all military assistance and all arms sales to Indonesia; for Human Rights.

DOC-EN\RE\302916

Document 26

European Union's Common Position on East Timor

The following is the text of the European Union's Common Position on East Timor which was cleared for publication on Tuesday, 25 June (1996):

COMMON POSITION CONCERNING EAST TIMOR The Council of the European Union,

Having regard to the Treaty on European Union, and in particular Article J.2. thereof,

HAS DEFINED THE FOLLOWING COMMON POSITION:

Article 1

The European Union, referring to its previous declarations on the situation in East Timor, intends to pursue the following aims:

1) to contribute to the achievement by dialogue of a fair, comprehensive and internationally acceptable solution to the question of East Timor, which fully respects the interests and legitimate aspirations of the Timorese people, in accordance with international law;

2) to improve the situation in East Timor regarding respect for human rights in the territory.

Article 2

To pursue the aims referred to in Article 1, the European Union:

1) supports the initiatives undertaken in the United Nations framework which may contribute to resolving this question;

2) supports in particular the current talks under the aegis of the United Nations Secretary-General with the aim of achieving the solution referred to in point 1) of Article 1, effective progress towards which continues to be hampered by serious obstacles;

3) encourages the continuation of Inter-Timor meetings in the context of this process of dialogue under the auspices of the United Nations;

4) calls upon the Indonesian Government to adopt effective measures leading to a significant improvement in the human rights situation in East Timor, in particular by implementing fully the relevant decisions adopted by the United Nations Commission on Human Rights;

5) supports all appropriate action with the objective of generally strengthening respect for human rights in East Timor and substantially improving the situation of its people, by means of the resources available to the European Union and aid for action by NGOS.

Article 3

The Council will be responsible for the follow-up concerning this common position.

Article 4

This common position shall apply from the date of its adoption.

Article 5

This common position shall be published in the official Journal.

Done at Luxembourg

For the Council
The President

Document 27

Letter to Javier Perez de Cuellar U.N. Secretary-General from Bishop Carlos Filipe Ximenes Belo, Apostolic Administrator of Dili, 6 February 1989

Please accept my sincere compliments of respect.

I am writing to your Excellency to bring to your attention that the process of decolonisation in Portuguese Timor has not been resolved by the United Nations and should not be allowed to be forgotten. We, the people of Timor, believe that we should be consulted about the future of our land.

As the person responsible for the Catholic Church and as a citizen of Timor I hereby request your Excellency to initiate a genuine and democratic process of decolonisation in East Timor to be realised through a referendum.

The people of Timor ought to be heard through a plebiscite on their future. Until now they have not been consulted. Others have spoken in their name. It is Indonesia which says that the People of East Timor have chosen integration but the people themselves have never said this. Portugal hopes that time will resolve the problem. But in the meantime we are dying as a people and as a nation.

Your Excellency, you are a democrat and a friend of human rights. I ask you to demonstrate by deeds respect for both the spirit and the letter of the UN Charter which gives to all peoples the right to decide their own destiny, freely, consciously and responsibly. Excellency, there is no better democratic way of knowing the supreme wishes of the Timorese people than by the conduct of a REFERENDUM promoted by the UN for the people of Timor.

Thank you for all your sympathy for the People of Timor.

Document 28

Announcement of the Norwegian Nobel Committee on Friday, October 11, 1996:

"The Norwegian Nobel Committee has decided to award the Nobel Peace Prize for 1996, in two equal parts, to Carlos Felipe Ximenes Belo and José Ramos-Horta for their work towards a just and peaceful solution to the conflict in East Timor,

"In 1975 Indonesia took control of East Timor and began systematically oppressing the people. In the years that followed it has been estimated that one-third of the population of East Timor lost their lives due to starvation, epidemics, war and terror.

"Carlos Belo, Bishop of East Timor, has been the foremost representative of the people of East Timor. At the risk of his own life, he has tried to protect his people from infringements by those in power. In his efforts to create a just settlement based on his people's right to self-determination, he has been a constant spokesman for non-violence and dialogue with the Indonesian authorities. Ramos-Horta has been the leading international spokesman for East Timor's cause since 1975. Recently he has made a significant contribution through the 'reconciliation talks' and by working out a peace plan for the region.

"In awarding this year's Nobel Peace Prize to Belo and Ramos-Horta, the Norwegian Nobel Committee wants to honour their sustained and self-sacrificing contributions for a small but oppressed people. The Nobel Committee hopes that this award will spur efforts to find a diplomatic solution to the conflict in East Timor based on the people's right to self-determination."

Document 29

Statement by the Spokesman of the UN Secretary-General on Award of 1966 Nobel Peace Prize

The Secretary-General welcomes the award of the 1996 Nobel Peace Prize to Monsignor Carlos Filipe Ximenes Belo and Mr. José Ramos-Horta, and congratulates the two recipients.

As is well known, the Secretary-General has been exercising, since 1983, his good offices to find a just, comprehensive and internationally acceptable solution to the issue of East Timor. In this capacity he has had the opportunity to consult on various occasions with Bishop Belo whose wisdom and commitment to peace and human rights has won him the respect of his people and of the international community. Both Bishop Belo and Mr. Ramos-Horta have participated actively in the All-inclusive Intra-East Timorese Dialogue facilitiated by the Secretary-General.

The Secretary-General hopes that this award will positively affect the continuing negotiations in the search for a lasting settlement.

New York
11 October 1996

Index

ABRI (see Indonesia, Armed Forces)
Alatas, Ali, 74, 86
Alkatiri, Mari, 48
Anderson, Ben, 17
Angola, 64. 85-6, 102 [Document 5]
Annan, Kofi (Secretary-General) [Document 11]
Araujo, Abilio, 48
Aristide, Jean-Bertrand, 103
ASEAN, 97
asylum seekers, 73-76
Australia, 2-3, 5, 10, 23, 80, 90-1, 97, Ambassador (Jakarta), 64, 67 business/defense links with Jakarta, 66-7 Foreign Ministry, 8, 63, 67, 83, 92 High Court, 68 Prime Minister, 5, 20, 58, 61, 66, 68 and World Court, 57-68 [Document 15 & 16]
Australian Council for Overseas Aid (ACFOA), 16-20

Baucau, 4-6, 25, 52, 78
Belo, Ximenes (Bishop and Nobel Peace Prize co-laureate), 13-14, 35, 45, 50, 53 [Document 27, 28 & 29]
Borsuk, Richard, 31
Bosnia, 85
Boutros-Ghali, Boutros (Secretary-General), 79, 84, 87
Budiarjo, Carmel & Liem Soei Liong, 17, 23-24
Bulog, 5-6, 19, 25
Burg Schlaining (Austria), 45-50 Declaration of, 45, 84 [Document 23 & 24]

Cambodia, 10, 16, 42, 83, 90-3, 103
Cape Verde [Document 5]
Carrascalão, João, 48
Carrascalão, Mario, 31
Catholic Relief Services (CRS), 15-18
Catholicism, 28-9, 52
Chinese, 5, 27, 29, 37, 54, 65
China, 77-82, 104
Chissano (President), 101
Chomsky, Noam, 98
Clark, Roger, S., 36
Cold War, 23, 99, 100, 104
coffee, 31-2
Conrad, Joseph, 3-4
Cyprus, 77, 82
da Cruz, Francisco Lopes, 47, 50
de Cuellar, Javier Perez (Secretary-General), 41-4, 68, 91, 96

death squads, 51-5
demography, 26-7
development, 9-40
Dhlakama, 101
Dili, 1, 6-7, 78 violence in, 52-3
Duarte regime, 98-9
Dutch, 2

East Timor Action Network (ETAN), 51-2
education, 13-15
Ekeburg, Hugh, 78
El Salvador, 97-9
elections, 11-12, 92, 95-6
Eritrea, 99-100, 103 Liberation fronts, 99-100
Escarameia, Paula, 79, 84
European, Community (Union) [Documents 6 & 26] Parliament [Document 25]

Evans, Gareth, 83, 85-6, 90 Evans plan, 90

Fanon, Franz, 35
Feith, Herbert, 30
Frelimo, 101-2
Freney, Denis, 7, 69-71
Fretilin, 6, 16, 34, 46, 53, 64, 69, 86, 96

Golkar, 11-12
Gomes da Costa, António (Mau Hunu), 3
Gonclaves, Guilherme, 50
Guinea-Bissau [Document 15]
Gusmão, (Xanana) José, 3, 9, 13, 34, 43, 48, 70 [Document 13]

Habibie, B.J., 47, 65
Haile Selasie, 99
Haiti, 103-4
Hamilton, John, 20
Hatano, Ruriko, 75
health, 10
Heininger, Janet E, 91
human rights, 55, 79, 81, 87, 99 [Documents 8 & 14]

immigrants, 2, 28, 103
Indonesia, 59-62, 63-8, Armed Forces (ABRI), 4-7, 10, 12, 19, 24, 51, 86 Embassies, 46-7 government, 10-11, 90 Foreign Ministry, 8, 43, 45-6, 59, 74, 86
International [Committee of the] Red Cross (ICRC), 15-19, 73, 95
International Court of Justice (see World Court)

Japan, 10, 23 business-links, 76 Embassy (Jakarta), 73-4 media, 73-6, peacekeepers, 102 war, 1, 76

Jenkins, David, 17

Kissinger, Henry, 94

language, 2, 5, 12-14
Lasso, Jose Ayala, 54
Lee, Jefferson, 83
Liberia, 97
Liquisa, 53-4, 78
Lloyd, Robert, B., 101-2
Lobato, Rogerio, 47
London meeting, 46-7

Macau, 13, 48, 77, 80
MacDougall, John, 42
Machel, Samora, 101
Marker, Jamsheed (UN Special Representative for East Timor) [Document 11]
malnutrition, 4, 18, 24, 32
maps, 77-82
Mengistu regime, 99-100
Mo, Timothy, 27
Morocco, 93-6
Mozambique, 7, 64, 85, 97, 101-2 [Document 5]
Muslims, 5, 28, 66

Namibia, 85, 88-90, 97
National Council of the Maubere Resistance (CNRM), 13, 21, 45
Nobel Peace Prize [Document 27, 28 & 29]
Nordland, Rod, 19
Ndiaye, Bacre Waly, 52-3, 65

Palau, 89
Partai Demokrasi Indonesia, 11
peace, building, 84 enforcement, 85 keeping, 84-5, 87, 98, 102, 104
petroleum, 58-9, 61-3, 80
Pontes, David, 93
Prabowo Subiato, 34, 85

Polosario, 95-6
Portugal, 7-8, 14, 36, 84, 97 Foreign Minister, 43, 45 Newsagency, 44 World Court, 57-68 **[Document 15 & 16]**
population control, 24-30
poverty, 10, 18, 32
press, 18-19, 52, 69-71

Ramos-Horta, José (Nobel Peace Prize co-laureate), 19, 45, 68, 70, 76, 81 **[Document 12, 28 & 29]**
Reagan, Ronald, 98
reconciliation, 45-50
referenda, 96
Renamo, 101-2
resistance, 13, 21
Robison, Richard, 24
Rodgers, Peter, 19
Romero, Oscar (Archbishop), 98

São Tome e Principe, **[Document 5]**
Santa Cruz (Dili) massacre, 1-2, 5, 14, 34, 41, 52 **[Document 5, 6, 7 & 8]**
self-determination, 10
Soares, Abilio, 33, 53
Soesastro, M. Hadi, 21-2, 30
South Africa, 88, 92
South Pacific Forum, 97
Spanish Sahara (see Western Sahara)
Stepan, Sasha, 96-7
Suharto (General/President), 13, 30, 46, 54, 58
Sukarno (President), 58
Surin Pitsawan, 18

Taiwan, 77-81
Taylor, 19
Tibet, 78-82
Timor Gap Agreement, 22, 44, 57-68 **[Document 15]**

tourism, 33-5
United Nations (UN), Committee on Decolonization, 79 **[Document 12]** General Assembly, 83-4, 87-8, 90, 94 **[Document 1 & 4]** Human Rights Commission **[Document 9, 10, 11 & 12]** Observer Mission in El Salvador (ONUSAL), 98-9 Operation for Mozamique (UNOMOZ), 101-2 Security Council, 78, 79, 87, 98 **[Document 2 & 3]** Secretary-General, 8, 84, 86 Statements on East Timor **[Document 17, 18, 19, 20, 21 & 22]** Special Rapporteur, **[Document 8]** Transitional Authority on Cambodia (UNTAC), 91-3 Transitional Authority on East Timor (UNTAET), 86-7, 84, 93, 103 Trusteeships, 88-9, 91
United States, 10, 23, 61, 99 AID, 15, 24 Ambassador, 16-17, 53 Embassy (Jakarta), 52, 75 Secretary of State, 94

Vietnam, 25-6, 31, 86, 90
violence, 51-5

Wako, Amos, 42
Webster, David, 80-1
Weiss, Thomas G., 8
Western Sahara, 77, 82, 85, 93-7
women, 30, 79
World Court, 44, 57-68, 88 **[Document 15 & 16]**
World War II, 1, 61, 76

Xanana (see Gusmão)

Zimbabwe, 101-2